ELITE SCHOOLS

Geography matters to elite schools—to how they function and flourish, to how they locate themselves and their Others. Like their privileged clientele they use geography as a resource to elevate themselves. They mark, and market, place. This collection, as a whole, reads elite schools through a spatial lens. It offers fresh lines of inquiry to the 'new sociology of elite schools'. Collectively the authors examine elite schools and systems in different parts of the world. They highlight the ways that these schools, and their clients, operate within diverse local, national, regional, and global contexts in order to shape their own and their clients' privilege and prestige. The collection also points to the uses of the transnational as a resource via the International Baccalaureate, study tours, and the discourses of global citizenship. Building on research about social class, meritocracy, privilege, and power in education, it offers inventive critical lenses and insights particularly from the 'Global South'. As such it is an intervention in global power/knowledge geographies.

Aaron Koh is Associate Professor of Literacy and English Education at Griffith University, Australia.

Jane Kenway is Professorial Fellow with the Australian Research Council, Professor of Education at Monash University, and an elected Fellow of the Academy of Social Sciences, Australia.

Education in Global Context
Series Editor: Lois Weis

Social Class and Education
Global Perspectives
Edited by Lois Weis and Nadine Dolby

Confucius and Crisis in American Universities
By Amy Stambach

Globalizing Educational Accountabilities
By Bob Lingard, Wayne Martino, Goli Rezai-Rashti, and Sam Sellar

Elite Schools
Multiple Geographies of Privilege
Edited by Aaron Koh and Jane Kenway

ELITE SCHOOLS

Multiple Geographies of Privilege

Edited by Aaron Koh and Jane Kenway

Routledge
Taylor & Francis Group

NEW YORK AND LONDON

First published 2016
by Routledge
711 Third Avenue, New York, NY 10017

and by Routledge
2 Park Square, Milton Park, Abingdon, Oxon, OX14 4RN

Routledge is an imprint of the Taylor & Francis Group, an informa business

© 2016 Taylor & Francis

The right of the editors to be identified as the authors of the editorial material, and of the authors for their individual chapters, has been asserted in accordance with sections 77 and 78 of the Copyright, Designs and Patents Act 1988.

All rights reserved. No part of this book may be reprinted or reproduced or utilised in any form or by any electronic, mechanical, or other means, now known or hereafter invented, including photocopying and recording, or in any information storage or retrieval system, without permission in writing from the publishers.

Trademark notice: Product or corporate names may be trademarks or registered trademarks, and are used only for identification and explanation without intent to infringe.

Library of Congress Cataloging in Publication Data
Names: Koh, Aaron, 1967- editor. | Kenway, Jane, editor.
Title: Elite schools : multiple geographies of privilege / edited by Aaron Koh and Jane Kenway.
Description: New York : Routledge, [2016] | Series: Education in global context | Includes bibliographical references and index.
Identifiers: LCCN 2015034961| ISBN 9781138779402 (hardback) | ISBN 9781138779419 (pbk.) | ISBN 9781315771335 (e-book)
Subjects: LCSH: Elite (Social sciences)--Education. | Upper class--Education. | Boarding schools. | Education--Social aspects--Cross-cultural studies.
Classification: LCC LC4931 .E55 2016 | DDC 373.22/2--dc23LC record available at http://lccn. loc.gov/2015034961

ISBN: 978-1-138-77940-2 (hbk)
ISBN: 978-1-138-77941-9 (pbk)
ISBN: 978-1-315-77133-5 (ebk)

Typeset in Bembo
by Saxon Graphics Ltd, Derby

CONTENTS

Series Editor's Overview	ix
Acknowledgements	xi

Introduction: Reading the Dynamics of Educational Privilege
Through a Spatial Lens   1
Aaron Koh and Jane Kenway

1   Becoming the Man: Redefining Asian Masculinity in an
Elite Boarding School   18
Wee Loon Yeo

2   Capitalising on Well-Roundedness: Chinese Students'
Cultural Mediations in an Elite Australian School   33
Yujia Wang

3   The Emergence of Elite International Baccalaureate
Diploma Programme Schools in China: A
'Skyboxification' Perspective   50
Moosung Lee, Ewan Wright, and Allan Walker

vi Contents

4 Elite Schoolboys Becoming Global Citizens: Examining
the Practice of Habitus 70
Chin Ee Loh

5 The Joy of Privilege: Elite Private School Online
Promotions and the Promise of Happiness 87
*Christopher Drew, Kristina Gottschall, Natasha Wardman,
and Sue Saltmarsh*

6 Old Boy Networks: The Relationship Between Elite
Schooling, Social Capital, and Positions of Power in
British Society 101
Shane Watters

7 Exclusive Consumers: The Discourse of Privilege in Elite
Indian School Websites 122
Radha Iyer

8 The Insiders: Changing Forms of Reproduction
in Education 139
Hugues Draelants

9 Can Geographies of Privilege and Oppression Combine?:
Elite Education in Northern Portugal 157
Eunice Macedo and Helena C. Araújo

10 "We Are Not Elite Schools": Studying the Symbolic
Capital of Swiss Boarding Schools 171
Caroline Bertron

11 Tourism, Educational Travel, and Transnational Capital:
From the Grand Tour to the 'Year Abroad' among
Sciences Po-Paris Students 188
Bertrand Réau

12 Schools and Families: School Choice and Formation of
   Elites in Present-Day Argentina   202
   Sandra Ziegler

13 The Economy of Eliteness: Consuming Educational
   Advantage   217
   Howard Prosser

Contributors   231
Index   235

SERIES EDITOR'S OVERVIEW

The series on Education in Global Context takes seriously the transnational migration of commerce, capital, knowledge, and peoples, and the implications of such for education and social structure. Globalization—in education, as in the world economy and patterns of human migration—affects all of us. The increasingly globalized and knowledge-based economy renders the linkages between education and social and economic outcomes empirically 'up for grabs' in a wide range of nations. Books in this series underscore the consequences of this 'new global' while stressing the importance and effects of a paradigmatic shift in our understanding of schooling and social/economic arrangements.

The changing nature of transnational migration patterns holds significant implications for this broad intellectual project. In a context where migrants—here defined as immigrants across class, race/ethnic, and religious background; refugees who comprise a range of national origins; and international students who similarly hail from a wide range of 'sending nations'—are positioned and work to reposition themselves inside new global circumstances, we can expect notable change in the nature of and engagement with knowledge, educational practices, and outcomes across the globe. This works to alter social structural arrangements both within and between nations.

Lois Weis

ACKNOWLEDGEMENTS

Jane expresses her deep appreciation to the Australian Research Council and to Monash University for the support provided to her for the five-year duration of the *Elite schools in globalising circumstances: a multi-sited global ethnography* research project. She also acknowledges with gratitude the contributions to her thinking made by the research team and the schools around the world in which the research for the project was conducted. As always, Lindsay Fitzclarence and Vashti Kenway have been her greatest inspiration and support.

Aaron is grateful to the Hong Kong Institute of Education and National Institute of Education for supporting his involvement in the five-year *Elite schools in globalising circumstances: a multi-sited global ethnography* research project. He also acknowledges the enduring friendship, love and unflinching support of George Chen, Jo-Marion Ng, and Victoria Carrington.

Finally, we acknowledge the team of reviewers we called on to review the chapters in this book. We thank them for taking their precious time to give feedback on the chapters. This edited collection has benefited from their generous critique.

INTRODUCTION

Reading the Dynamics of Educational Privilege Through a Spatial Lens

Aaron Koh and Jane Kenway

Elite schools are contentious institutions and elicit intense debate. They are seen to either represent schooling's gold standard and to produce highly educated luminaries who rightfully take their places at the apogee of all the institutions that matter. Or they are seen as socially isolated, luxury enclaves that breed and feed privilege and power and entrenched educational and social inequality and division. No matter where one stands in relation to such debates it is difficult to disassociate 'privilege' from elite schools. To ask in what ways elite schools are privileged invariably attracts predictable replies. They express privilege, it is frequently argued, through their high fees and thus their wealthy clientele, the grandeur of their grounds and buildings, their state-of-the-art learning facilities, their curricula and extracurricular range, their legions of famous alumni, and their powerful connections to elite universities and other significant institutions. And the list goes on especially when the focus shifts beyond such material and symbolic facets of privilege; what Daloz (2010, p. 94) calls "vicarious display". For then we get into the subtleties that researchers have been teasing out for some time. They show, not just how privilege is material and materialised, but how it is produced through an intricate array of practices, which adjust, over time, to suit changing economic, socio-cultural, and geo-political circumstances.

Even so, privilege is a slippery term often mobilised to speak to all sorts of individual and group advantage. The notion of privilege has been well explored and debated as Adam Howard, Aimee Polimeno and Brianne Wheeler (2014) illustrate in a useful overview of the literature where they link discussions of class privilege to other forms. They go on to show how affluent young people variously experience and express their privilege and the identity work involved. Interestingly quite a number of recent publications on elite schools have made the concept 'privilege' their leitmotif. Take another example. Utilising the concepts, "affect"

2 Aaron Koh and Jane Kenway

and "agency", Claire Maxwell and Peter Aggleton (2013) argue that privilege is a nested triadic relationship where "feelings and affect emerge as central to an understanding of the relation between agency and privilege" (p. 4). Affect and agency are seen to animate the spaces and discourses of privilege. Further, the triadic relationship between 'privilege', 'affect' and 'agency' are brought into an implicit conversation with Bourdieu's 'capitals'.

Along with many others we too are interested in the nature of privilege with regard to elite schools, its diverse forms, how it is gained, on what grounds and in whose particular interests. But further, looking behind the face of privilege leads to inquiries about its asymmetrical expression amongst the privileged themselves—how it is racialised, gendered, sexualised, and spatialised, for example. But why produce another book on elite schools and privilege? Is there anything more to be said? As we, and others, have been arguing for some time, there certainly is—not least around questions of *space, time, materiality and politics* and their entangled expressions. Certainly, the privilege that elite schools reflect and help to bring into effect has many such entanglements. Our overall focus in this collection is specifically on their multiple geographies—on the ways in which their privilege arises in different spaces and places and on various scales, occurs in different modalities, involves diverse mobilities, and arises in relation to assorted politics. A quick example illustrates such spatial thinking.

A recent article, published in the Singapore *Straits Times*, featured Raffles Institution, an elite independent school in Singapore known to produce many of the country's leaders. Titled "Raffles Institution now a 'middle-class' school, says principal" (Teng, 2015), it featured the principal's speech delivered on the school's 192nd Founders' Day. What appeared as an ordinary speech confined to an important occasion of the school's calendar suddenly became newsworthy and widely circulated on newsfeed in social media. Why? The principal touched a raw nerve in Singapore. Currently, elitism is a hot-button issue facing the school and the wider Singaporean polity. In the article, Mr Chan, the principal, is quoted as saying that "meritocracy in Singapore is working less well" and that "a long period of conditioning means that we often fail to see elitism even when it is staring at us in the face". He also admitted that the school "now largely caters to the affluent" and that taking pride in the school's many achievements and accolades "risk making it insular". Subsequently, the print press and then other social media amplified further critiques of the politics and spatiality of privilege. They pointed to the 'Bukit Timah belt'—an affluent area consisting of luxury housing where elite schools are concentrated thus also highlighting spatial disparities in Singapore's education system. Interestingly, the links between elite schools in Singapore, class, racial and spatial advantage and meritocracy are all offered as 'new' news.

But of course such links are not 'new' news. In all the countries where research on elite schools has been conducted, such research has consistently revealed that these schools underwrite, and sometimes help to rewrite, class, race and gender privilege and the associated relationships of power. The study by Lois Weis, Kristin Cipollone, and Heather Jenkins (2014) of schools in the USA is a particularly compelling example of the family intensities involved. They characterise the competition among parents vying for their child's admission to elite universities in the USA as "class warfare". What is relatively new, however, is that this is considered newsworthy in Singapore as a distinctive space.

Space always matters politically and analytically. An understanding of it is vital for an adequate interpretation of these news items and, indeed, for interpreting Mr Chan's reasons for speaking out in the manner he did. Understanding the space of the school and of the wider Singaporean polity is necessary. The latter includes the quite recent rise of anti-elitist sentiments in this country and the implications this has had for the policies of the governing People's Action Party (PAP). Until recently elite schools, like the Raffles Institution, gloried in their high status. In post-colonial Singapore they were specifically supported by the state to produce the new county's, largely Chinese, leaders. This was made explicit by the PAP and was largely accepted by the, usually compliant, people for some considerable time. Not any more. As we argue elsewhere:

> Recently the political field has become more contested. Increasingly the PAP is seen as aloof, detached and as losing touch with people's feelings and sacrifices. The May 2011 General Elections had the worst ever PAP result and was understood as a sign of its declining popularity. But its political capital has not necessarily diminished as the PAP hegemon is salvaging its political stranglehold post the 2011 election by addressing the discontents expressed by Singaporeans (demonstrated, for example, by the recent announcement of a 37% reduction in ministerial pay). Clearly, the state nobility is carefully manoeuvring within the (political) 'gaming space'.
>
> (Kenway & Koh, 2013, p. 273)

This narrative about Singapore points to the links between the politics of privilege and the intersecting geographies of the school, neighbourhood and state. As such it also highlights the central theme of this collection, which is concerned with such *geographical intersectionalities, multiplicities,* and *mobilities* and their relationship to elite schools and to privilege in different parts of the world. Such knowledge is important as it assists understandings of "what shapes the formation and maintenance of these [privileged] groups across local, national and global spaces" as well as "how class structures and practices are produced" (Maxwell, 2015, p. 15).

This raises matters of scale: of how analyses may involve extended or more limited scales. They may focus on the up-close or the more-distant, or on how the more-distant is expressed in, or constitutes, the up-close—or the reverse. Whatever the case a geographical analysis of privilege and elite schools calls attention to "the interaction of processes, structures and agents at different *scales*" (Murray, 2006, p. 19; emphasis added). Johannah Fahey, Howard Prosser, and

4 Aaron Koh and Jane Kenway

Matthew Shaw (2015) invoke something of this spirit in their collection of papers arising from a multi-sited global ethnography.

> Studying multiple schools in multiple countries that share a common status as elite schools means that we are able to consider a complex of 'small societies' across the globe and the ways in which they sustain each other, but also contemplate the ways in which these small societies are interdependent with a world beyond the school gates: with their localities, their regions and with contemporary globalization.
>
> (p. 8)

As this intimates, elite schools operate within local/neighbourhood, national and regional contexts and are also caught up in wider global forces.

Capitalism is one such global force (Harvey, 2014). In turn, its unfettered escalation has meant that on a global scale wealth is increasingly concentrated in the hands of a few, and that income inequality and the divide between the rich and poor is widening within nation states as well as between states and regions. For example, a recent OECD (2014) report aired concerns about the gross inequalities associated with contemporary global economic arrangements. And, a Credit Suisse study reported in the *Guardian* in 2014 shows that inequality is accelerating with the richest 1% owning more than 48% of global wealth (Treanor, 2014). Many similar studies point to the widening distances between both the rich and the rest and the exceptionally rich and ordinarily rich. This is the case within and between states and regions of the globe.

Such disparities between the rich and poor involve "contested geographies of wealth, privilege and exclusion" (Pow, 2013, p. 64). One important example of such contestation was the global mediatisation of the 'Occupy Wall Street' movement, whose slogan "We are the 99 percent" (that will no longer tolerate the greed of the 1 per cent) referred to the colossal wealth disparity between the rich and poor (Hay, 2013). This movement contributed to a heightened global consciousness of the multi-scalar politics of wealth, power and avarice.

Elite schools are intertwined in these 'contested geographies'. This is why the overall body of research on elites and their education needs to be multi-scalar. For as Stephen Ball (2015) argues it also needs to "'get close' to the work of social reproduction and the performance of elite-ness within families and education institutions" (p. 238). The essays collected here go some way towards advancing this multi-scalar requirement although not so much the notion of 'contested geographies' of privilege—a topic that requires much more attention.

But scale is not necessarily self-evident and standard approaches that nest smaller scales within larger are not always apt. Sometimes adopting a global/national logic can lead to restrictive either/or questions; for instance, do elite schools form global or national elites? It is more fruitful to explore the ways that elite schools are involved in various sorts of scale-making endeavours in the constitution of privilege and power. At certain times and in certain places they may emphasise one scale more than another. For example, Rachel Brooks and Johanna Waters' (2015) study of the websites of certain English schools shows how they mobilise meaning in relation to their "local community" as they project themselves into the wider world. In contrast, in his discussion of 'Asia rising' Fazal Rizvi (2015) shows how certain expensive schools are responding to this regional phenomenon. In both cases neither a national nor a global imaginary is invoked.

Sensitivity to varied scales and their intersections is crucial if we are to fully comprehend elite schools' multi-scalar geographies of privilege. Yet as Jean and John Comaroff (2007) observe, some scales are "awkward" and "difficult to capture" (Coleman & von Hellermann, 2011, p. 4). How scale links to mobilities, networks, de-territorialisation and virtual space is a matter for continued discussion.

Take the example of virtual geography. Via their websites, elite schools have a strong presence in virtual space. There is an obvious informational logic to this as the schools' websites are a major textual medium used to communicate the schools' corporate identity, values, educational philosophies, and commitment to students' development. But also the logic is economic. The competition for students in the global elite schools market is driving them to deploy more and more sophisticated advertising and branding techniques to attract potential clients from beyond the usual national or local pool. Such texts belong to "(semiotic) systems of representation" (Hall, 1997, p. 4), and are, of course, designed to represent the school in the most positive light. The notion of 'design' suggests that there is a preferred reading and thus, as such, those producing such texts undertake careful ideological work. Clearly then there is no necessary one-to-one correspondence between the schools' virtual spaces and the lived spaces of school life. But the scalar reach of such virtual spaces is only limited by the availability of the necessary technology. The school becomes a virtual spectacle that precedes and exceeds the school itself.

But, then, how might other concepts of 'space' be deployed to understand elite schools and their work of helping to produce privilege? Space, too, is an elusive and much debated concept. But once one acknowledges that spaces are not neutral territorial entities, then one also has to recognise that spaces are contested. As Lefebvre (1991 [1974]), and many number of his diverse followers argue, space is negotiated, fought over, and produced over time. This clearly leads to considerations of the processes concerned—of the ways in which particular spaces are made and made to mean and to matter. It leads to questions about the contests involved in the work of space making, mapping and imagining—to questions about how the self and the Other are positioned within and across space. Here space is understood relationally as involving "a myriad of connections and reconnections, alignments and realignments and various positionings in relations and diverse critical junctions" (Coleman & von Hellermann, 2011, p. 13). But such apparent fluidity has its limits. Wendy Brown

6 Aaron Koh and Jane Kenway

(2014) talks about the 'desire for walling' of contemporary states as challenges to their sovereignty mount. What she says about state walls might also be said about the walls of elite schools. "Walls … emerge from and figure in discourses, they become discursive statements themselves and they are crucial to the organization of power in and through space" (2014, p. 74). Of utmost significance, she says, is how walls are "perceived and experienced".

Elite schools' privilege, and that of their clients, is produced not just on multiple scales but also in and through intersecting and multiple spaces. In terms of their use of space they undertake space and boundary work to help them to constitute elitist/dominant class imaginaries and use their elitism to help them constitute space and boundaries (Prosser & Kenway, 2015; Shaw, 2014). Elite schools' walls, fences, gates, guards, security systems, entry rules and badges, and reception desks are bound to be 'perceived and experienced' differently according to one's location in relation to them. But from a critical geography perspective they represent these schools' social closure and enclosure; their self-protection and 'other' rejection. And, of course, the walls within elite schools also organise power, of a different order, 'in and though space'.

Obviously, then, space is not totally fluid or fixed. To Nigel Thrift (2003) space

> is the outcome of series of highly problematic temporary settlements that divide and connect things up into different kinds of collectivities which are slowly provided with the means which render them durable and sustainable.
>
> (p. 95)

His notion of "temporary settlements" highlights the links between geography and temporality. Space must be understood historically. But exploring the spatio-temporal, or what Jon May and Thrift (2001) call 'timespace', also involves considerations of such things as how time is lived, how it is part of the rhythms and routines of the every-day, how it is distributed and represented in space and place.

And what of elite schools' time/space? They use time in various ways. For example, they mobilise their traditions for reputational and promotional purposes. Urgency and intensity govern the everyday rhythms of school life. But equally the wealth of the schools' clients allows them to harness time in, and for, their own educational and other advancement in comparison to those who have neither sufficient money nor time. As Bourdieu (1986, p. 246) explains "Capital … takes time to accumulate … [and] is a force inscribed in the objectivity of things so that everything is not equally possible or impossible".

While elite schools certainly use time and space to represent themselves, they primarily promote themselves as places. It is thus also necessary to also engage them as such. But to do so involves the problem that the distinction between space and place is not at all clear and involves further theoretical dispute. The key issue is if and how space and place might best be distinguished from each other. Perhaps place is most readily understood as a particular type of space—one that is named and framed, activated, experienced and embodied in specific ways. Certainly place is often understood in small scale terms as more intimate, immediate and close-up than other spaces—as involving the micro-political. This has invited particular attention to its emotional, sensual and aesthetic geography. However, Massey (1993) develops the notion of a "progressive sense of place" to speak the spatial and the temporal. She argues that places can be understood as "particular moments" in the "articulation of social relations which necessarily have a spatial form" (1993, p. 60). Here, place is conceived as an inter-textual, or compiled, spatial form constructed through social relations with other places and objects. She sees place as porous. It involves links and interdependencies with other places, spaces and scales. It includes intimate and more distant 'power geometries' (Massey, 1993) together.

Elite schools are place-makers *par excellence*. They represent themselves to the world as places of distinction wherein affluence and influence are normalised. Landscaped gardens, extensive sports fields, architecture, busts, statues, icons, pictures of famous alumni, emblems, trophies, shields, logos are all mattering materials—in other words such materials are made to matter in particular ways. They are displayed as symbols of success, of tradition, of taste; they invite aspiration and emulation. But further, these schools represent themselves-to-themselves as places of 'community', of the school 'family', and of attachment and belonging in and over time. Those who populate them have long been encouraged to adopt such a humanistic, romanticised and 'apolitical' place-based perspective about their schools. And they have also been encouraged to adopt a very specific 'progressive sense of place' (Massey, 1993) through which they recognise that their schools, and thus they themselves, are connected to the other places and people who belong, or have belonged, to elite school systems and networks located nearby or in other national and global spaces. While these schools are centrally concerned with their own 'power geometries' (Massey, 1993) and the spatial extension of affluence and influence, theirs is not a critical sense of place as is Massey's. A critical sense of place and elite schools invites the sorts of analyses in the Fahey et al. (2015) collection which is evocatively called *In the Realm of the Senses: Social Aesthetics and the Sensory Dynamics of Privilege*. The chapters, vignettes, and photographic essays therein study privilege through the senses pointing to the materiality of the "sensory structures" which bear the stamp of privilege. A critical analysis of elite schools as places also requires a relational analysis of place and of educational inequality. Take this example from a discussion of elite schools in Geelong, Victoria, Australia.

> The educational and social segregation involved in their [the students'] school-based social cocooning mean that such students have little lived sense of life in wider Australia, let alone life on the bottom rungs. Such

8 Aaron Koh and Jane Kenway

schools can be thought of as 'purified spaces ... cleansed of variety and difference ... tame, sanitized'. Missing from such schools is 'The plurality and multi-vocality of the life setting' (Bauman, 2000, p. 99). This is a problem because as adults, they [the students] will exert a disproportionate influence over the lives of people right across the social spectrum.

(Kenway, 2013)

Our notion of multiple geographies of privilege helps to capture the intersectional power dynamics of scale, space and place as they relate to elite schools. Plainly then this notion does not simply refer to the fact that many countries are represented in this collection, namely, Australia (Chapters 1, 2 and 5), China (Chapter 3), Singapore (Chapter 4), UK (Chapter 6), India (Chapter 7), France (Chapters 8 and 11), Portugal (Chapter 9), Switzerland (Chapter 10), and Argentina (Chapters 12 and 13). This is not to say that national perspectives are unimportant; understanding national education systems as a whole, historically and currently, is crucial to an appreciation of how educational and class privilege are claimed systemically. Further, taking a national perspective potentially invites comparative analysis in relation to different national systems and historical periods and also explorations of the conceptual resources that best enable such comparative analysis. It potentially leads to differentiated understandings and multi-national perspectives: potentially, but not necessarily.

Such studies also run the risk of 'methodological nationalism'. This constructs the socio-political in national or international terms and, in turn, draws attention away from trans-nationalism, which Ong defines as "the condition of cultural interconnectedness and mobility across space—which has been intensified under late capitalism" (Ong, 1999, p. 4). This points to the important relationships between scales, spaces, places and '*scapes*'. Appadurai's (1996) notion of the disjunctive scapes of cultural globalisation is helpful here. These are ethno-scapes, media-scapes, ideo-scapes, techno-scapes, and finance-scapes and involve flows of people, ideas and ideologies, images, and imaginations and the technologies and money that facilitate and also drive them. Further, Kenway and Fahey (2010) have developed the concept *global emo-scapes* to attend to the attendant flows of emotions. As they are increasingly caught up in the global elite school market and as they also increasingly seek to globalise their practices all such scapes become ever more important to elite schools (Kenway & Fahey, 2014: Kenway, Fahey & Koh, 2013).

The chapters in this collection are *specifically not* intended as case studies of particular countries although, as individual chapters, some do not entirely escape possible charges of 'methodological nationalism' (Amelina et al., 2012). However, the collection as a whole, with its notion of multiple geographies of privilege as the overriding framework, hopefully works against such possible readings. It speaks to the fact that these different countries are plugged into the "uneven spatio-temporal development of capitalism" (Harvey, 2006, p. 115). Certainly, one way in which

Introduction **9**

such unevenness is expressed is *nationally* according to capitalism's particular connections to the geopolitics of such things as colonialism, post- and neo-colonialism, as well as contemporary neoliberalism. Another way in which such unevenness is expressed is *regionally*. Hence we have deliberately included a spread of chapters from, what are often called, the 'global North and South'—or the minority ('first') world and the majority ('third') world. These are clearly problematic terms but no less problematic than the others, which they often stand in for: 'third and first world', 'West and East', 'developed', 'developing' and 'underdeveloped', and so on. That said, despite the scalar span included here, the collection does not try, or claim, to be representative or to offer a complete global coverage.

Our overall contention is that it matters *where and when* 'privilege' is played out. Appadurai (2013) asserts that 'histories make geographies' but geographies also make histories. The specific geo-politico history and cultural politics at work in the national and regional space shape how privilege is articulated to elite schools as places. Collectively the chapters show that privilege is constituted in patterned but also diverse ways in such different spaces. It is relational and relative. So too are elite schools which, while having some shared generic characteristics, also differ. No blanket description is adequate. Overall, then, attention to multiple geographies requires what Hall calls a "conjunctural analysis" (Hall, 2010). This involves an analysis of a period during which "the different social, political, economic and ideological contradictions that are at work in [a] society [that] come together to give it a specific and distinctive shape" (Hall, 2010, p. 1). Such an analysis is evident in the chapters gathered here. They show the specificities of the scalar, spatial and place-based dynamics and politics of privilege and its close companion—elite schooling.

As with all publications, this book is implicated in power/knowledge geographies. Space and flow are highly relevant to elite education studies *per se*. Global power/knowledge geographies are central to the field's configuration. Let us count the ways. First, most of the educational research, published in the English language, has been about schools in England, the USA, Canada and Australia, although over recent times, and at long last, this is changing as studies from a diverse range of countries are now included in various English language edited collections (Gunter, Apple & Hall, 2016; Maxwell & Aggleton, 2016; Ball, van Zanten & Darchy-Koechlin, 2015; Kenway & McCarthy, 2014; Kenway & Koh, 2015; Howard & Kenway, 2015). Even so, the Anglophone literature is restricted in its overall purchase without access to that published in languages other than English. Second, scholars from non-English speaking countries often find that in order to gain a wider readership it helps if they publish in English language outlets. But this is very demanding and requires considerable conceptual and linguistic translation not to mention peer reviewer empathy as well as editorial support. These are not always forthcoming.

Thirdly, as Raewyn Connell has demonstrated in *Southern Theory* (2007), the flow of social science knowledge is often from the global North to the global

South, not the reverse, with those in the global South tending to feel the need to adopt or adapt European or North American theory and those in the global North largely disregarding studies and theories from the global South. This pattern is evident in studies of elite schools. Dialogue between studies from diverse locations, especially between studies in the global South, is occasional and gestural and comparative studies, in the best sense of the term (Dale & Robertson, 2009), are rare. Fourth, questions arise as to whether the commonly deployed conceptual resources from the USA or Europe adequately capture the nature of privilege and elite educational institutions in other locations around the world (Kenway & Koh, 2013). For example, the caste system in India is central to analyses of power and privilege there (Ambedkar, 2014/1936) and cannot be subsumed under class analysis, although there is a relationship between the two particularly as India becomes ever more caught up in global capitalism.

This asymmetrical geo-politics of knowledge production have led Connell to argue for the "global communication of knowledge" (Connell, 2007, p. xiii). This invites other forms of cross-fertilisation, in short, dialogues that transcend such power/knowledge geographies. A challenge for the field of elite education studies, as a whole, is to respond to Connell's invitation. Like other collections that seek to be more globally inclusive, this collection only goes some small way to addressing the issues involved. But, thinking through the lens of "multiple geographies" of privilege helps to achieve two things. It invites readers not to think about each chapter solely through the prism of the nation state from, or in relation to, which it is written. Secondly, the collection as whole reveals that while there are commonalities, there isn't a unitary narrative to the (re)production and expression of privilege and its politics. It shows that many modalities and mobilities are involved, grounded in and by the rich texture of geo-specific politico-histories. A feature of the 'new sociology of elite education' is its attention to the intersections of class/race/gender and, to a lesser extent, ethnicity and sexuality in, and in relation to, elite educational institutions. But this does not go far enough. We need to properly historicise and spatialise such inter-sectionality. In turn, this suggests that comparative analysis need not be restricted to the national scale and could, for instance, involve comparisons between different expressions of elite inter-sectionality in diverse locations.

Geographical Inter-Sectionalities, Multiplicities, and Mobilities

We now turn to the chapters and offer a taste of the manner in which each speaks to the matters we have outlined thus far.

'Western' theory is tested by Wee Loon Yeo in Chapter 1. He studied a group of 'Asian' boarders at St Andrew's School—an elite school located in Australia. This school understood itself in the tradition of the English/Australian 'public school'. Although the boarders were from diverse countries in Asia, they were also all Chinese. These boarders were Yeo's test-bed for theorising masculinity.

Yeo argues that in response to the 'hegemonic masculinity' observed in St Andrew's school culture, the Asian boarders enacted, and indeed manufactured, distinctive modes of Asian masculinity. To help him think this through, he introduces the theory of '*wen–wu*' Chinese masculinity to show how the Asian boarders negotiated, contested and constructed alternative masculinities. The fact that this Australian school culture actually produced a distinctive 'Asian' subjectivity complicates the links often made between place, identity and masculinity. Yeo's chapter draws attention to the ways that embedded geographical masculine privilege was disrupted by the alternative space-based identities that the boarders mobilised in order to re-articulate 'privilege' as an expression of elite Chinese masculinities.

The links that are often made between cultural cosmopolitanism and the global mobility of school students are problematised in Chapter 2 by Yujia Wang. She considers Chinese international students studying in an elite school in Australia. The theme of "well-roundedness" is the fulcrum of her analysis. As opposed to the generalising claim that students on-the-move, internationally, invariably develop cosmopolitan sensibilities, she argues for a more geographically grounded understanding of identities on the move in the transnational space of the global elite school market. The chapter shows how "Chinese-ness", as an identity marker, was disrupted in the contact zone of this very emplaced Australian school. In so doing she considers the cultural logics, mediations, and power dualities involved in these Chinese students' identity making processes. These involve, she argues, quite specific configurations of various geographical forces. And it is such configurations that make the actualisation of cosmopolitanism either possible or unlikely.

"Skyboxification" is a core concept mobilised by Moosung Lee, Ewan Wright, and Allan Walker in Chapter 3. They mobilise this metaphor to describe the increasing stratification of the Chinese schooling sector along with the growing class polarisation of Chinese society. This includes the tendency of elites to distance themselves from their host nation. They argue that the growing popularity of the International Baccalaureate Diploma Programme (IBDP) in international schools is linked to the politics of privilege in China. The provision of IBDP in schools is seen to deepen the class divide in part because of the homogenous profile and social isolation of students inside these schools. This, they claim, limits the cultivation of "open mindedness" and "intercultural understanding" that the IBDP learner profile endeavours to promote. They also suggest that, for parents and students in the Asian region, academic success has considerable priority over the IBDP learning profile that encourages students to balance their studies with Creativity, Action, Service (CAS) courses. As such they question whether the take-up of IBDP as the pinnacle of globally mobile curriculum is even appropriate for Asian students and parents.

Ace Institution in Singapore is an IBDP school and an elite government school with a long history associated with the Methodist church. In Chapter 4, Chin Ee

Loh explains that Ace created history in Singapore's education system by abandoning the GCE A level curriculum, which has been a cornerstone in the national education system, to take up the IBDP. But does Aces Institution prepare its students to be global citizens or do the strongly articulated national education imperatives of Singapore get in the way? Loh explores the tensions between the global IB curriculum and the Singaporean priority for nation building. She deploys Bourdieu's signature concept "habitus" to examine how students from Ace Institution are shaped by the school's institutional habitus to become global citizens. Yet, she shows how irreconcilable tensions interfere as "class, schooling, global and local imaginations intersect with institutional and individual habitus".

The relationship between joy and privilege in the virtual spaces of elite school websites and promotional materials is the focus of Christopher Drew, Kristina Gottschall, Natasha Wardman, and Sue Saltmarsh in Chapter 5. They examine such representations through discourse and semiotic analysis and non-representation theory and draw primarily from Sara Ahmed's theory of happiness. Happiness in these virtual spaces is represented as an index of, and as belonging to, a specific class, gender, and subjectivity. Drew et al. argue that the preferred reading to these virtual texts is that the joy of schooling is a privileged and exclusive enterprise not meant for all. And further the implication is that in all the nooks and crannies of the school, and at all times, everyone is entitled to, and has a responsibility to, be happy. This speaks both to the romanticisation of elite schools as places and to the significance of emo-scapes in the virtual elite school market. But it also leads to questions about the other emotional geographies of education (Kenway & Youdell, 2011) and how elite schools monopolise cheerfulness.

School websites are also the focus of Chapter 6 where Shane Watters analyses 28 old boys' networks in the UK. He uses close content analysis and Bourdieu's social capital theory to unearth and explain the extent and nature of the influence of these networks. Overall he points to the resources, connections and power that reside within them. More specifically, his study illustrates that "the majority of schools sampled showed signs of structuring their networks towards particular employment destinations". He also shows that these networks are not restricted to the UK but are transnational, denoting the movement of transnational elites. This virtual space of the network both represents and helps to mobilise valuable relationships between the powerful *in situ*. Socialising and networking help those in the network to accrue capitals that are recognised and can be translated into favoured career prospects and/or positions in high places.

Radha Iyer's Foucauldian discourse analysis, in Chapter 7, of 21 elite school websites in India offers a sense of the spatialisation of privilege in this part of the world in very different types of schools. Iyer points out that a distinctive feature of elite schools in India is that their 'eliteness' and 'privilege' are symbiotically linked to the history of colonialism. This history left a legacy that highly prized Western education and knowledge. These sediments of colonialism help to constitute the identity of current elite schools in India and can be found in the different types of discourses mobilised by the schools in virtual space. Additionally, though, Iyer draws on the fivefold category system developed by Rubén Gaztambide-Fernández to define an elite school and transfers his categories to these Indian schools to assess their relevance across space. Despite the spatial and scalar differences she finds that all his elements are represented in the 21 elite school websites that she analysed. Additionally and importantly, though, these are variously combined with discourses of the global and of postcolonial nationalism.

Bourdieu's theory of the inheritance of cultural capital as a main resource for the reproduction of educational and social advantage is challenged by Hugues Draelants in Chapter 8. Writing also from France, but over 30 years after Bourdieu's (1986) key work on "capitals", he proposes the spatial concept "insiders" as opposed to "inheritors" as more relevant. His premise is that cultural capital shifts with time. He supports this argument by focusing on school choice in France as an example of a new form of cultural capital that requires parents to have *insider* knowledge about possible educational pathways for their children. He argues that it is this specific knowledge that allows them to skilfully navigate education systems and to propitiously channel their various resources to their greatest advantage. "Privilege" is therefore not about 'inheriting' cultural capital because what is inherited may not be recognised as a useful capital. Rather, becoming an "insider" allows one to have access to knowledge resources and networks that can readily be converted in space/time.

When and how geographies of educational privilege have emerged in Portugal is explored by Eunice Macedo and Helena Araújo in Chapter 9. They explain that Portugal's national education system is currently organised around a centralised educational regime and that it is tainted by the global forces of neoliberalism, marketisation, and commodification. In this context the demand for elite private education has soared and the politics associated with class, elitism, hierarchies and deepening inequalities have intensified. Their study of an elite school in Portugal brings to light the life-style limits placed on students due to the hyper-competitive politics of performativity, individualism, consumerism, as well as the gender constraints that arise and constrain the lives of privileged girls and boys. These are the blights of privilege. They focus on such forms of subjugation amongst the well off themselves but also identify students' highly judgemental views of those outside their social and educational citadel.

Certain elite boarding schools in Switzerland are quite distinctive in that they are owned and run by families and are passed down from one generation to another as Caroline Bertron explains in Chapter 10. While the three schools she studied are essentially prestigious family enterprises, they resist being called a "business" or "elite". Instead, they turn to national and historical legacies to construct their own identity and brand. Bertron mobilises Bourdieu to show how elite boarding schools in Switzerland actively brand themselves with various forms of symbolic capital. For example, as a strategy of mobilising the "[local/

national] symbolic capital of recognition", these expensive boarding schools capitalise on the grandeur and the picturesque landscapes of the Swiss Alps. They market place as a way of marketing themselves. The curriculum also strongly emphasised local Swiss "pedagogues". This is despite their claim to embrace globalisation and internationalisation. Indeed, while these elite Swiss boarding schools sell and brand themselves as schools with opportunities for cosmopolitan learning, Bertron argues that "the symbolic economy of territorial identification" is accorded priority.

The travel of the affluent is the topic examined by Bertrand Réau in Chapter 11. He presents a historical engagement with different types of educational travel in Europe; the *peregrinatio academica*, the Grand Tour, and the ERASMUS programme via the elite French Sciences Po. He shows how such travels relate to the accumulation of social capital and thus class/elite formation. Réau's study shows that much like the Grand Tour, which was undertaken by privileged classes, the travel associated with the ERASMUS programme is undertaken by middle- and upper-middle-class young people who are already well travelled. Social and class backgrounds are central, he argues, to explaining what students gain from joining study abroad programmes. Such travel is a form of capital accumulation intended to facilitate yet more capital accumulation on the global stage.

The relationship between elite schooling, school choice and educational advantage is the theme explored in Sandra Ziegler's Chapter 12. She studied three elite schools concentrated in the prosperous urban spaces of the city of Buenos Aires in Argentina and illustrates how 'choice' is manifest in this locale. Here affluent parents actively seek out suitable elite schools that will ensure that their children will mix with those of similar class background—everyday social and spatial segregation is regarded as rational and as nothing out of the ordinary. Admission to these schools, she points out, does not include academic grades or so called merit. Instead, the deciding factors include the family's background including job title, schools attended, the surnames of families, and interviews with adults. Such advantage secures further advantage without even the veneer of 'merit' which is often a filter used, along with fees, by other elite schools (Koh, 2014).

Through the concept "economy of eliteness", Howard Prosser, in Chapter 13, advances how 'privilege' is understood. He developed this term from a historical and ethnographic study of an elite high fee school in changing Argentina. Conceptually, an "economy of eliteness" exposes the market logic that operates in this economy. "Elite", as a label, has enormous exchange value within the variously scaled but linked up economy of elite schools. Parents and students buy an elite education because 'status' and 'prestige' are the symbolic capitals associated with it. Importantly, parents have come to believe that this symbolic capital also has exchange value in the market place of work; an investment in elite education promises the economic return of a high paying/high status career. His concept draws attention to the economic relations that exist outside elite schools; to those workplaces where the powerful make the money that enables them to purchase elite education. It also calls attention to the finance-scapes involved in the buying and selling of elite education. Prosser insists that such exchange value defines the very essence of privilege, how it is acquired and by whom, and how class gets reproduced.

Together the chapters gathered here indicate the multiple ways in which geography matters in the constitution of privilege though education. They show that educational privilege is enmeshed in power dynamics on various scales and in different but intersecting spaces and places. These intercept global flows and forces in specific ways, which have their own peculiar densities. As such they point to the relativity and relational geographical dynamics of privilege.

References

Ambedkar, B. R. (2014/1936). *Annihilation of caste*. London and New York: Verso.
Amelina, A., Nergiz, D., Faist, T., & Schiller, N. (2012). *Beyond methodological nationalism: Research methodologies for cross-border studies*. New York: Routledge.
Appadurai, A. (1996). *Modernity at large: Cultural dimensions of globalization*. Minneapolis: University of Minnesota Press.
Appadurai, A. (2013). *The future as cultural fact: Essays on the global condition*. London: Verso.
Ball, S. (2015). Elites, education and identity: An emerging research agenda. In S. J. Ball, A. van Zanten & B. Darchy-Koechlin (Eds.), *World yearbook of education 2015: Elites, privilege and excellence: The national and global redefinition of educational advantage* (pp. 233–240). London: Routledge.
Ball, S. J., van Zanten, A. & Darchy-Koechlin, B. (Eds.) (2015). *World yearbook of education 2015: Elites, privilege and excellence: The national and global redefinition of advantage*. London: Routledge.
Bauman, Z. (2000). *Liquid modernity*. Cambridge: Polity Press.
Bourdieu, P. (1986). The forms of capital. In J. G. Richardson (Ed.), *Handbook for theory and research for the sociology of education* (pp. 241–258). New York: Greenwood.
Brooks, R. M., & Waters, J. L. (2015). The hidden internationalisation of elite English schools. *Sociology*, 49, 212–228.
Brown, W. (2014). *Walled states, waning sovereignty*. New York: Zone Books.
Coleman, S., & von Hellermann, P. (2011). Introduction: Queries, collaborations, calibrations. In S. Coleman & P. von Hellermann (Eds.), *Multi-sited ethnography: Problems and possibilities in the translocation of research methods* (pp. 1–15). New York: Routledge.
Comaroff, J., & Comaroff, J. (2007). *Ethnography on an awkward scale: On qualitative method in the social sciences*. Boulder: Paradigm Publishers.
Connell, R. (2007). *Southern theory*. Malden, MA: Polity Press.
Dale, R., & Robertson, S. (2009). Beyond methodological 'ISMS' in Comparative Education in an era of globalisation. In R. Cowen & A. M. Kazamias (Eds.), *International handbook of comparative education: Part One* (pp. 1113–1129). London and Wisconsin: Springer Science + Business Media.

Daloz, J.-O. (2010). *The sociology of elite distinction: From theoretical to comparative perspectives.* London: Palgrave Macmillan.

Fahey, J., Prosser, H., & Shaw, M. (Eds.) (2015). *In the realm of the senses: Social aesthetics and the sensory dynamics of privilege.* Singapore: Springer.

Gunter, H., Apple, M., & Hall, D. (Eds.) (2016). *Elite schools and education policy.* New York: Routledge.

Hall, S. (1997). The work of representation. In S. Hall (Ed.), *Representation: Cultural representations and signifying practices* (pp. 1–13). London: Sage.

Hall, S. (2010). In conversation with Doreen Massey: Interpreting the crisis. *Strategic Practice.* Retrieved August 2015 from http://www.strategicpractice.org/commentary/hall-and-massey-interpreting-crisis

Harvey, D. (2006). *Spaces of global capitalism: Towards a theory of uneven geographical development.* London: Verso.

Harvey, D. (2014). *Seventeen contradictions and the end of capitalism.* London: Profile Books.

Hay, I. (2013). Establishing geographies of the super-rich: Axes for analysis of abundance. In I. Hay (Ed.), *Geographies of the super-rich* (pp. 1–25). Cheltenham, UK: Edward Elgar.

Howard, A., & Kenway, J. (2015). Canvassing conversations: Obstinate issues in studies of elites and elite education. *International Journal of Qualitative Studies in Education*, 28(9), 1005–1032.

Howard, A., Polimeno, A., & Wheeler, B. (2014). *Negotiating privilege and identity in educational contexts.* New York: Routledge.

Kenway, J. (2013). Challenging inequality in Australian schools: Gonski and beyond, *Discourse: Studies in the Cultural Politics of Education*, DOI:10.1080/01596306.2013.770254. Available at: http://dx.doi.org/10.1080/01596306.2013.770254

Kenway, J., & Fahey, J. (2010). Is greed still good? Was it ever? Exploring the emoscapes of the global financial crisis. *Journal of Education Policy*, 25(6), 717–727.

Kenway, J., & Fahey, J. (2014). Staying ahead of the game: The globalising practices of elite schools. *Globalisation, Societies and Education*, 12(2), 177–195.

Kenway, J., Fahey, J., & Koh, A. (2013). The libidinal economy of the globalising elite school market. In C. Maxwell & P. Aggleton (Eds.), *Privilege, agency and affect: Understanding the production and effects of action* (pp. 1–12). London: Palgrave/Macmillan.

Kenway, J., & Koh, A. (2013). The elite school as a 'cognitive machine' and 'social paradise'?: Developing transnational capitals for the national 'field of power'. *Journal of Sociology*, 49(2–3), 272–290.

Kenway, J., & Koh, A. (Eds.) (2015). Special Issue: New sociologies of elite schooling: Theoretical, methodological and empirical explorations. *British Journal of Sociology of Education*, 36(1), 1–192.

Kenway, J., & McCarthy, C. (Eds.) (2014). Special Issue: Elite schools in globalising circumstances: New conceptual directions and connections. *Globalisation, Societies and Education*, 12(2), 165–320.

Kenway, J., & Youdell, D. (2011). Emotional geographies of education. *Emotion, Space and Society* (Special issue), 4(3), 131–199.

Koh, A. (2014). Doing class analysis in Singapore's elite education: Unravelling the smokescreen of 'meritocratic talk'. *Globalisation, Societies and Education*, 12(2), 196–210.

Lefebvre, H. (1991 [1974]). *The production of space* (translated by Donald Nicholson-Smith). Oxford: Blackwell Publishing.

Massey, D. (1993). 'Power-geometry' and a progressive sense of place. In J. Bird, B. Curtis, G. Robertson & L. Tricker, L. (Eds.), *Mapping the futures: Local culture, global change* (pp. 59–69). London: Routledge.

Maxwell, C. (2015). Elites: Some questions for a new research agenda. In A. van Zanten, S. J. Ball & B. Darchy-Koechlin (Eds.), *World yearbook of education 2015: Elites, privilege and excellence: The national and global redefinition of educational advantage* (pp. 15–28). London: Routledge.

Maxwell, C., & Aggleton, P. (2013). Introduction: Privilege, agency and action—Understanding the production and effects of action. In *Privilege, agency and affect—Understanding the production and effects of action* (pp. 1–12). London: Palgrave Macmillan.

Maxwell, C., & Aggleton, P. (Eds.) (2015). *Private and elite education: Global debates.* London: Routledge.

May, J., & Thrift, N. (Eds.) (2001). Introduction. In *Timespace: Geographies of temporality.* London: Routledge.

Murray, W. E. (2006). *Geographies of globalization.* London: Routledge.

OECD. (2014). All on board: Making inclusive growth happen. Available at http://www.oecd.org/inclusive-growth/All-on-Board-Making-Inclusive-Growth-Happen.pdf#page=1&zoom=auto,-100,615

Ong, A. (1999). *Flexible citizenship: The cultural logics of transnationality.* Durham: Duke University Press.

Pow, C.-P. (2013). 'The world needs a second Switzerland': Onshoring Singapore as the liveable city for the super-rich. In I. Hay (Ed.), *Geographies of the super-rich* (pp. 61–76). Cheltenham, UK: Edward Elgar.

Prosser, H., & Kenway, J. (2015). Distinguished spaces: Elite schools as cartographers of privilege. In J. Fahey, H. Prosser & M. Shaw (Eds.), *Social aesthetics of elite schools: The sensory dynamics of privilege* (pp. 31–57). Singapore: Springer.

Rizvi, F. (2015). The discourse of 'Asia Rising' in an elite Indian school. In S. J. Ball, A., van Zanten & B. Darchy-Koechlin and (Eds.) *World yearbook of education 2015: Elites, privilege and excellence: The national and global redefinition of educational advantage* (pp. 126–140). London and New York: Routledge.

Shaw, M. (2014). The Cyprus game: Crossing the boundaries in a divided island. *Globalisation, Societies and Education,* 12(2), 262–274.

Teng, A. (2015) Raffles Institution now a 'middle-class' school, says principal. Retrieved August2015fromhttp://www.straitstimes.com/singapore/education/raffles-institution-now-a-middle-class-school-says-principal

Thrift, N. (2003). Space: The fundamental stuff of geography. In S. Holloway, S. Rice & G. Valentine (Eds.), *Key concepts in Geography* (pp. 95–108). London: Sage.

Treanor, J. (2014, October 14). Richest 1% of people own nearly half of global wealth, says report. *Guardian.* Retrieved from http://www.theguardian.com/business/2014/oct/14/richest-1percent-half-global-wealth-credit-suisse-report

Weis, L., Cipollone, K., & Jenkins, H. (2014). *Class warfare: Class, race, and college admissions in top-tier secondary schools.* Chicago and London: The University of Chicago Press.

1

BECOMING THE MAN

Redefining Asian Masculinity in an Elite Boarding School

Wee Loon Yeo

"I never saw our school as an elite school or one of those 'preppy' schools. To me, it is a home where I lived and hung out with my friends during those years. It never once crossed my mind that the school is considered elite. In fact, I only realised how much the school shaped me until much later on," Zach revealed during a conversation we had two years ago. Our paths first crossed when he was a final year student at St Andrew's School, an elite private boys' boarding school, where I conducted fieldwork as part of my Doctoral dissertation in 2007. Six years on, Zach had since graduated from university and just started working in the family business when we caught up again.

Zach's oblivion on his alma mater being considered elite is not entirely surprising given the myriad definitions and confusing representations (Walford, 1991). While elite boarding schools have been discussed in various works and defined in disparate ways, Gaztambide-Fernández (2009a) suggests five constitutive traits that make an elite boarding school: They must be typologically, scholastically, historically, demographically, and geographically elite. When seen in light of these traits, St Andrew's School, a private boarding school for boys in Perth, Western Australia, should be regarded as elite. In the public eye, the school was renowned for not only being consistently among the top performing schools in the state tertiary entrance exams, their students also excelled in non-academic fields such as sport and debating. Geographically, the school has been located along the river in a premium residential suburb in Perth since it was founded in the early 1900s. These characteristics, Gaztambide-Fernández (2009b) would argue, contribute to the process by which students "construct elite identification and internalise their privilege" (p. 28). Hence, elite boarding school, with its all-inclusive routine and holistic regulation of the lives of its occupants, acts as a social system for the acceptance of new cultural values. Living and participating in activities within such close proximity of each other helped to construct and reinforce traits shared by most members of the group. These qualities could be observed through embodied practices, vital for creating and maintaining a sense of being in the presence of other groups in the school community (Koh & Kenway, 2012). This approach is apparent in Allan and Charles' (2014) study of feminine identity in a private girls' school. They explored how 'classed feminism', an intrinsic part of the students' identity, was produced and articulated against the backdrop of a long-established and privileged context. This study, like others who examined gender identities, put forward schools as key social sites where these contestations and representations could be explored. From Willis' (1977) study on the cultures and sub-cultures of working class 'lads' to Renolds' (2004) account of boys who shaped their masculinities against the ideal categories perpetuated by the school, these studies often emphasised the plurality and hierarchical nature of masculinities (Connell, 1989). Such studies traced the collective and dynamic character of masculinity through immersive research methods. Similarly, this chapter situates the discussion of masculine identity in the boarding school but through the perceptions and expressions of Asian boarders in St Andrew's School.

Such discussions remain relevant as schools evolve their social purposes in a rapidly globalised landscape (Kenway & Fahey, 2014). These changes can be seen as responses and adaptations to new cultural discourses which result in new definitions and expressions of gender identities. Rapid globalisation can also be witnessed in the changing dynamics within the elite boarding school community. International students are now mainstays in many Australian private schools. Recent data from Australian Education International (AEI, 2014) revealed more than 500,000 international students have studied in Australian schools since 2008.

Australian Education International or AEI uses 'international students' as an umbrella term to include all foreign-born students who are studying in Australia on a student visa regardless of their country of birth. Australian citizens and permanent residents are excluded from this group. In most cases, international students are not eligible for Australian Government subsidies and have to pay full fees. In St Andrew's School the term 'overseas students' was used broadly to refer to students who did not hold an Australian passport or did not have permanent residency. This group of students included three Anglo-Saxon boarders who were born in Europe and Canada, but the overwhelming majority were from Southeast Asia. In St Andrew's School, staff members commonly used the term 'Asian boarders' to describe students who came from Asia and had the appearance of an 'Asian'. Zach and 43 other students came under this banner when they were boarding in St Andrew's School during 2007.

Drawing on the experiences of the Asian boarders, this chapter sets out to illustrate how this group of boys shaped and positioned their masculine identity as they resided in an elite boarding school setting. The first section of the chapter explores the ideal notions of masculinity portrayed and projected by the boarding school staff members through the school's publicity materials. The remainder of the chapter examines the creative extent to which the Asian boarders managed to negotiate and maintain alternative masculinities. Central to this discussion is their privileged background and unique position as the minority. My analysis recognises that the Asian boarders were active in their resistance and conformity to hegemonic masculinity. Through these processes, they gained clearer definitions of their Asian identity.

Hegemonic Masculinity: The St Andrew's School Man

Masculinity does not exist as an ontological given, but comes into existence through deliberate construction and constant reinforcing. Hence, schools are often seen as sites where masculine identities are shaped and articulated (Connell, 1989; Gilbert & Gilbert, 1998; Greene, 2007). This section examines idealised forms of masculinity upheld by the school as embodied in the 'St Andrew's School Man' through staff members. This model is then contrasted with the Asian boarders' perception of 'Asian masculinity'.

In St Andrew's School, most of the boarding staff were males. Their ascribed role was to look after the residential welfare of all boys in their respective year level and formally supervise the boys throughout the week and on weekends, as well as help with excursions and other activities within the community. Another additional obligation that might not be entirely apparent was that they were put forward as the model of masculinity upheld by St Andrew's School.

Cookson and Persell (1985) noted that the key element their researched school sought when hiring new boarding staff was "balance", where successful applicants were required to have "academic skills, sports skills, artistic skills, as well as personal characteristics as gender, experience, morality, and last but by no means least, enthusiasm" (p. 90). While every school's conception of balance may vary, staff members were certainly promoted to the public as well-rounded individuals who not only had the academic qualifications to carry out their duties; they also possessed other qualities that epitomised the school's ideology of masculinity. Analysis of the publicity materials and school website offers insight into the definition and certain essential qualities that the St Andrew's Man must possess. Students in the boarding community therefore do not need to look far to find examples of the masculinity to which they should aspire. The staffing patterns and structure within the boarding community also served as examples of the expected conduct of the St Andrew's Man.

In a typical school publication, they began by detailing the role and responsibilities of that particular staff member:

> Matt is the Year 10 Coordinator and is the primary contact for all our Year 10 boarding parents. He is responsible for the leadership, pastoral care, spirit and morale, security, supervision and discipline of all boarders, in such a way as to promote their growth and well-being. He is charged with

the task of ensuring that the residential experience of a St Andrew's School boarder is an engaging and rewarding one. The aim is to empower boarders to take charge of their own lives by developing them to be confident and capable young men in an atmosphere of warmth, support and care.

One could comment that most aspects of the job were difficult to measure but what these terms mapped out was the social learning and atmosphere the boarding community could provide for the boarders. By reiterating lofty qualities such as 'leadership', 'spirit and morale', and 'empowering', the school presented what Connell (1990) calls an 'ideological framework' which embodies key traits that all conceptions need to align with.

The description would go on to present the credentials of the staff member, beginning with their educational background, followed by their relevant experiences as a teacher:

> Matt graduated from the University of Queensland with a Bachelor's degree in Arts with Honours. After relocating to Perth, he attained a Graduate Diploma in Education from the University of Western Australia.
> At the start of his teaching career, Matt spent nine years working at agricultural schools around Western Australia as a teacher of Social Science and English, he taught at Pasture School in rural Kalgoorlie. Matt joined the St Andrew's School in 1995 as a teacher of English and Social Science. Last year, he joined the boarding house as a Year Coordinator.

From this description, we can infer that the first element crucial in the St Andrew's School concept of masculinity was that a man should possess academic ability and intellect. This emphasis was stated as one of the school's aims "to enable boys to grow in knowledge, skills and understanding". The boys were inculcated in the values of working hard to develop and refine their intellectual ability. They must also value and take responsibility for their educational endeavours.

Having established intellectual ability as the most important quality, the introduction went on to highlight other qualities the institution perceived as required from young men of the school:

> An accomplished hockey player, Matt competed in State level competitions. In the co-curricular domain, Matt has coached hockey and tennis. He is currently the Teacher in Charge of Hockey.

In another example, talent of a different nature is described:

> Having a keen interest in music, Stephen teaches piano lessons on the weekends, plays in a jazz ensemble once a week and plays the piano recreationally.

The above description resonates with Cookson and Persell's (1985) observation that the ideal staff member and student should have balance. Therefore, by including the other interests or as the school termed it, "special talents" of the staff members, the school upheld the ideal of a balanced man with multiple skills, particularly in sports or music. The school positively encouraged these interactions and hoped that through them a set of practices that construct models, ideas, activities and relations to promote particular forms of masculinity could be imparted (Gilbert & Gilbert, 1998, p. 114). Through increased contact with staff members, the boarders could perceive the staff members as not only teachers but as individuals endowed with additional abilities. It was common to see staff members join the boarders in an impromptu game of soccer or basketball after school. Qualified staff members willingly offered pointers to the boarders on how to improve aspects of their game. Interactions such as these added to the respect the boarders had for the staff members. Furthermore, boarding staff members often had to volunteer as coaches in the various sports teams. Hence, training sessions and games provided opportunities for interaction. Staff members had many opportunities to establish more personal and open relationships with boarders than the formal classroom might allow. Such shared experiences between student–teacher led to 'deep bonding' (Gaztambide-Fernández, 2009b, p. 142), consequential for reinforcing institutional ideologies.

The final aspect often featured in the introduction to the school was personal information on a staff member, especially those regarding his family:

> He lives with his wife Mary and two boys Peter and Jonathan in the boarding House, which is attached to the accommodation for the boarders.

The inclusion of this information is interesting because of the various connotations, both overt and veiled, conveyed through this short description. These discourses conveyed undertones of masculinity implying that a man's responsibilities are to his family and with that the mandate to be the provider, leader and protector. Mac an Ghaill (1996) suggests that if schools are perceived as active agents in the cultural production of masculinities, a teacher's role should be identified as being important to this notion since teachers 'actively produce a range of masculinities' and femininities that are made available for students collectively to negotiate and occupy (p. 385). In other words, the efforts of the school in presenting the boarding staff members as family men endorsed and provided a conceptual map to begin to explore the range of masculine formations required of students.

Summarising the qualities essential for the quintessential St Andrew's School man, he must be accomplished in three main areas: intellect, physical abilities, and character. All three qualities contribute to what Honey (1977) terms as "an air of self-confidence in knowing that he can accomplish greatness" (p. 43). Various investigations into traditional boarding school ideology reveal similar emphasis on individuals being "well-adjusted" and possessing "prep poise"

(Cookson and Persell, 1985, p. 54). According to research in gender studies, the variation of meanings could be attributed to how masculinity is historically and socially constructed (Atkins, 2005; Connell, 2000). These qualities are certainly embodied in the school's depiction of staff members. However, it is necessary to consider how masculine identities are constituted in relation to other identities. For instance, cultural background could ascribe different meaning to status, virtues, and expectations. Connell and Messerschmidt (2005), in their discussion of 'hegemonic masculinity', noted that masculinity could be expressed and experienced differently by diverse cultural groups. Connell (1990) defines hegemonic masculinity as 'the culturally idealised form of masculine character' which is characterised by male heterosexuality and physical, social, and economic power. Connell (1990) argues that idealised forms of masculinity become hegemonic when it is widely accepted in a context and when that acceptance reinforces the dominant gender ideology of the context. Connell (1996) asserts that although the hegemonic form of masculinity may be what many males aspire to achieve, alternate forms of masculinity could vary according to cultural setting. Hence, she suggested that two diametric processes are likely to be taking place; first, the promotion of one's own form of masculinity and secondly, the active defence against the competing form. Similarly, the Asian boarders actively reinforced notions of masculinity from their home countries as they were confronted with the different cultural forms of masculinity present in a boys' school in Australia. These previous notions of masculinity inevitably shaped the ways they related to each other and promoted their group identity.

In the next section, I discuss the Asian boarders' own constructions of masculinity and consider its implications in terms of the school's notion of the 'St Andrew's School man'.

The *Wen–Wu* of Asian Boarders' Masculinity

Masculinity is often overlooked in the context of educational research and Asian students have largely been ignored in Australian research. Luke (1997) highlights the awkward treatment of Asian masculinity in Australian research because Asians are "without any of the defining characteristics of dominant masculinity—white skin, hairy chests, beards and facial hair, big arms and big muscles" (p. 32). Kam Louie (2002), in his book *Theorising Chinese Masculinity*, suggests an alternative model for understanding Asian masculinity. He adopts the indigenous theoretical construct of a Chinese warrior and scholar (*wen–wu*) to analyse Chinese masculinity and suggests that "the dynamic tension between the poles of *wen* and *wu* permits the production of a varied number of possible expressions of male self" (p. 20). He argues that all forms of masculinity should be valued and viewed cross-culturally, stressing the need to know their "meanings, implications and significance" (p. 165). I described earlier the centrality of 'balance' and 'all-rounder' to the 'St Andrew's School Man'. In similar ways, an ideal man, as described by Kam (2002) would embody a balance of *wen* and *wu*. Similar to the commonly invoked Chinese paradigm of *yin–yang*, he puts forward that "both essences are regarded as being in constant interaction where *yin* merges with *yang* and the *yang* with the yin in an endless dynamism" (p. 9). He uses this paradigm to demonstrate how the seeming opposition between wen, the mental or civil, and *wu*, the physical or martial, should be perceived to be essential for men of substance because it invokes both the authority of the scholar and the bravery of a warrior. The following discussion seeks to juxtapose the earlier representation of the St Andrew's man with the Asian boarder's expression of masculinity. Kam's (2002) model of *wen–wu* masculinity forms the framework I have adopted to investigate the various articulations by the Asian boarders.

The Asian Warrior

The characteristics of *wu*, according to Kam Louie (2002), are easier for western culture to identify as masculine traits because of their association with behaviour such as "bravery, mateship and physical strength" (p. 23). Sport is predictably an arena where these qualities are demonstrated. Connell (1990) notes the connection of sport with "hegemonic masculinity", which is defined as "the culturally idealized form of masculine character" that emphasises "the connecting of masculinity to toughness and competitiveness" (p. 83). Building on this, sport becomes hegemonic because it inevitably presents an idealised form of masculinity that is widely accepted in a culture and that can also vary between cultures.

Sport

Like the Australian boarders, the Asian boarders enjoyed playing and following sport. Table tennis and badminton are examples of sports popular in most Southeast Asian countries, where their luminaries are widely admired in similar ways to sports stars in Australia. However, unlike the Australian emphasis on toughness and aggression, qualities such as tactical acumen, respect towards opponents, and finesse are revered in the Southeast Asian variant. Wang (2000) highlights the association between Chinese masculinity and qualities such as kinship, decorum, and humility. Yet set against the western interpretation of masculinity, those qualities would be labelled as 'effeminate and passive, and thus unmanly' (p. 117). Many of the Asian boarders were already actively involved in sport and had a keen interest in certain games. These games continued to be played with much enthusiasm in the boarding house as the school provided table tennis tables and badminton courts that were the site of many intense duels during weekends and after school lessons.

Sport, as Whannel (2002) comments, "confers and confirms masculinity" (p. 10) and various studies have drawn the connection between sports stars and the construction of gendered identities (e.g., Martino, 2000; Burgess, Edwards &

Skinner, 2003). Connell (1990) emphasised the qualities of "toughness and competitiveness" as core components of the "culturally idealized form of masculine character". The Asian boarders constructed a hybridised version of 'warrior' masculine traits by piecing together the positive aspects of Chinese sporting constructions such as humility, teamwork, and tactics with western representations that involved individual heroism, dominance, and flair. These constructions also appeared to influence their views of other forms of masculinity in the school as demonstrated by their strongly dismissive attitudes towards Australian Rules football, a game many Australian boarders play. When Aran, an avid soccer fan, was asked about his views on soccer and how it compared to Australian Rules football, he replied:

> Soccer requires so much more skill, why would they call it the beautiful game? Aussie rules is fucked up, such a stupid game ... requires no intelligence to play it but playing soccer, you need more brains and tactics.

He further elaborated that greater mental finesse was required to appreciate the skills in soccer rather than the spectacle of many more goals as in Australian Rules football. When I asked Chingy, an outspoken boarder from Malaysia, he revealed a deeper level of analysis of Australian culture through Australian Rules football:

> Aussie rules footy do not have any rules. It is just a combination of American football and Rugby. Very much like the Aussies ... they don't have their own culture but more of an amalgamation of American and English culture. Aussie rules are played by a bunch of poofters in tight shorts.

From these statements, we observe the Asian boarders' dismissive attitude towards Australian Rules football and tendency to distance themselves from the qualities the game embodied. At the same time, they projected their disdain for the sport onto Australian culture. This indicates that sport was such a significant dimension of the Asian boarders' lives that it became a constant basis for their interpretations and judgements about cultural differences in their boarding experience. Since the group was made up of boarders, all of the sport they participated in occurred within the confines of the school. Yet, masculine identity is not constructed as some abstract idea, which is then imposed on the boarders, nor is it confined to the walls of the school. Masculinity is always constructed in relationships and situations, which are brought about by other dimensions of boarding life including activities outside of boarding school.

The next section describes another unique conduit through which the Asian boarders framed and expressed their masculinity. Again, this version of masculinity involves competitiveness and embodied the spirit of *wu* masculinity. Since this activity took place during weekend city leave and beyond the limits of the school, it offers an alternative vision of how their masculinity was constructed.

26 Wee Loon Yeo

Let's Go Tuning!

During the weekends, the Asian boarders usually spent their afternoons at Timezone. Timezone is a trendy arcade gaming centre where patrons can pre-purchase credits and indulge in an eclectic range of video arcade games. The Asian boarders only played one game: 'Wangan Midnight Maximum Tune' (MT) or as they called it, 'Tuning'. The premise of this game is relatively simple: a player can pick from a selection of sports cars and then challenge other players to street races through various virtual landscapes and courses. Upon completion of the race, the player will be awarded points according to their finishing position. These points can then be accumulated and used to 'tune' their cars through a variety of upgrades such as engine modifications, 'dressing up' the car through supplementary accessories and loud paint jobs. Each player has a magnetic card that stores game data such as car modifications and game levels. The great appeal of this game to the Asian boarders was that through it they could imagine their dream cars, customise them according to their tastes, and compete with other players.

Keen to find out more about MT's appeal, I asked Tin, an avid gamer, what he enjoyed about the game:

> It is very exciting, you know, challenging other people and yourself. The graphics are very cool also. Uh. Almost like you are really driving. I've always read manga [Japanese comics], especially those car racing. Tune is good because it gives me a chance to be like one of those drivers. I love the cars. My favourite one is the 180SX [Nissan]. I put in a lot of effort to improve it. The body work also. People look at it; they know this car is me.

Reflecting on this dialogue with Tin, he maintained a strong emotional attachment to his virtual car. Driving it offered him feelings of liberation and empowerment. To Stradling (2002, citing Sheller, 2002), part of the attraction for the young in driving a car is the 'sense of displayed personal identity it conveys' (p. 11). Several studies have drawn on this very observation and conceptualised the term 'Car Culture' where a vehicle is not simply a rational economic choice but can be perceived as an extension of the self, or "a device for performing gender" (p. 17). In the case of the Asian boarders who enjoyed MT, their vehicles might have only been virtual simulations but the feelings for their cars were deeply felt. These feelings bore similarities to the young working-class men described in Walker's (1998) study on masculinity and motor vehicle use. In both instances, the focus was on performance and demonstration, crucial to a process of "making masculinity" (p. 24). As Tin revealed, the boys perceived the MT races as a channel through which to establish and compete for positions in the hierarchy of masculinities. It follows then that a priority for them was to possess a car admired by their peers, the most important elements being speed and performance. However, sheer horsepower and electrifying livery were not enough to gain victory. Tin needed to invest time and money to hone his driving skills. The money spent on this game was quite significant. Most of them revealed spending more than one to two hundred dollars on MT per month. This amount, they admitted, was hefty to spend on an arcade game but justifiable because it provided reprieve from boarding life and reinforced their collective notion as Asian men.

Linking this with Kam's (2002) discussion of masculinity and *wu* attributes, a warrior is not one who exercises military strength impulsively but one who also possesses the wisdom and restraint to know when and where to deploy it (p. 14). Walker (1998) makes a similar argument when pointing out that driving prowess combines physical, intellectual, and psychological elements. All these factors contributed to the Asian boarders' attraction to MT and, at the same time, provided an outlet for their expression of masculinity. The trait of using a car as a form of articulation was unlikely to change as they often discussed the types of car they hoped to drive once they had left school and obtained their licence.

Drawing together the contents of their discourse, it was not surprising that the cars of their yearning did not deviate from the invented forms in MT. The characteristics of their dream cars were largely similar: they were Japanese, characterised by speed, sleek bodywork and interior, flamboyant paintjobs, and embellished with light-emitting diodes. Most of the Asian boarders were able to tell me specifically the make and model of their dream cars: Nissan (180SX, Fairlady Z, Skyline GT-R), Mitsubishi (Evolution), and Subaru (WRX). After all, the aim of 'car culture' is to be noticed and to this end, their car needs to stand out from the rest (Walker, Butland & Connell, 2000). Their continual emphasis on Japanese cars is interesting not because of the vociferous manner in which they conveyed this desire but because of the attached social meaning. Japanese sports cars, to the Asian boarders, reflected their 'Asian pride'. Don articulated this clearly:

> It shows that we can be just as good if not better than the Aussies. You see those Japanese cars. They are faster, lighter, powerful and a lot more fuel efficient. Not just brute force and power but must have control and style.

Through this excerpt, we can tell that a car to the Asian boarders was not merely an inanimate object to fulfil specific functions such as transportation but a desire for difference. This desire was driven by different motivations. As Sheller (2002) expresses it, "Car consumption is never simply about rational economic choices, but is as much about aesthetic, emotional and sensory responses to driving, as well as patterns of kinship, sociability, habitation and work" (p. 2). To the Asian boarders, their MT car and conception of their dream car was a medium that reflected their perception of masculinity, their dreams for the future, an imagined lifestyle where "goods are imagined and dreamed about before they are purchased"

28 Wee Loon Yeo

(Carrabine & Longhurst, 2002, p. 187). For the Asian boarders, gaining a driver's licence and possessing a sports car was the ultimate expression of maturity and manhood. I noticed these aspirations were eventually realised after they left St Andrew's School. All of them attained a driving licence during university and most of them owned a car. This was evident on online social media where photos of their cars were shared and discussed. Earlier, I highlighted Tin's penchant for Nissan sports cars. He eventually owned a black Honda Accord with customised livery and light strips.

While immersing in car culture represented a physical emblem of maturity and embodied qualities such as control and mental ability for the Asian boarders, it could also be seen as an externalisation of their elite position. The continuity of overt cultural forms from their time at St Andrew's School was apparent and realised as they progressed in their elite futures.

The Asian Scholar

Possessing a powerful car is only half the race won. Earlier I touched on the Asian boarders' reflection that possessing control and the mental capability to win races were just as crucial as horsepower. Kam (2002) classifies these 'genteel' and 'refined' qualities as those associated with a person who is accomplished in *wen*: 'cultured men' (p. 14). These qualities bear close resemblance to St Andrew's School's conception of an educated man. Within this construction, educational accomplishments were an expression of St Andrew's School masculinity, particularly in the way they measured and vied with each other academically. Most of the Asian boarders also placed great emphasis on education. After all, they were sent to Perth to further their studies and viewed the classroom as a competitive space.

The Asian boarders knew who among them were the good students and this knowledge did not appear to hinder their friendships with each other. The Asian boarders, irrespective of school performance, lived together and went out together. During these times of communication, there was usually no mention of academic performance nor did the high achievers form a clique. This was no different during assessment periods. Often the high achievers would be at their busiest not because of their exam revisions but because the other boarders would pester them for help with work questions. Since the 'high achieving' Asian boarders often compared results, one would expect the high achievers to be vexed by these constant approaches which interrupted their own work, but that was not the case. I witnessed many occasions where the high achievers willingly obliged their peers. Ken was one such example who was known around the school as a mathematics and science 'whiz'. It was not uncommon to see some boys knocking on his room door during prep time seeking his input on studies, and Ken usually obliged. The following reflection provided a clue to his willingness to help others:

I was a mediocre student in my school in Singapore. So I know how it feels to need help but not getting it. Now that I am in the position to help others, why not? It feels good too that others know that you are good and come to you for help. I, of course, must help because we all should do well together.

Ken's thoughts were similar to Tin's revelation as to why he enjoyed playing Maximum Tune. Both disclosed that recognition from their peers made them "feel good". These positive feelings came from affirmations from members of the group as well as the recognition that they could contribute back to the group. Willis (1977) in his study of working-class youth in Hammertown, found that during their secondary school years, the lads changed their collective attitudes to class work and orientated themselves more to their peer group. This desire to fit in with the 'lads' undermined any conspicuous efforts of working hard in school. As Gilbert and Gilbert (1998) put it, there is a "potential stigma associated with doing too well at school" (p. 140). Hence, even the more competent boys in Willis' study were swayed into disruptive behaviour to demonstrate their sense of solidarity with the group.

For Ken and the Asian boarders, the opposite was observed as the more able students were willing to help their weaker peers. Ken's desire to help his peers was driven by similar motivations to the Hammertown lads but instead of using disruptive behaviour to fit in as a collective, he desired his peers to work hard as a collective to gain pride for the Asian boarders. This strong belief in collective learning was also observed in Kuriloff and Reichert's (2003) study on elite schools. By adopting this stance, they underplayed the failings of the low achievers, leading to greater group homogeneity. While being a scholar is an important aspect of *wen* masculinity, for the Asian boarders, it was not competition or domination but group camaraderie that took precedence. A central marker of masculinity for the Asian boarders was the potential benefits that excelling as a group could bring. After all, they were in the school with the aim of excelling in their studies, progressing to university and ultimately, seeking a road to a lucrative career path.

This fits with another articulation of *wen* masculinity: through successfully negotiating the examination system, the scholar gains a foothold for realising high-ranking posts which in turn translates to wealth, power, and status (Kam, 2002, p. 60), bringing to mind the school's construction of a man's responsibility as a provider. Indeed, an important marker of masculinity for the Asian boarders was a lucrative career path, which strongly implies their ability to be the sole provider for and protector of their family. Most of them were ambivalent about their future spouses working and indicated that women should care for the family and look after household tasks. The following statement by Ivan illustrated this attitude.

I want to have a good job that pays well. It's good because I can enjoy life like eating out and going out to buy, like, stuff. Plus being the guy, I should earn more than my gf [girlfriend] or future wife.

While this respondent first referred to the more immediate aspirations of living life in the fast lane, his latter views were defined in terms of "the logic of a patriarchal gender system" (Connell & Messerschmidt, 2005, p. 832). Their views on gender roles were clearly influenced by the patterns of practice they had observed in their own households. Most families in the Asian boarders' home countries consisted of mothers who were full-time homemakers and fathers who pursued profitable careers. The importance of hard work was therefore emphasised as central to their perceptions of themselves as successful males who would become providers, protectors and guardians. The progression implied by most of the Asian boarders was that good grades in education could lead to a high paying job. Embarking on a lucrative career path would facilitate the acquisition of wealth essential for being a good provider—a marker of elite Asian masculinity.

Conclusion

This chapter opened with Zach's reflection that his years spent in St Andrew's School profoundly shaped his life and gave him clearer definition of his identity. When I met Zach last year, he had recently become engaged to a lady he met while at university; he was being groomed to helm the family business, still played badminton regularly, and was driving a sports coupe. He could, in many ways, embody the qualities of the St Andrew's School Man. The St Andrew's School Man was put forward as an ideal type in the school's attempt to produce and transmit dominant notions of masculinity. Juxtaposing this portrayal with the Asian boarders' conception, the chapter drew parallels between the two and at the same time highlighted variations in what they considered masculine. To this end, it discussed the discourses of masculinity within this small group of Asian boarders.

While being an 'all rounder' who is accomplished in both intellect and physical pursuits is also esteemed in the context of Asian *wen–wu* masculinity, the Asian boarders also found unique channels of expression. Although it is not possible to generalise from the themes that have emerged, my findings suggest that it was the interaction between the boys' notions of masculinity from their home culture and the school construction that shaped their group identity.

References

Allan, A., & Charles, C. (2014). Cosmo girls: Configuration of class and femininity in elite educational settings. *British Journal of Sociology of Education*, 35(3), 333–352.

Atkins, G. L. (2005). My Man Fridae: Re-producing Asian masculinity. *Seattle Journal of Social Justice*, 4, 67–100.

Australian Education International (AEI). (2014, June 13). *About AEI.* Retrieved 5 December 2014 from https://internationaleducation.gov.au/about-aei/pages/default.aspx

Burgess, I., Edwards, A., & Skinner, J. (2003). Football culture in an Australian school setting: The construction of masculine identity. *Sport, Education and Society*, 8, 199–212.

Carrabine, E., & Longhurst, B. (2002). Consuming the car: Anticipation, use and meaning in contemporary youth culture. *The Sociological Review*, 50, 181–196.

Connell, R. W. (1989). Cool guys, swots and wimps: The interplay of masculinity and education. *Oxford Review of Education*, 15, 291–303.

Connell, R. W. (1990). An iron man: The body and some contradictions of hegemonic masculinity. In M. A. Messner & D. F. Sabo (Eds.), *Sport men and the gender order: Critical feminist perspectives.* Champaign, IL: Human Kinetics.

Connell, R. W. (1996). Teaching the boys: New research on masculinity, and gender strategies for schools. *Teachers College Record*, 98(2), 206–235.

Connell, R. W. (2000). *The men and the boys.* Cambridge, MA: Polity.

Connell, R. W., & Messerschmidt, J. W. (2005). Hegemonic masculinity: Rethinking the concept. *Gender & Society*, 19, 829–859.

Cookson, P. W., & Persell, C. H. (1985). *Preparing for power: America's elite boarding schools.* New York: Basic Books.

Gaztambide-Fernández, R. (2009a). What is an elite boarding school? *Review of Educational Research*, 79, 1090–1128.

Gaztambide-Fernández, R. (2009b). *The best of the best: Becoming elite at an American boarding school.* Cambridge, MA: Harvard University Press.

Gilbert, R., & Gilbert, P. (1998). *Masculinity goes to school.* London: Routledge.

Greene, R. (2007). Understanding the world of high school sociology: Views from an insider. *The American Sociologist*, 38, 211–220.

Honey, J. R. D. S. (1977). *Tom Brown's universe: The development of the public school in the 19th century.* London: Millington.

Kam, L. (2002). *Theorising Chinese masculinity: Society and gender in China.* Cambridge: Cambridge University Press.

Kenway, J., & Fahey, J. (2014). Staying ahead of the game: The globalising practices of elite schools. *Globalisation, Societies and Education*, 12(2), 177–195.

Koh, A., & Kenway, J. (2012). International education. Cultivating national leaders in an elite school: Deploying the transnational in the national interest. *International Studies in Sociology of Education* (Special Issue), 22(4), 291–311.

Kuriloff, P., & Reichert, M. C. (2003). Boys of class, boys of color: Negotiating the academic and social geography of an elite independent school. *Journal of Social Issues*, 59(4), 751–769.

Luke, A. (1997). Representing and reconstructing Asian masculinities: This is not a movie review. *Social Alternatives*, 16, 32–34.

Mac an Ghaill, M. (1996) What about the boys?: Schooling, class and crisis masculinity. *The Sociological Review*, 44, 381–397.

Martino. W. (2000). Mucking around in class, giving crap, and acting cool: Adolescent boys enacting masculinities at school. *Canadian Journal of Education/Revue canadienne de l'éducation*, 25(2),102–112.

Martino, W. (2003). *So what's a boy?: Addressing issues of masculinity and schooling.* Milton Keynes, UK: Open University Press.

Renolds, M. (2004) 'Other' boys: Negotiating non-hegemonic masculinities in the primary school. *Gender and Education*, 16(2), 247–265.

Sheller, M. (2004). *Automotive emotions: Feeling the car.* Department of Sociology, Lancaster University. Retrieved October 2015 from http://www.comp.lancs.ac.uk/sociology/soc124ms.pdf

Stradling. S. (2002). Persuading people out of their cars. Presented to the ESRC Mobile Network. Retrieved 15 October 2014 from http://www.its.leeds.ac.uk/projects/MobileNetwork/downloads/StradlingESRCMobNetPleasureDec02.doc

Walford, G. (1991). *Private schooling: Tradition, change and diversity.* London: Paul Chapman.

Walker, L. (1998). Under the bonnet: Car culture, technological dominance and young men of the working class. *Journal of Interdisciplinary Gender Studies*, 3, 23–43.

Walker, L., Butland, D., & Connell, R. W. (2000). Boys on the road: Masculinities, car culture, and road safety education. *Journal of Men's Studies*, 8, 153–169.

Wang, A. (2000). Asian and white boys' competing discourses about masculinity: Implications for secondary education. *Canadian Journal of Education*, 25, 113–125.

Whannel, G. (2002). *Media sport stars: Masculinities and moralities.* London: Routledge.

Willis, P. (1977). *Learning to labour: How working class kids get working class jobs.* Farnham, UK: Ashgate Publishing Company.

2

CAPITALISING ON WELL-ROUNDEDNESS

Chinese Students' Cultural Mediations in an Elite Australian School

Yujia Wang

Introduction

There is a trend among elite schools that increasingly seeks to market their peculiar forms of social, cultural and physical capital to ensure the production and reproduction of advantage and privilege among students (English, 2009; Forbes & Weiner, 2008; Horne et al., 2011; Kenway & Koh, 2013; Weenink, 2008). In the new sociology of elite schooling how these forms of capital work to shape student identities has attracted scholarly attention.

Among the studies of elite schools, a recent body of literature approaches elite education from a transnational perspective. This body of work investigates how international students choose to take up and experience an elite education overseas. Particular attention is paid to explore how students' cultural practices and identities are shaped by the 'formative possibilities' of overseas elite schooling (Matthews & Sidhu, 2005; Rizvi, 2005; Waters & Brooks, 2011; Weenink, 2008). However, the existent work fails to explore the link between international students' uses and experiences of overseas elite education as a transcultural space in their explorations of cultural identities in transnational mobility.

Theoretically engaging with and in an attempt to enhance cultural cosmopolitan theses, this chapter employs the notions of cultural logic and mediation to investigate the processes of students' cultural identities. It relates to the question of what constitutes a good life intersected with personal cultural choices in transnationality. It seeks to go beyond the deconstruction of a territorialised notion of culture and engage with the de-territorialising of geographies of meanings, values and ethics under the geographies of power regimes and forces.

In this chapter, I use interview data to test out and extend notions of mobile identities with a specific focus on well-roundedness as a potential form of elite cultural capital. I want to explore how well well-roundedness travels among Chinese international students and the implications of this travel in elite education. In so doing, I examine the students' perceptions of this notion, their related cultural practices and mediations behind such practices. By focusing on well-roundedness as the selling point of the elite school, I aim to explore, from a transnational perspective, the theoretical connections between Chinese students' cultural interpretations of well-roundedness, cultural practices and cultural identities. Generally speaking, I intersect my interest in elite schools with a transnational perspective to contribute to the theorisation of youthful cultural identities.

This chapter begins by proposing an analytical framework. The notions of cultural mediation and cultural logic will be introduced and enhanced, with a discussion of the usefulness of cultural cosmopolitanism theses in cultural identities theorisation. Schoolteachers' construction of the well-roundedness ethos will follow. My analysis then turns to students' interpretations and cultural practices in relation to this notion of well-roundedness and the school-orchestrated co-curricular programmes. I conclude this chapter by reviewing my findings, theoretical development and implications for elite schools.

Theoretical Frameworks

I draw on Mazzarella (2004) and Ong (1999) to initiate the theorisation of personal cultural identity. Mazzarella (2004, p. 345) conceptualises individual cultural identity as a process and subject to mediation. Mediation is 'a social act' and 'a constitutive process in social life': an individual's cultural identity is the outcome of processes of mediation.

I delineate Mazzarella's notion of mediation into three modes to clarify the processual nature of an individual's cultural identity. The starting point for mediation is 'cultural difference', which is identified by individuals by means of their "reified schemes of cultural identity and cultural difference" (Mazzarella, 2004, p. 360). Cultural difference is important in the process of mediation, as it is understood as "a potentiality, a space of indeterminacy inherent to all processes of mediation, and therefore inherent to the social process per se" (Mazzarella, 2004, p. 360). It offers the node of mediation for individuals. In the first mode of mediation, values and meanings are "produced" through "nodes of mediation" (Mazzarella, 2004, p. 346).

The second mode of mediation involves individuals' contestations about values and meanings that are newly deciphered "more or less self-consciously, in the name of culture" (Mazzarella, 2004, p. 346). That is, new meanings and values extracted from cultural difference are conceived, received and made sense of in terms of culture. This mode of mediation manifests the individual cultural choice making in the form of cultural practices of either rejection or incorporation. Individuals' cultural practices are demonstrative of the outcome of their personal cultural choice.

In Mazzarella's thesis, an individual's cultural identity process needs the third mode of mediation for him/her to make sense of his/her cultural choice in terms of his/her formerly formed or shaped identity, or sense of a cultured self. This mediation involves the act of reflexively realigning an individual's cultural choice in terms of a cultured sense of self, as

> Mediation is the process by which the self recognizes itself by returning to itself, renewed and once removed.
>
> (Mazzarella, 2004, p. 357).

Mazzarella's notion of mediation is a useful tool for me to use to analyse Chinese international students' cultural identity as processes in transnationality, especially through my demarcating the three modes of cultural mediation. However, it seems that Mazzarella regards cultural mediation, meanings and values as neutral and power free. Here I find Ong's (1999) cultural logics/power duality most useful to be engaged with.

This duality manifests her epistemological departure from that of Mazzarella's in understanding culture, cultural practices, cultural logics, and individual cultural identity. Culture, she argues, cannot be teased out of rationality regimes, as it is inseparable from 'rational' institutions or power regimes, such as "the economy, the legal system, and the state" (Ong, 1999, p. 23). Cultural practices in the form of "little routines and scenarios of everyday life" embody, enact and are reciprocal and reflexive of rationalities calculated out of specific geographical configuration of power. Cultural logics are cultural rationalities. Therefore, for Ong, cultural values, meanings and norms are far from being neutral. Instead, they are manifestations of rationalities shaped within "relations of domination" and "relations of reciprocity and solidarity" (Ong, 1999, p. 5).

Mazarella's understanding of mediation as a neutral social act, with neutral values and meanings, now contradicts with Ong's power-laden conceptualisation of culture. I meld Mazzarella's neutral notion of mediation with Ong's power approach to rationalities as mediation/power duality. That is, here I strike off neutrality in Mazzarella's mediation/values duality, bring in Ong's rationalities/power duality and blend them in a new mediation/rationalities duality. In so doing, mediation is no longer neutral. Rather, it is subject to power regimes and it produces rationalities towards values, meanings, and norms. This mediation/power duality is the conceptual tool I employ in this chapter.

Engaging with the Cultural Cosmopolitan Theses

With my theoretical tools of mediation/power and cultural logics of transnationality, I am concerned about how to work with, and in an attempt to develop further, theories of cosmopolitan identities that have been widely used to theorise identities in today's life world of mobilities and flows. However, the term cosmopolitanism or cosmopolitan identity "continues to escape easy definition" (Skrbiš & Woodward, 2013, p. 2). Skrbiš and Woodward (2013) regard cosmopolitanism as something of a project or process, and identify its four basic dimensions, namely, the cultural, political, ethical, and methodological. In this chapter, I focus on the cultural dimension of this term in transnational contexts.

Skrbiš and Woodward stress that the "leitmotif of contemporary cosmopolitan identity" is openness or "the practice of openness to cultural difference" (Skrbiš & Woodward, 2013, p. 14). Likewise, Hannerz (1990, p. 239) observes that cosmopolitanism "must entail relationships to a plurality of cultures understood as distinctive entities", although cultures, territorially defined in terms of nations, regions, or localities, "tend to overlap and mingle" and are not "easily separated from one another as the hard-edged pieces in a mosaic". He highlights an open attitude to the practices of incorporating other cultures or nation-state demarcated cultural contrasts. This conception emphasises an active practice taken towards cultural diversity rather than towards cultural uniformity. Cultural cosmopolitanism, therefore, can be used to refer to the state of cultural 'co-existence' in relation to the native/non-native culture nexus.

Although cultural cosmopolitanism theses contribute to the line of argument that challenges conventional understandings of a nation-state bounded notion of identities, the nation-state remains a defining feature of the ideas of cosmopolitanism. Thus, the nation-state is further reinforced as a bounded and legitimate cultural marker. This introduces a line of confusion into these cosmopolitan theories. In contrast, it is argued, from the vantage point of cultural globalisation studies, that the nation-state as the bounded unit of culture is de-territorialised, and, consequently, culture begins to lose its distinctiveness as a national marker as a result of flows of cultural goods, media, technology, and information (Featherstone, 1995; Appadurai, 1996). These flows and mobilities, to varying degrees, homogenise national cultures along the nation-state lines. Concurring with this argument, I further read these flows as a component of new geographies of forces that compete with the forces exerted by national cultural regimes. Therefore, I argue that the homogenisation dimension of national cultures cannot be ignored in the cultural cosmopolitanism thesis by an overemphasis on transnational cultural contrasts.

In addition, Hannerz (2006) cautions that whereas there are those who can be labelled 'cosmopolitan', there are also those who are 'un-cosmopolitan'. Here, cosmopolitan as an adjective describes the outcome of the processes of cosmopolitanisation. Hence, the distinction between cosmopolitanism as a process and being cosmopolitan as an outcome is introduced. Thus, several questions are called into attention. What happens in the processes of cosmopolitan encounters that may enable cultural openness or result in cultural closure? What comes after the cultural mixing, co-existence or cultural closure? Skrbiš and Woodward (2013) point out the need to engage empirically with the way in which cosmopolitan encounters produce meaning and impact on personal identities.

To answer their call, in this paper I focus on exploring the link between cosmopolitan encounters, cosmopolitan engagement and the formation of a cosmopolitan or un-cosmopolitan identity. I develop cosmopolitan theses along the axis of rationalities associated with cosmopolitanisation processes within a more complicated configuration of power, or the geographies of forces in transnationality. The theoretical tools—mediation/power duality and cultural logics—are thus employed to explore the specific configuration of individual geographies of forces, to locate and identify the cultural logics/rationalities of Chinese international students.

Methodology

To tackle the theoretical questions listed above, this study employed semi-structured, in-depth interviews as the major data collection method. In my interviews, I explored Chinese students' and school teachers' construction of school ethos, and, in particular, the Chinese students' use and experience of elite school culture and its well-roundedness tenet in Melbourne.

From December of 2010 to May 2011, I interviewed 12 Chinese students and seven staff members from the senior sector of the school. Teachers were interviewed once, for up to 30 minutes. The Chinese international students were interviewed two or three times, with each interview running from 40 to 60 minutes. Students were asked about their schooling experiences, in particular, their involvement in school sport and other co-curricular activities, and their interactions with their local peers.

I also used other data collection methods to complement, further inform and elucidate these interviews. For these Chinese international students, I organised a focus group discussion before individual interviews started. After finishing all individual interviews with students, I asked them follow-up questions via phone calls and emails.

In what follows, I will start with teachers' understanding of its well-roundedness school ethos. Then the focus will move to Chinese students' mediations of this ethos and the school orchestrated cultural space.

Teachers' Construction of the Well-Roundedness Ethos

Beachton Grammar is a co-educational school about 20 kilometres from Melbourne's central business district. It offers programmes from kindergarten to Year 12. When I carried on this study at the end of 2010, Beachton Grammar had 1,197 students and charged an annual fee of $21,358 per annum for local students in Years 11 and 12. In the same year level, for international students, the annual fees were $27,222. Contrasting these fees, in Australia, the minimum wage was $30,643 and the median income was $44,146 in 2010 (Kenway, 2013, p. 16).

Apart from being a high-fee independent school, Beachton Grammar's index of community socio-educational advantage (SEA) can be categorised as a high SEA status. The official national government website *My school*, established by the Labor Government to make school profiles transparent and accessible to all, outlines four SEA statuses, namely, top quarter, second top quarter, bottom quarter and second bottom quarter. According to *My School*, 59% of its total enrolments came from the top quarter, and 87% were in the top half, with only 3% coming from the bottom quarter.

On its official website, Beachton Grammar presents itself as a school offering a well-rounded education. This is featured by an emphasis on strong academic programmes as well as extensive co-curricular choices in sport, arts, debating, music, and drama. In my interviews with six teachers and the school principal, well-roundedness is frequently mentioned. For example, Natasha, the Marketing Manager, gives quite a representative explanation of the school's ethos of 'well-roundedness',

> What our school is trying to do is that it looks at the whole person, not just somebody who is a student, like a person who's learning something, in terms of in the classroom writing, reading, arithmetic, that's important, that's a given. You just have to do that. What this school tries to do is that all that learning, plus all the other things make up a really great person which is personal self-satisfaction, maybe sport, art or music. Everybody has a talent, whether it is inside or outside the classroom ... I would say welfare and wellbeing of the children are paramount.

This notion of 'well-roundedness' capitalises on "the whole wellbeing of the child". It firstly prescribes the cultural way of being a "really great person", who is supposed to be capable of "all the other things", namely a talent in co-curricular programmes of sport, art or music, as well as academic learning. In other words, the school's 'well-roundedness' legitimates certain cultural practices, such as sport and music.

According to the teachers, 'well-roundedness' also involves a reflexive self-appreciation of these cultural attainments or cultural inculcation in terms of 'personal satisfaction', a link between legitimated cultural practice and the introspection of the self. Instead of emphasising what English (2009, p. 99) calls 'co-curricular cultural capital' as a selling point, Beachton Grammar weaves these coercive, middle-class cultural practices of inculcation into attractive narratives of 'pastoral care' and self-care imperatives. Self-care, according to Sonia, a staff member working in the area of school publications, is about the students "with a really broad knowledge of who they are" and are "confident in who they are".

Another important aspect of this well-roundedness ethos is about 'life skills'. Beachton Grammar encourages its students to experience life, to better understand the self and be better prepared for an independent life. 'Life skills', overlapping with self-care skills, such as time-management and leadership capacity, are all marketable skills that can advantageously position students to compete in the job market. The emphasis on cultivation by students of self-care skills is embedded in and communicates a neoliberal moral ethics that stresses the importance of self-responsibility for market-oriented self-making.

To enforce and inscribe the school ethos of well-roundedness, Beachton Grammar relies on its well-structured co-curriculum as a culture-imposing operation. It strictly monitors students' participation in such programmes. The school's practice supports Bourdieu's (1984) argument that the co-curriculum constitutes the very fabric of the non-scholastic, legitimated, school culture. In some studies, schools' curricula and co-curriculum offer manifest a neoliberalising, market logic (English, 2009; Horne et al, 2011). That is, schools assign significant market value to the knowledge and skills they are to impart and cultivate in students, positioning students advantageously for future professional success. Although the teachers I interviewed do not hint at this logic behind their construction of the well-roundedness ethos, on the school's website, such a link between well-roundedness and future career success has been made.

Several questions are thus called into attention: How do Chinese students interpret the tenet of well-roundedness? How do they construct the usefulness of the cultural space Beachton Grammar purposefully carves and strictly monitors? How do they experience this cultural space and explore these cultural activities and programmes? The following section will focus on answering these questions.

Students' Cultural Mediation of Well-Roundedness and Cultural Identities Constructed

A Coherent Geographically Embedded Cultural Identity Consolidated

Rose and **Cindy** come to Australia to fulfil their respective university dreams. They never link co-curricular activities at Beachton Grammar to the idea of well-roundedness. They simply have to attend Physical Education (PE) class and Saturday sport, believing that sports are for fun and for keeping fit. In addition, they regard their involvement in sport as the only compulsive venue to communicate, socialise, and play with their local peers, and they see it as the only window through which to have a glimpse of the local culture. According to them, in Beachton Grammar, the Chinese international students and local students tend to separate and mix with their own group on other occasions. In one word, their cultural logic is to use sports to achieve their socialising goal and to incorporate some non-native culture along the way.

Equating sport fields to the socialising arena, they feel that they are excluded. Their node of mediation revolves around the experience of exclusion. Cindy says of her basketball class,

> Like we play basketball in PE class, local students exclude overseas students. Even when they see you, they treat you as if you were not in their team, and pass the ball to their other teammates. Feels like they think we are no good players, actually we aren't. If they happen to pass me the ball unexpectedly, I immediately pass it to someone else.

Cindy and Rose construct a notion of local sport culture to understand and explain their experience of basketball court exclusion. The local sport culture is mediated in terms of values and meanings, such as that local girls are serious in sport, doing their best and are motivated to win. Consequently, Cindy and Rose see their failure to contribute to the team as a shame on themselves. But it has a cost for them to take up these values. The sheer bodily gap in stamina and strength built on different sport trajectories overwhelms Cindy and Rose. What is more, the local girls' sport culture makes them worry about their safety on the sport field.

> Rose: Like we played soccer in class, they asked me to defend the goal. One girl shot the ball and it hit my legs several times and sprang back. My legs hurt like crazy!

> Cindy: Sometimes when these girls run, they have difficulty stopping and end up bumping into you. They just run with all their might.

Cindy and Rose's mediation of a sport-crazy and tough-bodied sort of Australian youthful femininity as a new set of values bring about knowledge, but not necessarily endorsement. Even identifying with these values will not change the fact that they are virtually excluded from cultural participation at school. Out of safety concerns, embarrassment for not being able to contribute and awkwardness felt from being excluded, Cindy and Rose retreat from joining local peers in combative sports. They choose sport that they are comfortable with and they feel good at playing. But this gives rise to another concern for Cindy,

> Sometimes in PE class, the teacher suggests that we play badminton. But the local girls react like, why badminton? We want to play footy … China takes the lead in these sports [badminton and table-tennis] and Australia is not keen on them.

It is worth noting that in this school, co-curricular programmes are culturally hierarchical around the local/overseas distinction. Sports are nationalised as 'mainstream Australian sports', and as 'Chinese sports'. This labelling of sport becomes a commonsensical practice which the interviewed students, local and overseas alike, are quite aware of. This local/overseas sport hierarchy can be demonstrated in local students taking the initiative in sport choice in PE class,

Capitalising on Well-Roundedness **41**

while international students are at the bottom of this bargaining power hierarchy. The school's differentiation of sport in terms of nationality and the prioritisation of local sports on the basis of a sport cultural hierarchy assign local sport a form of symbolic capital. When the school favours 'local' over 'overseas', it exercises an act of 'symbolic violence' (Bourdieu, 1984) to Chinese international students who are disadvantageously positioned in this cultural hierarchy. This is where the national espoused sport and sport culture is rendered structural to Cindy and Rose.

Such PE class interactions prevent Cindy and Rose's cultural participation, obstruct their cultural mediation and endorsement, and contribute to sport field exclusion along national lines. The girls are forced to fall back on their favourite Chinese sport. A process of cultural membership labelling happens in a two-way fashion and reinforces the Chinese–Australia dichotomy.

When the sheer cultural difference takes the form of cultural hierarchies along national lines and is structurally felt, cultural rationalities revolving around the fairness of the cultural system flare. Emotions erupt. Transcultural communications fail. Accordingly, Chinese/local dichotomy is constructed and a sense of nationality has been awakened. Their Chinese identity has been reinforced. Deprived of cosmopolitan conditions, Cindy and Rose have nothing to add to their cultural identities but the reified sense of cultural difference carved out of national dichotomy.

Frank understands that a well-rounded student should not only excel at academic performance but also have some hobbies and interests. In his definition, a hobby is a pastime. It is for fun, for self-satisfaction, for inner peace, for friendship, and for adding a talent to his profile. In particular, a hobby stands for personality, free choice, self-motivation, and taking initiatives. But in Beachton Grammar, Frank finds that his personal hobbies are strictly monitored. He elaborates,

> Sometimes I play basketball just because it is a fine day, or because I am bored and want to have some fun with my classmates … Before when I played basketball with my classmates, we decided when and where to play it. But our school is like, you must do this and you cannot do that. When you have your freedom constrained, your hobbies are the prices you pay … This school offers us some music programmes, but there are too many conditions attached … Like you have to practise in your spare time at least twice or three times a week. You have to perform to compete with other students. That's far from what I really want. I enjoy the process of learning to play a musical instrument, but I have no interest in performing in front other people or in winning an award … Once you are bundled by these 'treaties', your hobbies turn out to be a commitment, a responsibility, and a must.

42 Yujia Wang

Frank believes that the school uses 'hobbies' to lure students into commitment traps. Deprived of freewill and initiative, he feels coerced to participate in the school orchestrated cultural space. He is strongly against the competitiveness and exhibitionism associated with what he believes to be a personal or even a private hobby. His cultural decipher and problematisation result in ethical negation rather than endorsement or appreciation.

His experience in sport involves a lot of cultural deciphering, too. Frank endorses the 'fit' body as part and parcel of Australian youthful masculinity. But sports field encounters turn his appreciation of the strong bodies into negation of the local masculinity. He problematises the way local boys use their strong bodies as an advantage and how the Australian basketball rules unfairly prioritise bodily toughness. He complains,

> The local boys are sturdy and tough … However good our basketball techniques, we are no match because they go charging around the court. I had six pairs of glasses broken … The way local boys play basketball is similar to the way they play footy. The referee takes it for granted. So when charging happens, the referee seldom gets his whistle out. When the referee does blow the whistle, the penalty is too light. Basketball is an imported sport in Australia, so the rules of a basketball match are not strictly carried out. But in China we don't take them lightly … The local boys are wild and they seem to have an untamed and uncivilised strength in their bodies. Sometimes it turns out to be a physical bully on the sports field. It's just like when an intellectual confronts with a soldier, and there is no room for reasoning. In the end they have to fight each other physically.

This is an example of how different basketball culture and nationed masculinities have entered the cultural hierarchy scheme and become a structure-laden issue. Frank's cultural logics turn ethical when challenging the Australian basketball culture as a form of structural inequality. The value clashes regarding different versions of masculinities and sports culture become a dead-end structural issue which he rejects without hesitation.

Is Frank cosmopolitanised? He demonstrates the ability and competence to decipher another culture, which is the capacity to learn about other cultures highlighted by Hannerz (2006). But, he lacks what Hannerz calls 'the core of cultural cosmopolitanism', namely "the ability to make one's way into other cultures, and the appreciative openness toward divergent cultural experiences" (Hannerz, 2006, p. 13). Contrary to Rizvi's (2005) argument that transnationality cosmopolitanises, in Frank's case, transnationality is a re-territorialising process.

Frank's case highlights the limitations of cosmopolitanisation. In the cultural space manipulated and monitored by Beachton Grammar, Frank interprets the intercultural difference as different cultural ethics. China and Australia are constructed as cultural units of irreconcilable opposites. He problematises this space as a localised cultural hierarchy. Consequently, for Frank, the intercultural difference becomes a site of problematisation, leading to his informed cultural rejection. Frank retains a coherent Chinese cultural identity, as China is mobilised as legitimated cultural and ethical moorings of his sense of self.

A Simultaneous Cultural Identity

Without giving a thought to well-roundedness, **Jack** enjoys co-curricular programmes provided by the school. He uses this cultural space to fulfil his basketball dream. School sport can be considered as 'masculinity vortexes', and in particular, competitive team sports "are important in the wider culture as symbols of masculinity" (Connell, 2008, p. 137). Jack's mediation node catches a different form of masculinity,

> The difference is that in China we play basketball with our brains, while in Australia, the locals play basketball with their muscles. They do not value basketball techniques.

The dyad *wen–wu* (cultural attainment–martial valour) advanced by Louie (2002) can be used to understand Jack's dichotomised constructs of masculinities between the Chinese males and his Australian counterparts. According to Louie (2002, p. 4), "*wen* refers to a whole range of attributes such as literary excellence, civilised behaviour, and general education while *wu* refers to just as many different sets of descriptors, including powerful physique, fearlessness and fighting skills". He argues that different manifestations and implications of the *wen–wu* dyad are "a defining feature of Chinese masculinity" subject to socio-historical change (Louie, 2002). Jack acknowledges this brainy-type of Chinese masculinity. In the meanwhile, he comes to terms with the "muscle" type of Australian masculinity, which Connell (2008, p. 140) observes as involving "a certain level of physical confrontations and (legal) violence".

To cope with the bodily confrontations on the basketball court, Jack resorts to a heavy bodybuilding project. He spends an average of two hours playing basketball and extra hours on exercises such as push-ups, sit-ups, and squats to build up his muscles. In pursuit of his basketball dream, he also ventures out of his cultural comfort zone, joining the school basketball team as the only Chinese international student and, indeed, as the only Asian background student. He immerses himself in the micro basketball team life congested with language barriers, different basketball cultures and some taunts and jibes once in a while.

Therefore, Jack's processual cultural identity project involves cultural endorsement and incorporation. His cultural cosmopolitanisation takes place in his act of fearless, consistent, cultural participation.

Natalie and **Jane** are confident high-achievers. They use the school's co-curricular programmes and activities as a venue to socialise with their local

44 Yujia Wang

peers. They aspire for a harmonious social life, wanting to fit in the new cultural landscape and making local friends. However, their intercultural communication is not smooth. The poignant sense of inadequacy and inability in their transcultural communications is revealed in their talk about their partying experiences with local friends, which resonates so much with their socialising experiences with local peers at school.

> Natalie: I attended a friend's birthday party. She was born here so she has many local friends. I went to such local parties a couple of times. It is really boring and frustrating, just cannot find the topic. I am a very extroversive, easy-going girl, always ready to talk. But I suddenly become the most reticent one among the Aussie girls.

> Jane: Yes, it is really because of the cultural difference. Their topics simply cannot match ours. Boys crack strange jokes that we just don't get them. They will talk about footy. Girls love talking about their friends, just gossips. We don't have a clue whom they are talking about. Just cannot communicate.

Their statements demonstrate the difficulty of in-depth cosmopolitanisation. The intimate cultural knowledge about jokes, social mores and joint friendship circle constitutes a big barrier to their cultural cosmopolitanisation in intercultural socialising arenas. To make matters worse, Jane and Natalie seldom engage with Australia's media culture as a source of intercultural input. They show little interest in Australian media culture.

Jane's and Natalie's case prompts us to ask, how far can cultural cosmopolitanisation go? Intercultural communication involves more than a 'banal' form of cosmopolitanism, like tasting non-native food. Intercultural barriers and differences do exist. Such differences beg for intercultural competence and knowledge. And, strong emotions are involved in intercultural communications. The two girls feel culturally alienated, totally out of place, frustrated, and their Chinese cultural identities are consequently awakened and reinforced on the route to cosmopolitanisation. I argue that cultural cosmopolitanisation and the assertion of cultural membership co-exist in this case; the more they try to cosmopolitanise, the more aware they are of their cultural roots and moorings.

Phil has always been a versatile student. He is a straight A student with a lot of talents in sport and music. But in China his talents went unnoticed because his school only cared about students' academic performance. He believes in well-roundedness and embodies this ethos in his self-making project. He finds the co-curricular programmes at Beachton Grammar an appealing stage to showcase his talents. It is worth noting that Phil possesses some talents such as in music composition, singing, and swimming, which are transferable in the Australian context. More importantly, he takes pride in showing his talents, which gives him great self-satisfaction.

Phil also uses this school orchestrated cultural space to learn non-native cultural knowledge and making local friends. His cultural logic is that any culture, whether Chinese, global, or Australian, is knowledge. There is no sense of right or wrong, or cultural superiority in culture itself. He treats culture as neutral, and the cultural take-up is only personal preference. He believes that cultural learning facilitates interpersonal communications, but it is not necessary to go to great lengths to follow suit or take up others' cultural preference or tastes. This view is particularly self-evident in his co-curricular choices at school,

> I never play footy; it's too dangerous. I do soccer, [but] basketball no, maybe because of the height (laugh). I love going to gym both here and in China. I love swimming because I used to be part of a local swimming team [in China] ... I specialise in butterfly stroke. I am just showing off [to my Aussie classmates].

Phil also uses co-curricular activities as an opportunity to accumulate non-native cultural capital or cosmopolitan capital. In the meanwhile without dwarfing his native cultural capital he uses these cultural activities as a venue to showcase his unique Chinese talent and turn his Chinese cultural capital into a cosmopolitan form of cultural capital. He regards this intercultural difference as a form of knowledge, even when they are framed in China/Australia duality,

> We (Chinese students) are good at sports like pingpong [and] badminton. We know how to use small techniques to be faster, to be better. So I teach my Aussie friends how to use these techniques.

Believing in cultural learning, Phil is eager to de-construct the Australia/Chinese dichotomy. In his process of cultural learning, similarities can be shared, and differences can be exchanged. His intercultural communication is a two-way process that involves both cultural learning and cultural teaching between him and his local peers in the school.

In addition, the global youth culture also facilitates Phil's two-way inter-cultural communication. His geographically transferable skills in piano and butterfly stroke draw him close to his local peers. As 'scaped' pop culture cosmopolitanises young people globally, he and his local peers share common media consumption tastes. Unlike Jane and Natalie, the inter-cultural barriers are not salient in Phil's case. He feels that local boys, rather than his Chinese counterparts at the elite school, are more like-minded persons.

Phil's cultural identity undergoes intercultural cosmopolitanisation. Cosmopolitanisation is extended in this sense beyond Szerszynski and Urry's (2002) notion of cosmopolitanism as a way of learning through cultural take-up

46 Yujia Wang

and cultural absorption or incorporation. Cosmopolitanisation is a two-way process involving cultural dissemination as well. In addition, Phil's view of culture as a form of knowledge makes his cultural emplacement a neutral one, free of conflicts and problematisation. Therefore, his cultural identity takes the form of 'simultaneity', a harmonious combination and incorporation of two nationed cultures.

To sum up, Jane, Natalie, Jack and Phil embrace the idea of being open to other cultures. However, their attitude originates from different but not necessarily self-conscious rationalities. For Jane and Natalie, their in-depth cultural cosmopolitanism involves the processes of value deciphering, negotiation, and mediation in making sense of their former cultured self. Their case supports the argument that transnational cultural difference, when deciphered in terms of values, poses questions for the intimate or committed cosmopolitanism because value incorporation is not always frictionless. For Jack, his practices of cultural incorporation are unconscious, without mediation among specific power registers. For Phil, cultural cosmopolitanism is free from power registers, as non-native culture is approached as knowledge. Jane, Natalie, Jack, and Phil are therefore in varied processes of cultural cosmopolitanisation, which is featured by cultural identity transformation and reification by both detachment from and attachment to their Chinese cultural anchoring. Their cultural incorporation does not necessarily come with their giving-up or negation of their Chinese cultural anchorage.

Conclusion

My analysis focused on exploring students' cultural logics in relation to how they *use and experience* the well-roundedness ethos and the school culture orchestrated by an elite Australian school. It is revealed that well-roundedness as a form of elite capital and as a tenet that guides and orchestrates Beachton Grammar's co-curricular programmes and school culture is linked to a sense of middle-classness by teachers. But these teachers do not link this middle-class cultural reproduction to an ongoing, secured class privilege in the job market.

I also engaged with the question of how far this elite form of cultural capital can go in the transnational context. I asked whether elite school cultural capital can be de-contextualised and stripped of its cultural embeddedness of geographically located education and assumed to be 'universal'/'global' knowledge or a form of cosmopolitan capital (Weenink, 2008). Obviously, Chinese students regard the well-roundedness ethos as a localised practice complemented by a prioritised Australian cultural programme. As Chinese students do not make direct connections between well-roundedness and a future class privilege, nor do they harbour a geographical mobility future aspiration, they fail to take a capital approach to well-roundedness.

In response to the theoretical linkage between sport-related capital such as strong, competitive, healthy bodies and future class privilege (Bourdieu, 1984;

Connell, 2008; Horne et al., 2011; O'Flynn & Lee, 2010; Shilling, 2004; Warde, 2006), neither teachers nor students in my study make such a direct connection. In particular for Chinese students, school co-curricular programmes provide them an arena for fun, for relaxation, for forging friendship and for being part of the school community. Although some students decipher and appreciate the well-roundedness ethos, they mediate it more in an ethical lens than in an instrumentalist perspective.

In relation to the theorisation of youthful cultural identities in geographical mobility, I hinged on the question of how students react to intercultural difference in transcultural immersion. In so doing, I not only examined the question of non-native culture incorporation by attending to the rationalities and emotions involved in such practice of incorporation, but investigated the rationalities and emotions of non-native culture rejection as well.

I enhanced the cultural cosmopolitan theses by demarcating a range of nuanced rationalities. Theoretically, along with the humanity perspective and the instrumentalist cultural logics, I added an ethical perspective that relates to the question of what constitutes a good life intersected with personal cultural choices in transnationality. In this way, I developed the theorisation of cultural cosmopolitanism along the cosmopolitanism/power duality. I also put forward the notion of in-depth cosmopolitanism against Hannerz's (1990) theorisation of cultural cosmopolitanism, by revealing the mediation processes of cultural cosmopolitanisation.

Furthermore, I drew attention to the question of 'cosmopolitanisation failures', pointing out the structural factors involved in transcultural contexts, highlighting the emotions and rationalities behind such non-native cultural rejection. I paid heed to the difficulty and cultural needs of in-depth cosmopolitanisation.

To do so, I delineated cultural difference in terms of cultural contradictions, cultural dissimilarity (dissimilar but not oppositional), or cultural add-ons (having no equivalent counterpart in the culture of origin) from an individual's past cultural repertoire, to highlight the process of cultural cosmopolitanisation.

Lastly, I have extended Ong's notion of cultural logics by delineating the uses of culture and the experiences of culture and made an analytical linkage between the two. This chapter theoretically goes beyond the deconstruction of a territorialised notion of culture and engages with the de-territorialising of geographies of meanings, values and ethics under the geographies of power regimes and forces. I have delineated the geographies of forces exerting influences at national and global levels, and checked whether Chinese students could break loose from the power wielded by their nation-state of origin and the nation-state of displacement.

In so doing I enhanced the cultural cosmopolitanism thesis, while most importantly, developed theorisations of cultural identities through differentiating between the forces that exert their effect within and beyond nation-state boundaries. I have led the theorisation of cultural identities to the frames of geographies of cultural identity to understand fully the cultural identities in transnational mobility.

References

Appadurai, A. (1996). *Modernity at large: Cultural dimensions of globalization*. Minneapolis, MN: University of Minnesota Press.

Bourdieu, P. (1984). *Distinction: A social critique of the judgment of taste*. Cambridge, MA: Harvard University Press.

Connell, R. (2008). Masculinity construction and sports in boys' education: A framework for thinking about the issue. *Sport, Education and Society*, 13(2), 131–145.

English, R. (2009). Selling education through 'culture': Responses to the market by new, non-government schools. *Australian Educational Researcher*, 36(1), 89–104.

Featherstone, M. (1995). *Undoing culture: Globalization, postmodernism and identity*. London: Sage.

Forbes, J., & Weiner, G. (2008). Under-stated powerhouses: Scottish independent schools, their characteristics and their capitals. *Discourse: Studies in the Cultural Politics of Education*, 29(4), 509–523.

Hannerz, U. (1990). Cosmopolitans and locals in world culture. *Theory, Culture & Society*, 7(2–3), 237–251.

Hannerz, U. (2006). *Two faces of cosmopolitanism: Culture and politics*. Documentos CIBOD, Serie: Dinamicas Interculturales Numero 7.

Horne, J., Lingard, B., Weiner, G., & Forbes, J. (2011). 'Capitalizing on sport': Sport, physical education and multiple capitals in Scottish independent schools. *British Journal of Sociology of Education*, 32(6), 861–879.

Kenway, J. (2013). Challenging inequality in Australian schools: Gonski and beyond. *Discourse: Studies in the Cultural Politics of Education*, 34(2), 1–23.

Kenway, J., & Koh, A. (2013). The elite school as a 'cognitive machine' and 'social paradise'?: Developing transnational capitals for the national 'field of power'. In T. Bennett, J. Frow, G. Hage & G. Noble (Eds.), Working with Bourdieu: Antipodean Cultural Fields. *Journal of Sociology* (Special Issue), 49(2–3), 272–290.

Louie, K. (2002). *Theorising Chinese masculinity: Society and gender in China*. Cambridge: Cambridge University Press.

Matthews, J., & Sidhu, R. (2005). Desperately seeking the global subject: International education, citizenship and cosmopolitanism. *Globalisation, Societies and Education*, 3(1), 49–66.

Mazzarella, W. (2004). Culture, globalization, mediation. *Annual Review of Anthropology*, 33, 345–367.

O'Flynn, G., & Lee, J. (2010). Committed young men and well-balanced young women: Private schooling, physical activity and the classed self. In J. Wright & D. Macdonald (Eds.), *Young people, physical activity and the everyday* (pp. 59–74). London: Routledge.

Ong, A. (1999). *Flexible citizenship: The cultural logics of transnationality*. Durham: Duke University Press.

Rizvi, F. (2005). International education and the production of cosmopolitan identities. In A. Arimoto, F. Huang & K. Yokoyama (Eds.), *Globalization and higher education* (pp. 77–92). Hiroshima: Hiroshima University.

Shilling, C. (2004). Physical capital and situated action: A new direction for corporeal sociology. *British Journal of Sociology of Education*, 25(4), 473–487.

Skrbiš, Z., & Woodward, I. (2013). *Cosmopolitanism: Uses of the idea*. London: SAGE.

Szerszynski, B., & Urry, J. (2002). Cultures of cosmopolitanism. *The Sociological Review*, 50(4), 461–481.

Warde, A. (2006). Cultural capital and the place of sport. *Cultural Trends*, 15(2/3), 107–122.

Waters, J., & Brooks, R. (2011). 'Vive la différence'? The 'international' experiences of UK students overseas. *Population, Space and Place*, 17(5), 567–578.

Weenink, D. (2008). Cosmopolitanism as a form of capital: Parents preparing their children for a globalising world. *Sociology*, 42(6), 1089–1106.

3

THE EMERGENCE OF ELITE INTERNATIONAL BACCALAUREATE DIPLOMA PROGRAMME SCHOOLS IN CHINA

A 'Skyboxification' Perspective

Moosung Lee, Ewan Wright, and Allan Walker

Introduction

In this chapter we focus on International Baccalaureate (IB) schools as an emerging sub-sector of elite schooling in China. Over the past decade, IB schools, in general, and International Baccalaureate Diploma Programme (IBDP) schools, in particular, have expanded rapidly across countries in Asia. As examples, in China and India the number of IBDP schools has rapidly increased from below 10 in 2000 to 67 and 99 in 2014, respectively (IB, 2014a). While there are a number of factors that have shaped such a fast growth of IBDP schools in the region, one of the key factors seems to be that IBDP schools have succeeded in creating a brand that presents high-quality preparation for university entrance and international mobility through a rigorous curriculum and progressive pedagogy. This organisational image has been increasingly accepted by stakeholders such as students, parents, universities, and the mass media more broadly in the region (see Doherty, 2009).

At the same time, the brand of the IB as a form of elite schooling offering high-quality preparation for entrance to internationally reputable universities is more than just an image. Indeed, the high performance of IBDP graduates in university entrance has been evidenced in recent studies. For example, our study (Lee et al., 2014) targeting the vast majority of IBDP schools in China found that three out of four IBDP graduates during the period between 2002 and 2012 were admitted to one of the world's top 500 universities, while almost one-third (30.0%) were admitted to one of the top 50 ranked universities. This high performance of IBDP graduates in China in relation to university entrance can be applauded and appreciated, given the relatively short history of IBDP schools in China compared to that of other countries or regions.

The Emergence of Elite IBDP Schools in China **51**

Nevertheless, there are growing concerns emerging from such a success. IBDP schools that equip students with the tools for potential entry to prestigious universities worldwide are increasingly an option in China *only for those who can afford it*. While the exclusiveness of elite schools has been well researched in settings such as the USA (Weis, Cipollone & Jenkins, 2014), the UK (Donnelly, 2014) and Singapore (Koh, 2014), there remains a gap in the literature exploring the emergence of elite international IBDP schools in China. This is significant given that IBDP schools remain accessible to an especially selective population in China in terms of legal and financial perspectives.[1] Specifically, IBDP schools in China are an option only for foreign passport holders who can afford to pay approximately US$30,000 per student for an annual tuition fee, plus additional charges such as annual capital fees (Wright & Lee, 2014a).

Given that the gross national income per capita in China was US$5,720 in 2012 (World Bank, 2014a), arguably, students in and graduates from IBDP schools in China are very selective sub-populations. Indeed, this chapter will suggest that many international IBDP schools in China can be identified as elite schools due to sharing characteristics identified in the existing literature on elite schools. This includes selective admission procedures, provision of first-rate educational resources, emphasis on character development, and social prestige (see Gaztambide-Fernández, 2009) that enable their students to "stay ahead of the game" in university applications and labour market transitions (Kenway & Fahey, 2014, p. 177).

The concern—i.e., educational advantage to small, selective sub-populations— gets more serious when we consider potential or real divides between those IBDP schools in China and people and communities in the host society. Our recent studies (Lee et al., 2014; Wright & Lee, 2014b) found that the potential of the IBDP to foster so-called 21st-century skills such as inter-cultural understanding and open-mindedness, which are core goals of the IB, among IB students and other social, cultural and economic groups in China could be substantively constrained. While IBDP schools are equipped with the IB Learner Profile and Creativity, Action, Service (CAS),[2] teachers, administrators, and students recognise tensions when it comes to the implementation of these components of the programme in results oriented school cultures of international IBDP schools in China.

In this chapter, we have two goals. First, we aim to demonstrate the aforementioned findings in detail with empirical data—i.e., by tracking the extent to which IBDP graduates in China have been successful in university entrance and identifying if IBDP graduates are disconnected and separated from their host society. Second, more importantly, we aim to draw implications of such socio-economic, cultural, and physical divides between IBDP schools and the host society with the conceptual lens of 'skyboxification'. As we will discuss in detail, Michael Sandel (2012) coined the term of skyboxification in order to describe the polarisation of American life caused by marketisation of public and civic spheres where people of diverse backgrounds rarely interact. As Sandel (2012) noted, in an increasingly market-based society—where money can buy more and more things—people from different socio-economic and cultural backgrounds are living increasingly separated civic lives, including in the realm of education (cited in Wright & Lee, 2014a). Within this context, we aim to explore how we can conceptualise the emergence of elite IBDP schools in China from the perspective of Sandel's skyboxification.

This chapter consists of four parts. First, we will briefly review elite schooling in China to establish the context of this study. This will be followed by an introduction of the concept of skyboxification. Second, we will outline empirical data, based on four different types of datasets. Third, drawing from the multiple data sources, we will demonstrate substantial divides between elite international IBDP schools and local schools and communities in China with regards to organisational status and practices. Finally, we present a number of implications of the findings for research, practice and policy.

Elite Schooling in China

Over the previous decade China has overseen a rapid expansion of secondary level education. Between 2002 and 2012 the percentage of the relevant age group enrolled in secondary education increased from 59% to 89% (World Bank, 2014b). While this expansion has undoubtedly increased educational opportunities, recent years have also witnessed a growth of elite schools in both the national and international schooling sectors. This has important implications for educational equity and for the promotion of inter-cultural understanding and open-mindedness among students in China.

Firstly, at the national level elite schooling includes a concentration of investment in a limited number of what have been termed "key schools" (OECD, 2011) or "exemplary schools" (Zhao, 2014). These elite schools are often given preferable treatment by educational authorities in terms of being offered "additional resources and assigned better teachers" (OECD, 2011, p. 95) and having priority over "matriculation of top-performing students on standardized assessments" (Wu, 2014, p. 2).

Reflecting this, studies have shown that students in elite schools are more successful relative to 'ordinary schools' in terms of overall academic achievement, applications to top ranking universities, and over the course of their working careers (Lin, 2009; OECD, 2011; Zhang, 2013). There is often, therefore, fierce competition to gain admission to elite schools. This process remains largely determined by student performance in high stakes assessments, location of residence, and by lottery systems of admission (Zhang, 2013). Nevertheless, there have been reports about a high concentration of students from high socio-economic groups from urban areas in elite schools (Wu, 2014; Zhang, 2013; Zhao, 2014). For instance, Zhao notes that elite schools are largely limited to those with the financial and social capital to navigate the admissions process, for example by purchasing property in elite school catchment areas (Zhao, 2014).

The Emergence of Elite IBDP Schools in China **53**

Secondly, another growth area of elite schools in China has been in the international schooling sector. There is ongoing debate about how international schools should be defined (see Hayden & Thompson, 2008) with evidence of increasing diversity among international schools around the world (see Bunnell, 2014). For the purpose of this chapter, the IBDP schools under investigation are deemed international schools due to their student demographics, English medium of instruction, and offering of an international educational programme (i.e., the IBDP). As previously noted, the number of schools offering the IBDP in China has grown at a rapid pace in recent years. For example, the first IBDP was implemented at the International School of Beijing in 1991. As of 2014, the number of schools authorised to run the IBDP in China reached 67, representing a sevenfold increase since 2014.

On the one hand, this expansion of IBDP schools, alongside other types of international schools in China, has been facilitated by a relaxation of government policy, especially since the turn of the 21st century. Notably, China's National Outline for Medium- and Long-Term Education Reform and Development (2010–2020) outlined efforts to increase cooperation with international education providers, including attracting international schools (Ministry of Education, 2010, p. 36).

On the other hand, the strong presence of international schools reflects growing demand for these schools from populations in China. In contrast to other parts of East Asia where this demand increasingly stems from the *local* socio-economic elite (see Brummitt & Keeling, 2013; Hayden & Thompson, 2008; Kenway & Koh, 2013), in China growth has been driven by non-Chinese nationals. This reflects legal restrictions on international schools enrolling Chinese passport holders (KPMG, 2010). As a result, international school students in China are predominantly globally mobile expatriates or students of Chinese heritage with overseas passports (Lee et al., 2014).

However, in both cases the attraction is largely due to a perception that international schools offer a distinct and superior education to national schools. This includes many of the perceived benefits offered by national elite schools around the world such as selective admissions procedures, provision of first-rate educational resources (i.e., facilities, teacher–student ratios, highly trained and qualified staff, and extra-curricular activities), emphasis on character development (i.e., communication and leadership skills) and social prestige (see Gaztambide-Fernández, 2009). In addition, the research has identified that the international nature of such schools is perceived to offer further advantages to national schools in terms of an English medium of instruction (Brummitt & Keeling, 2013), liberal educational approaches (Ng, 2013), 'transnational capital' associated with a globalised student body and orientation (Kenway & Koh, 2013), and access to international programmes, such as the IBDP (Lee, Hallinger & Walker, 2012a).

Arguably, elite international schools are more likely than national elite schools in China to have a student body consisting of those from high socio-economic backgrounds. This is because, as will be outlined in this chapter, school fees charged by international schools in China are among the highest in East Asia, if not the world. A consequence is that access to international schools remains limited to a small and relatively elite minority of the population.

The implications of the concentration of students from high socio-economic backgrounds at both national and international elite schools in China are potentially serious. This includes reinforcing societal inequalities by providing wealthy students with greater opportunities for educational success and admissions to prestigious higher education institutions (Khan, 2013). Research has consistently shown that such educational trajectories are often followed by entry to "the power elite" (Mills, 1956) in China (Qian & Walker, 2011), the USA (Hayes, 2012), and indeed globally (Sklair, 2001). Moreover, the implications of this point are arguably given additional weight as such students from elite schools may have limited opportunities to interact and to develop inter-cultural understanding with students from other backgrounds (Heyward, 2002; Kenway, 2013; Pearce, 1994). The following sections of this chapter will build on this latter point to discuss the potential ramifications of this with reference to elite international IBDP schools in China.

A Skyboxification Perspective

As previously noted, we aim to tap the potential utility and value of Sandel's term of skyboxcification in deepening our understanding of the emergence of elite schooling, particularly international IBDP schools in China. To explain Sandel's concept of skyboxification, let us begin with his personal narrative:

> When I went to see the Minnesota Twins play in the mid-1960s, the difference in price between the most expensive seats and the cheapest ones was $2. In fact, for most of the twentieth century, ball parks were places where corporate executives sat side by side with blue-collar workers, where everyone waited in the same lines to buy hot dogs or beer, and where rich and poor alike got wet if it rained. In the last few decades, however, this has changed. The advent of skybox suites high above the field of play has separated the affluent and the privileged from the common folk in the stands below.
>
> (2012, p. 173)

Sandel's concern is that this kind of segregation between the elite (and/or the affluent) from the rest of the public has been found throughout the American society. He calls this the 'skyboxification of American social life'. The impetus of this wide-ranging skyboxification stems from rapid marketisation of public spheres where "[t]he more things money can buy, the fewer the occasions when people from different walks of life encounter one another" (p. 202). In other

The Emergence of Elite IBDP Schools in China **55**

words, in such a market based society "people of affluence and people of modest means lead increasingly separate lives" (p. 203).

Drawing from moral and political philosophy, Sandel proposes two fundamental objections against the phenomenon of skyboxification driven by the market society. Firstly, he raises a concern about fairness and inequality in social life, fostered by marketisation:

> In a society where everything is for sale, life is harder for those of modest means. The more money can buy, the more affluence (or the lack of it) matters. If the only advantage of affluence were the ability to afford yachts, sports cars, and fancy vacations, inequalities of income and wealth would matter less than they do today. But as money comes to buy more and more—political influence, good medical care, a home in a safe neighborhood rather than a crime-ridden one, access to elite schools rather than failing ones—the distribution of income and wealth looms larger.
>
> (p. 8)

Secondly, Sandel points out "the corrosive tendency of markets" (p. 9). He argues that putting a high price on goods, especially belonging to civic and public life such as admission to elite secondary schools and prestigious universities, erodes the value and alters the nature of such social goods. As examples, legacy admission, widely practised in prestigious liberal arts colleges and research universities, without transparency is detrimental to the value of diplomas and the integrity of university communities. Also, charging high tuition and other supplementary fees such as capital levies that enable only 'super-rich' parents to secure a place for their children in elite international schools could alter the nature of education as a social good—i.e., educational activities, including teachers' passion and professionalism, in those schools are downgraded to something that can be purely transactional.

From our perspective, Sandel's idea of skyboxification is well suited to capture tensions and concerns about the rapid emergence of elite international IBDP schools in China, since our data tell a story of physical, socio-economical and cultural divides between students in IBDP schools in China and the host society. In the following sections, we will show how IBDP schools in China can be identified as a case of skyboxification and discuss the implications in terms of educational research, practices and policy.

Methodology

Research Design

We planned a multi-method study, the phases of which are analytically separate but conceptually integrated, for the purpose of exploring elite IBDP schools in

China from the perspective of skyboxification. The mixed methods study employed a sequential explanatory design based on four different datasets gathered from 2012 to 2013. Specifically, the mixed-method approach included (1) descriptive statistical analysis of archival data on financial costs of IBDP schools in East Asia, (2) descriptive statistical analysis of archival data on university destinations of IBDP graduates from China, (3) qualitative analysis of interview data from five elite IBDP schools in China, and (4) quantitative analysis of one of the key attributes in the IB Learner Profile—i.e., open-mindedness.

Data Collection

We utilised four different datasets gathered from three different research projects on the IB in East Asia. The first dataset was mainly from the IB website and IB school websites in order to trace the relative financial costs of attending IBDP schools in Asia. We investigated school fees charged by all IBDP schools across 12 metropolitan cities. The cities included Bangkok, Beijing, Ho Chi Minh, Hong Kong, Jakarta, Kuala Lumpur, Manila, Seoul, Shanghai, Singapore, Taipei, and Tokyo. To this end, we identified the annual tuition fees charged and additional fees such capital levies for the IBDP students in the 2012/13 academic year. The schools were identified using the "Find an IB world school" resource on the IB website (IB, 2014a). To obtain details of relevant school fees, the research team undertook a detailed investigation of each of the schools' websites and contacted school admissions departments directly when required.

To build the second dataset, focusing on the university destinations of IBDP graduates from China, a mass email was sent out to all IBDP schools operating in China as of 2012 (i.e., 43 IBDP schools). As a result of a follow-up through email correspondence, registered mail letters, and long distance phone calls over a period of three months, we obtained information about university destinations of 1,612 IBDP graduates from 14 schools in China during the period between 2002 and 2012 (cf. Lee et al., 2014).

Following the data collection of university destinations, we collected interview data from administrators, teachers, and students in five high-performing IBDP schools in China. In total, 44 interviewees were involved in this data collection. This included individual semi-structured interviews with head teachers and IBDP coordinators at each of the five schools, followed by focus groups with a total of 17 students and 17 teachers. The schools were selected due to sharing common characteristics in terms of being among the leading IBDP schools with regards to examination results in China, being IBDP-only schools (i.e., not offering the Primary Years Programme or the Middle Years Programme), and being located in the metropolitan cities of Beijing and Shanghai. The primary goal of data collection was to understand how the IBDP is implemented and how it contributes to university entrance and preparation for students in both academic and non-academic domains (e.g., inter-cultural understanding) (cf. Lee et al., 2014).

The final dataset was partially borrowed from another large-scale study on the IB schools in East and South-East Asia, including China (cf. Walker, Bryant & Lee, 2014). This large-scale study consisted of a pilot study, including 976 IBDP students from 18 schools and a follow-up main study, including 758 IBDP students across 29 schools in East Asia. We used the validated survey data of the IB Learner Profile Questionnaire (IBLPQ) from the pilot study in order to compare IBDP students in China and other countries in East Asia in terms of the perception of their capacity to be 'open-minded', one of the key IB Learner Profile attributes reflecting students' capacity of inter-cultural understanding (Walker, Lee & Bryant, forthcoming).

Data Analysis

For quantitative data, we used a series of descriptive statistical analyses including frequency analysis, t-test, and ANOVA. For qualitative data, we developed a coding scheme based on patterns emerging from the interviews, which were later reduced into a smaller number of analytical units based on similar themes (Miles & Huberman, 1994). Nvivo 10 was used for cross-case analysis.

Findings

IBDP Schools as a Vehicle for Entrance to World-Class Universities[3]

Our archival data showed that the most common university destination for IBDP graduates was the USA, with over half of the IBDP graduates (51.1%) from 2002 to 2012 attending US universities, followed by the UK (11.4%) and Canada (10.7%). In terms of university destination by language (i.e., universities in English speaking countries versus universities in non-English speaking countries), a vast majority of the IBDP graduates (83.1%) chose universities in English speaking countries (e.g., USA, UK, Canada, and Australia), and a much smaller proportion (11.5%) went to university in non-English speaking countries, while 5.4% were classified as 'others' or 'missing'.

Our case study data indicated that university destinations in part reflected the nationality of the students due to tuition-fee incentives and existing social support networks. Nevertheless, the popularity of US universities also reflected a geographical concentration of academically strong institutions that were attractive to globally mobile IBDP graduates. Indeed, our archival data revealed that 71.6% of IBDP graduates attended top 500 universities worldwide.[4] Further analysis of the data showed that 30.0% of IBDP graduates enrolled at one of the top 50 ranked universities worldwide and 7.7% entered a top 15 ranked university. Moreover, the high performance of IBDP schools in China in terms of university entrance was very stable over 10 years; the median ranking of universities where IBDP graduates studied was 71. While simplified notions of university rankings

58 Moosung Lee, Ewan Wright, and Allan Walker

as a proxy for quality have been widely criticised (see Marginson, 2007), such highly ranked institutions certainly have strong global reputations and can be understood as the elite brands of higher education.

School Fees in IBDP Schools in China

Despite the high performance of IBDP schools in terms of university entrance of their graduates to world-class universities, a concern emerges from their high school fees that are far beyond ordinary people's affordability in China. Specifically, Table 3.1 shows the tuition fees across IBDP schools in East and Southeast Asia. Of the 12 metropolitan cities in East and Southeast Asia, IBDP schools in Beijing and Shanghai charge the highest tuition fees whereas international IBDP schools in Manila, Hong Kong and Indonesia charge the lowest tuition fees. Notably, IBDP schools in Beijing and Shanghai charge more than their counterparts in Hong Kong, Singapore, and Tokyo, which are some of the most prosperous places in the world, as is indicated by country-level gross national income statistics. That is, if we consider the aspect of average incomes, the tuition fees charged by IBDP schools in Beijing and Shanghai appear to be relatively more expensive than the face value.

TABLE 3.1 Tuition fees of IBDP schools in major Asian cities (2012–2013)

Rank	City	Median tuition fees of IBDP schools (US$)	Number of schools	Country GNI per capita (US$)
1	Beijing	30,486	11	5,720
2	Shanghai	29,019	16	5,720
3	Seoul	26,399	2	22,670
4	Kuala Lumpur	23,000	4	9,820
5	Ho Chi Minh	20,475	6	1,550
6	Singapore	22,014	17	49,710
7	Taipei	18,348	2	N/A
8	Tokyo	18,000	5	47,870
9	Bangkok	17,661	7	5,210
10	Manila	16,075	5	2,500
11	Hong Kong	14,764	26	36,560
12	Jakarta	10,418	9	3,420

Notes: In this compiled information, several schools were not included due to data inaccessibility; specifically, two schools in Tokyo, one school in Bangkok, one school in Manila, and four schools in Jakarta. In addition, we acknowledge that city level IBDP school tuition fee data is not directly comparable to country-level gross national income statistics.

Source: World Bank (2014a).

The Emergence of Elite IBDP Schools in China **59**

In addition, the majority of the IBDP schools in Beijing and Shanghai charge fees in addition to tuition fees. This includes application fees, registration fees, deposits, and various forms of non-refundable capital levies. Indeed, if we take into account these additional charges, the median school fees of IBDP schools in Beijing and Shanghai for the 2012/13 academic year reached US$36,936 and US$29,345, respectively. Given that, as Table 3.1 shows, the gross national income per capita in China equalled US$5,720 in 2012, it is clear that the IBDP remains accessible to a very small minority of families who not only hold foreign passports but also have high socio-economic status (cf. Wright & Lee, 2014a). As a result, IBDP students in China may have limited opportunities to interact with students from other socio-economic and cultural backgrounds during their schooling. Moreover, this could be extended to their out-of-school lives by the language barriers faced by some non-Chinese nationals and that wealthy expatriates often reside in particular gated communities which can act as 'foreign enclaves' (Wang & Lau, 2008).

The Skyboxification of School Life in Elite IBDP Schools in China[5]

A central objective of the IBDP is to ensure that graduates are provided with an internationally validated route to higher education institutions around the world (IB, 2014d). As has been outlined in this chapter, the IBDP in China has been successful in this regard over the preceding decade. Indeed, further studies have identified that the IBDP is held in high esteem by leading universities in countries including Australia and New Zealand (Coates, Rosicka & MacMahon-Ball, 2007), the UK (Jenkins, 2003) and the USA (Gehring, 2001).

Yet, in addition to this largely instrumental function, the IB also claims that the IBDP is about providing a uniquely holistic and progressive education. Notably, the mission statement of IB states that the core purpose is "to develop inquiring, knowledgeable and caring young people who help to create a better and more peaceful world through *intercultural understanding* and respect" (IB, 2014e, emphasis added). The IB notes that this statement is "translated" into everyday school life through a set of ten Learner Profile outcomes promoted through the structure of the IBDP curriculum and pedagogical approaches. These include inquirers, knowledgeable, thinkers, communicators, principled, open-minded, caring, risk-takers, balanced, and reflective (IB, 2014b).

Reflecting this dual objective, there is a growing literature highlighting that there are considerable tensions between such a progressive educational philosophy and more instrumental concerns regarding university admissions, especially as the IB continue to expand into new educational contexts globally (see Brunold-Conesa, 2010; Doherty, 2009; Tarc, 2009).

60 Moosung Lee, Ewan Wright, and Allan Walker

Building on this work, our multi-site case study of five elite IBDP schools shed light on the relative success of the IB to implement the mission statement and the Learner Profile in the context of China. Above all, there was consensus among interviewees across the five case study schools that the Creativity, Action, Service (CAS) course had significant *potential* to promote Learner Profile outcomes such as balanced, caring, communicators, and open-minded. CAS is a compulsory IBDP course assessed by a pass/fail binary that the IB maintains offers a "refreshing counterbalance to academic studies". The 'Service' component of CAS is argued to provide students with opportunities for community engagement through projects such as "helping children with special needs, visiting hospitals and working with refugees or homeless people" (IB, 2014c).

Moreover, it was frequently noted that Learner Profile outcomes were related to the development of inter-cultural understanding that was deemed to have become highly important for academic and career-related success in an increasingly integrated world. In this regard, it was reported at three schools that CAS could be especially valuable for students at elite schools in terms of negating the potentially negative implications of a 'skyboxed' education by promoting inter-cultural understanding among students and other cultural, economic and social groups in society. As one teacher argued:

> Some of the projects involve working in orphanages and migrant schools. For our students these are really important because they are very privileged and could lack understanding of how the other half of the world lives—which is one of the most important things we need to make sure we teach them.
>
> (Teacher 4, School 3)

Despite this positive narrative, there were concerns about the *implementation* of CAS in the context of IBDP schools in China. Above all, this was thought to stem from the highly competitive and results-oriented culture of the five case study schools. For example, in describing the students, respondents variously reported that, "It is cool to work hard at school, that is definitely the culture here" (Coodinator, School 1), "It is all about taking the next step and entering the right university so passing the exam is the priority" (Headteacher, School 2), and "Our kids are not here to go to any kind of tertiary education that isn't somewhere not in the top 100 universities in the world" (Coodinator, School 4).

This academic environment was deemed to lead to tensions in the promotion of authentic engagement in CAS activities. Firstly, while there were examples of successful CAS projects, it was reported in four of the case schools that students often neglected CAS relative to other parts of the programme that were perceived to have a greater bearing on progression to higher education. Indeed, administrators, teachers and students all reported that many students reduced CAS to a "box-ticking" exercise and completing the course was often motivated by a desire to bolster applications as part of "the university admissions game". As one student described:

The Emergence of Elite IBDP Schools in China **61**

> I know a lot of students who do CAS because of CAS. I think that is the main disadvantage of CAS because everyone thinks 'does this activity count as CAS?' or 'how many hours can I get from this activity?' So it is more about getting credit and wanting to pass the IBDP.
>
> (Student 4, School 1)

Secondly, such tensions in implementing CAS in a result-oriented culture were reported to be heightened by difficulties in assessing student performance in CAS activities. As a result, it was argued that there were often limited ramifications if students were suspected of failing to engage in CAS in an authentic manner. Consequently, the interviewees reported that the benefits of CAS, which include tackling potentially negative implications of a 'skyboxed' education, could not be guaranteed through participation in the course. As was noted by one headteacher:

> You can be suspicious but if someone says, 'I really enjoyed working with those disabled kids and it has really changed the way I look at the world around me,' what are you going to say, 'I don't believe you'?
>
> (Headteacher, School 2)

In addition, respondents in three schools reported that difficulty in promoting student commitment to CAS was exacerbated by higher education institutions under-prioritising CAS in the admissions process. An implication of this was that some students could gain admission to elite higher education institutions without engaging in CAS in an authentic manner. As one coordinator argued:

> Just today one of our students was threatened to have the Diploma removed from him at this very, very late stage because his CAS portfolio was in an absolute mess … Now this student, and this brings up the whole idea of what's important to universities, got an offer from Oxford. It makes a point there.
>
> (Coordinator, School 4)

The IBDP and Open-Mindedness in China

To supplement our case study findings, we used the validated survey data of the IB Learner Profile Questionnaire (IBLPQ)[6] based on the findings of a pilot study (i.e., Walker et al., 2014). This enabled us to compare IBDP students in China with five different countries in terms of the perception of their capacity to be 'open-minded', one of the key IB Learner Profile attributes reflecting students' capacity for inter-cultural understanding of other cultural, economic, and social groups.[7] We compared 67 IBDP students in China with 82 IBDP students in five different countries in East Asia (Indonesia, Laos, Philippines, Singapore and Korea). Results showed that IBDP students in these countries indicated moderately high levels of perceptions of their capacity to be open-minded, given that the measure was based on a six-point Likert scale: mean = 4.41, SD = 0.81 for IBDP students in China and mean = 4.84, SD = 0.84 for IBDP students in the five countries. At the same time, however, there was a noticeable group difference in students' perceptions of their capacity to be 'open-minded'. A t-test indicated that IBDP students in China perceived a relatively lower level of 'open-minded' than their peers in other East Asian societies: $t(147) = -3.21$, $p = 0.002$.

Discussion

In recent years there has been heightened interest in documenting and explaining a global upturn of income and wealth inequality since the late 20th century (Krugman, 2013; Piketty, 2014; Stiglitz, 2012). Looking specifically at China, research has identified that income inequality now ranks among the highest globally and that inequality is particularly pronounced compared with countries with a similar or higher level of economic development (Xie and Zhou, 2014). A common response to such concerns is that the *distribution* of income and wealth is not necessarily a problem in its own right. Instead, it is often argued that the focus should be on reducing overall levels of poverty and increasing standards of living (see Feldstein, 1999, 2014). In this regard, China has been remarkably successful with World Bank data showing levels of "extreme poverty" have declined from 84% of the population in 1981 to 12% of the population in 2010 (Olinto et al., 2013).

Yet, the work of Sandel (2012) illuminates that a serious implication of economic inequality, in conjunction with an expansion in the realm of markets, is the 'skyboxification' of everyday life. Sandel posits that in increasingly unequal societies "we live and work and shop and play in different places. Our children go to different schools" (p. 203). As a result, Sandel believes that there are fewer places where "people of different backgrounds and social positions bump up against one another, in the course of everyday life" which he argues is essential to enabling citizens to "learn to negotiate and abide our differences" (p. 203). Put another way, as intra-societal inequality grows, people from different socio-economic backgrounds live increasingly isolated lives that, in turn, can restrict the development of inter-cultural understanding and open-mindedness within society.

In this section we aim to link what we have found from our data of international IBDP schools in China to this perspective of skyboxification. We argue that China represents a noteworthy case of skyboxification of an elite schooling system, given both the rapid expansion of IBDP schools over the past decade and their status as highly exclusive elite schools to Chinese people and also to some expatriates who are relatively less affluent relative to their counterparts in China. Specifically, even compared to IBDP schools in more economically developed neighbouring countries/societies in the region, IBDP schools in China charged

The Emergence of Elite IBDP Schools in China **63**

the highest school fee on average. Furthermore, the face value of such fees would be comparatively higher, given the living costs and annual income of ordinary people in China. That is, owing to both financial and legal restrictions on enrolment, access to international IBDP schools in China remains mostly limited to an elite minority of non-Chinese nationals from high socio-economic backgrounds.

While the high performance of IBDP schools in China in terms of university preparation and entrance to internationally reputable universities is applauded, the elite status of those IBDP schools indicates that such educational benefit (i.e., access to world-class universities) is enjoyed exclusively by those who can afford high school fees. Probably, one may counter-argue to justify this divide, based on market principles of selling and buying goods by saying "what's wrong with purchasing goods using my personal fortune?" Indeed, there is nothing wrong in this 'transaction' activity *per se*; selling and buying a civic good such as a place in an elite school is not illegal at least. However, several moral or justice-related concerns are overlooked in the transaction of a civic good, such as education.

First, if people can sell and buy something belonging to social public spheres, then the transaction can alter the essential quality or nature of such a good. For example, if a place in IBDP schools is regarded as something that can be transactional *only* for those who are able to afford it, educational activities including teaching and learning in IBDP schools can also be viewed as a part of such a transaction package; the affluent may think that they can buy teachers' time, teachers' professionalism, passion of teaching or even they may think that they can privatise experiences and activities offered by schools. Such a perception of teacher–student social relations as an economic transaction has been identified as part of a wider trend of the commodification of teaching practices (see Luke, 2004). We wish to argue that accommodating such transactions as a normal educational practice has a corrosive component that erodes the value or nature of education as a civic good—i.e., teaching and learning as part of a transactional package. If education is something that can be transactional, especially for only a selected group of parents in a society, without a base of any acceptable meritocratic components, such an education system can be viewed as merely an apparatus for reproducing or maintaining those selected groups' socio-economic status. In other words, it could be argued that such an education system cannot be regarded as entirely fair or just.

Another concern is pedagogical. Despite a rich cultural mix of student and faculty nationalities at IBDP schools in China, students may have limited scope to interact and develop inter-cultural understanding with host communities. Both of our qualitative and quantitative data highlight this concern. Indeed, without counter-balancing measures which successfully promote inter-cultural understanding and open-mindedness among students, the expansion of the IBDP across China could result in students being schooled in a relatively elitist "cultural bubble" (Pearce, 1994), which could also extend to their out-of-school lives due to language barriers and the concentration of wealthy expatriates in gated communities which function as "foreign enclaves" (Wang & Lau, 2008).

Specifically, our case study in five high performing schools indicated such dilemmas embedded in the implementation process of IB Learner Profile and CAS. These findings were given additional weight by our quantitative data analysis that shed light on the limited capacity of IB students in China to demonstrate open-mindedness relative to IB students in five other countries. Although the quantitative analysis has a limitation in terms of generalisability given its non-random sampling and small sample size, the finding is indicative that our concern of skyboxification is legitimate.

While the IBDP's high performance in terms of university preparation and entrance can be celebrated, we need to think about how such benefit can be more widely distributive to the rest of the public. In terms of policy, therefore, it seems necessary to expand access to IB programmes to public schools with systematic support. This would not be without precedent. For example, a vast majority of IBDP schools in the USA are public schools. Indeed, prior research has shown that IBDP schools in the USA can function as a springboard for the college admission of students of colour from low-income families (cf. Mayer, 2008). Unlike the US situation, we note that a majority of IBDP schools located in China and other countries in East Asia operate in the private schooling sector (Hallinger, Walker & Lee, 2010; Lee et al., 2014; Lee & Wright, 2015). According to Hallinger et al.'s (2010) study based on data from the IB gathered from 232 IB programme coordinators around the world, 87.3% of IB coordinators working in East Asia were from private schools whereas 48.5% of IB coordinators working in the rest of the world were from private schools. The finding from this proxy measure is consistent with the observations of others. For example, as of 2010, international education programmes located in Thailand were serving more than 100,000 students and *all* were located in private schools (Khaopa & Kaewmukda, 2010 cited in Lee et al., 2012a). This tendency of IB schools to operate predominantly in the private international schooling sector is salient in China where only the affluent have access to such educational opportunities. This resonates with the concerns about skyboxification; the fairness and meritocracy issues discussed above.

We think that the IBDP is equipped with the potential to become a model for schooling in the 21st century, given its progressive pedagogical approaches, innovative curriculum components and deep philosophical underpinnings. At the same time, however, reflecting all the tensions and concerns discussed in this paper, as critical supporters for IB schools, we argue that elite international IBDP schools in China need to pay more attention to the authentic implementation of CAS and the IB Learner Profile. We are aware that many of the interviewed teachers and principals strive for such authentic educational activities, despite various organisational challenges (cf. Lee et al., 2014; Lee et al., 2012a; Lee, Hallinger & Walker, 2012b). However, if IB schools are to succeed in becoming

The Emergence of Elite IBDP Schools in China **65**

a model for 21st-century schooling, rather than being a forerunner among elite schooling systems, the concerns raised in this chapter must be taken seriously in terms of school improvement and organisational development.

Finally, we believe that this chapter demonstrates how Sandel's concept of skyboxification can serve as another lens to deepen our understanding of the elite schooling system in particular and the marketisation of schools in general. Above all, we believe that the skyboxification perspective enables researchers to take a closer look at the moral limits of the rapidly growing elite international schooling system in East Asia, which to date has been primarily driven by market impetus that potentially erodes public and civic life for many of us.

Notes

1   While the vast majority of IBDP schools in China operate in the international schooling sector, there are a small number of 'local' schools in China that offer IB programmes.

2   The IB defines the Learner Profile as the "set of learning outcomes for the 21st century" which are promoted through IB programmes. The learning outcomes include balanced, caring, communicators, inquirers, knowledgeable, principled, open-minded, reflective, risk-takers, and thinkers (IB, 2014b). CAS is a compulsory part of the IBDP that is geared towards offering students a "refreshing counterbalance to academic studies". The IB states that projects for the Service component of CAS could involve "helping children with special needs, visiting hospitals and working with refugees or homeless people" (2014c).

3   Some findings are reconstructed from our recent research (Lee et al., 2014). For more details of this section, see Lee et al. (2014).

4   Specifically, to generate the first group of universities, we used three major university ranking tables published in 2011/12: Academic Ranking of World Universities (ARWU) offered by Shanghai Jiao Tong University, QS World University Rankings, and the Times Higher Education World University Rankings.

5   Some parts of this section were reconstructed from our previous work (i.e., Wright & Lee, 2014a).

6   For more details about the statistical procedures and psychometric properties of the IBLPQ, see Walker et al. (2014). Regarding the question of items for measuring open-minded, the following items were used: (1) Critically examine your own cultural values and beliefs. (2) Critically explore the ways different individuals and cultures see the world. (3) Learn about the values and beliefs of different cultures. (4) Examine your own values and beliefs through learning how people from other cultures think and act. (5) Consciously seek more knowledge about different cultures. (6) Encourage others to learn about different countries and cultures.

7   In this comparison, we excluded the samples from Hong Kong since a vast majority of the sampled students were from Hong Kong—i.e., 827 out of 976 (85%)—for a more balanced comparison in terms of the sample sizes of the subgroups.

References

Brummitt, N., & Keeling, A. (2013). Charting the growth of international schools. In R. Pearce (Ed.), *International education and schools* (pp. 25–36). London: Bloomsbury Academic.

Brunold-Conesa, C. (2010). International education: The International Baccalaureate, Montessori and global citizenship. *Journal of Research in International Education*, 9(3), 259–272.

Bunnell, T. (2008). The exporting and franchising of elite English private schools: The emerging 'second wave'. *Asia Pacific Journal of Education*, 28(4), 383–393.

Bunnell, T. (2014). *The changing landscape of international schooling: Implications for theory and practice*. Oxon: Routledge.

Coates, H., Rosicka, C., & MacMahon-Ball, M. (2007). *Perceptions of the International Baccalaureate diploma programme among Australian and New Zealand universities*. Melbourne: Australian Council for Educational Research Press.

Doherty, C. A. (2009). The appeal of the International Baccalaureate in Australia's educational market: A curriculum of choice for mobile futures. *Discourse: Studies in the Cultural Politics of Education*, 30(1), 73–89.

Donnelly, M. (2014). The road to Oxbridge: Schools and elite university choices. *British Journal of Educational Studies*, 62(1), 57–72.

Feldstein, M. (1999). Reducing poverty, not inequality. *The Public Interest*, 137(Fall), 33–41.

Feldstein, M. (2014, May 14). Piketty's numbers don't add up. *The Wall Street Journal*. Retrieved 23 June 2014 from http://online.wsj.com/news/articles/SB100014240527 0230408180457955766417691 7086

Gaztambide-Fernández, R. A. (2009). What is an elite boarding school? *Review of Educational Research*, 79(3), 1090–1128.

Gehring, J. (2001). The International Baccalaureate: 'Cadillac' of college prep programs. *Education Week*, 20(32), 19.

Hallinger, P., Walker, A., & Lee, M. (2010). *A study of successful practices in the IB program continuum*. Hong Kong: Asia Pacific Center for Leadership and Change, Hong Kong Institute of Education.

Hayden, M., & Thompson, J. (2008). *International schools: Growth and influence*. Paris: UNESCO.

Hayes, C. (2012). *Twilight of the elites: America after meritocracy*. New York: BroadwayBooks.

Heyward, M. (2002). From international to inter-cultural: Redefining the international school for a globalized world. *Journal of Research in International Education*, 1(9), 9–32.

International Baccalaureate Organization. (2014a). Find an IB World School. Retrieved 1 May 2014 from http://www.ibo.org/school/search/

International Baccalaureate Organization. (2014b). IB Learner Profile. Retrieved 1 May 2014 from http:// www.ibo.org/programmes/profile/

International Baccalaureate Organization. (2014c). Diploma Programme Curriculum – Core Requirements. Retrieved 1 May 2014 from http://www.ibo.org/diploma/ curriculum/core/cas/

International Baccalaureate Organization. (2014d). University Recognition. Retrieved 1 May 2014 from http://www.ibo.org/recognition/university/

International Baccalaureate Organization. (2014e). Mission and Strategy. Retrieved 1 May 2014 from http://www.ibo.org/mission/

Jenkins, C. (2003). *Perceptions of the International Baccalaureate Diploma Programme: A report of an inquiry carried out at UK universities and institutions of higher education.* United Kingdom: International Baccalaureate Organization.

Kenway, J. (2013). Challenging inequality in Australian schools: Gonski and beyond. *Discourse: Studies in the Cultural Politics of Education,* 34(2), 286–308.

Kenway, J., & Fahey, J. (2014). Staying ahead of the game: The globalising practices of elite schools. *Globalisation, Societies and Education,* 12(2), 177–195.

Kenway, J., & Koh, A. (2013). The elite school as 'cognitive machine' and 'social paradise': Developing transnational capital for the 'national field of power'. *Journal of Sociology,* 49(2–3), 272–290.

Khan, S. R. (2013). Elite identities. *Identities: Global Studies in Culture and Power* (Special Issue: Re-launch Issue: Mapping Identities), 19(4), 477–484.

Koh, A. (2014). Doing class analysis in Singapore's elite education: Unravelling the smokescreen of 'meritocratic talk'. *Globalisation, Societies and Education,* 12(2), 165–176.

KPMG. (2010) *Education in China.* Amstelveen, The Netherlands: KPMG International Cooperative.

Krugman, P. (2013, December 15). Why inequality matters. *The New York Times.* Retrieved 16 June 2014 from http://www.nytimes.com/2013/12/16/opinion/krugman-why-inequality-matters.html?_r=0

Lee, M., & Wright, E. (2015). Elite schools in international education markets in East Asia: Emerging patterns, successes and challenges. In Hayden, M., Levy, J. & Thompson, J. (Eds.). *The Sage handbook of research in international education* (pp. 583–597). Thousand Oaks, California: Sage.

Lee, M., Hallinger, P., & Walker, A. (2012a). Leadership challenges in international schools in the Asia Pacific region: Evidence from program implementation of the International Baccalaureate. *International Journal of Leadership in Education,* 15(3), 289–310.

Lee, M., Hallinger, P., & Walker, A. (2012b). A distributed perspective on instructional leadership in International Baccalaureate (IB) schools. *Educational Administration Quarterly,* 48, 664–698.

Lee, M., Leung, L., Wright, E., Yue, T., Gan, A., Kong, L., & Li, J. (2014). *A study of the International Baccalaureate Diploma in China: Program's impact on student preparation for university studies abroad.* Hong Kong: Education Policy Unit, Faculty of Education, The University of Hong Kong.

Li, H., Meng, L., Shi, X., & Wu, B. (2012). Does attending elite colleges pay in China? *Journal of Comparative Economics,* 40(1), 78–88.

Lin, J. (2009). Emergence of private schools in China: Contexts, characteristics and implications. In E. Hannum & A. Park (Eds.), *Education and Reform in China* (pp. 44–63). Oxon: Routledge.

Luke, A. (2004). Teaching after the market: From commodity to cosmopolitan. *Teachers College Record,* 106(7), 1422–1433.

Marginson, S. (2007). Global university rankings: Implications in general and for Australia. *Journal of Higher Education Policy and Management,* 29(2), 131–142.

Mayer, A. (2008). Expanding opportunities for high academic achievement: An International Baccalaureate Diploma Program in an urban high school. *Journal of Advanced Academics,* 19(2), 202–235.

Miles, M. B., & Huberman, A. M. (1994). *Qualitative data analysis: An expanded sourcebook* (2nd ed.). Thousand Oaks, CA: Sage.

Mills, C. W. (1956). *The power elite*. London: Oxford University Press.

Ministry of Education. (2010). *The Outline of China's National Plan for Medium and Long-term Education Reform and Development (2010–2020)*. Retrieved 6 June 2014 from https://www.aei.gov.au/news/newsarchive/2010/documents/china_education_reform_pdf.pdf

Ng, V. (2013). The decision to send local children to international schools in Hong Kong: Local parents' perspectives. *Asia Pacific Education Review*, 13(1), 121–136.

OECD. (2011). *Strong performers and successful reformers in education: Lessons from PISA for the United States*. Paris: OECD Publishing.

Olinto, P., Beegle, K., Sobrado, C., & Uematsu, H. (2013). *The state of the poor: Where are the poor, where is extreme poverty harder to end, and what is the current profile of the world's poor?* Washington, DC: World Bank.

Pearce, R. (1994). International schools: The multinational enterprises' best friends. *CBI Relocation News*, 32, 8–9.

Piketty, T. (2014). *Capital in the twenty-first century*. Cambridge. MA: Harvard University Press.

Qian, H., & Walker, A. (2011). The 'gap' between policy intent and policy effect: An exploration of the interpretations of school principals in China. In T. Huang & A. W. Wiseman (Eds.), *The impact and transformation of education policy in China* (pp. 187–208). Bingley: Emerald Group Publishing Limited.

Sandel, M. (2012). *What money can't buy: The moral limits of markets*. New York: Farrar Strauss Giroux.

Sklair, L. (2001). *The transnational capitalist class*. Oxford: Blackwell.

Stiglitz, J. (2012). *The price of inequality: How today's divided society endangers our future*. London: W. W. Norton & Company.

Tarc, P. (2009). *Global dreams, enduring tensions: International Baccalaureate in a changing world*. New York: Peter Lang.

Walker, A., Bryant, D., & Lee, M. (2014). *The International Baccalaureate continuum: Student, teacher and school outcomes*. Hong Kong: Asia Pacific Center for Leadership and Change, Hong Kong Institute of Education.

Walker, A., Lee, M., & Bryant, D. (forthcoming). Development and validation of the International Baccalaureate Learner Profile Questionnaire (IBLPQ). *Educational Psychology*. DOI: 10.1080/01443410.2015.1045837

Wang, J., & S. S. Y. Lau (2008). Forming foreign enclaves in Shanghai: State action in globalization. *Journal of Housing and the Built Environment*, 23(2), 103–118.

Weis, L., Cipollone, K., & Jenkins, H. (2014). *Class warfare: Class, race, and college admissions in top-tier secondary schools*. Chicago: The University of Chicago Press.

World Bank. (2014a). GNI per capita, Atlas method (current US$). Retrieved 18 June 2014 from http://data.worldbank.org/indicator/NY.GNP.PCAP.CD

World Bank. (2014b). School enrollment, secondary (% gross). Retrieved 18 June 2014 from http://data.worldbank.org/indicator/SE.SEC.ENRR

Wright, E., & Lee, M. (2014a). Elite International Baccalaureate Diploma Programme schools and inter-cultural understanding in China. *British Journal of Educational Studies*, 62(2), 149–169.

The Emergence of Elite IBDP Schools in China **69**

Wright, E., & Lee, M. (2014b). Developing skills for youth in the 21st century: The role of elite International Baccalaureate Diploma Programme schools in China. *International Review of Education*, 60(2), 199–216.

Wu, X. (2014). *School choice in China: A different tale?* Oxon: Routledge.

Xie, Y., & Zhou, X. (2014). Income inequality in today's China. *Proceedings of the National Academy of the United States of America*, 111(19), 6928–6933.

Zhang, H. (2013). The mirage of elite schools: Evidence from lottery-based school admissions in China. Retrieved 18 June 2014 from http://www.sole-jole.org/13050.pdf

Zhao, Y. (2014). *Who's afraid of the big bad dragon?: Why China has the world's best and worst education.* San Francisco, CA: Jossey-Bass.

4

ELITE SCHOOLBOYS BECOMING GLOBAL CITIZENS

Examining the Practice of Habitus

Chin Ee Loh

In *The Credential Society*, published in 1979, Randall Collins (1979) suggests that educational credentials rather than grades and occupational skills are more likely predictors of occupational success. He argues that despite the increasing emphasis on education and greater access to credentials in the US context, there has been little change in relative stratification, since "the children of the higher social class have increased their schooling in the same proportions as the lower social classes have increased theirs" (p. 183). Collins' prediction of an expansion of credentialism holds true in today's neoliberal economy where education continues to be seen as the route to an economic and social mobility no longer limited by the national market. The credential competition has intensified to include not just the accumulation of better grades but also better portfolios that demonstrate abundance of talent (in the form of sporting or artistic ability) and character (in the form of leadership, participation in community involvement projects and the accumulation of varied experiences beyond one's nation). After all, the world is an oyster for those who demonstrate the ability to flexibly engage in knowledge production work, who are able to become "symbol-analysts" (Reich, 1991) or "ideal global workers" (Resnik, 2008) able to engage in economically rewarding work at national and international levels.

Elite schools with their rich histories, connections and funding are excellent breeding grounds for developing students' portfolio of dispositions, grades and connections required for global mobility. In this chapter, I focus on how elite schoolboys construct global identities, on how they *become* elite through the acquisition of various desirable dispositions that allow for a flexible citizenship in various nation-states, and at transnational level (Ong, 1999). As cosmopolitans, these elite students would become what Hannerz calls "'the new class' people with credentials, decontextualized cultural capital" (Hannerz, 1990, p. 246) whose influence rested on *whom* they know rather than *what* they know. Yet, the role of elite schools is not just to provide students with the know-how for international profit-making. Rather, the ideological role of elite schools in producing national leaders (Koh & Kenway, 2012) and international agents of social change (Bunnell, 2010) forms much of the agenda of the elite schools. In the context of the International Baccalaureate (IB) schools, Bunnell suggests that the expansion of IB schools could lead to the emergence of a group of business-oriented 'class-for-itself' individuals or to more compassionate, socially responsible global citizens. In the same way, the complexity of elite schooling is played out in the everyday lived experiences of students from this study, with the myriad of school organised events such as extra-curricular activities and overseas enrichment programmes inculcating twin desires of advancement and service.

The work of elite schools in reproducing advantage has been one key concern of educational sociologists since the seminal work of Bourdieu and Passeron (1990) in France and Bowles and Gintis (1976) in the USA. More recently, there has been another wave of research and scholarship on elite schools in Anglophone contexts such as the USA (Demerath, 2009; Howard & Gaztambide-Fernández, 2010; Khan, 2012), France (Draelants & Darchy-Koechlin, 2011), Australia (Meadmore & Meadmore, 2004). The five-year study by an international team "Elite Independent Schools in Globalising Circumstances: A Multi-sited Global Ethnography" (2010–2014) has also done much to expand our understanding of elite schools in former British colonies such as South Africa, Singapore, and India (e.g., Epstein, 2014; Fahey, 2014; Kenway & Koh, 2013). "Studying up" (Howard, 2010b) can provide critical insight into how advantage (and thus, disadvantage) is reproduced. Moreover, in an increasingly globalised world where issues of mobility and (in)equity extend beyond national boundaries, scholars have also began to explore the impact of globalisation on elite schooling: how do elite schools reposition themselves in global educational markets (Courtois, 2015; Rizvi, 2014), how do elite schools educate students for global professional futures (Forbes & Lingard, 2015; Kenway & Koh, 2013), how do elite students move across national borders and for what purposes (Waters, 2006; Ye & Nylander, 2015)?

Becoming an elite student involves the complex interplay of home and school habitus (Bourdieu, 1984) where the individual learns particular dispositions and habits associated with being elite. Habitus, or the embodiment of an individual's life experiences, including his or her family background, schooling, and educational credentials, serves as a form of distinction for elite students to distinguish themselves from the perceived masses. In this chapter, I focus on how the individual habitus of a group of elite schoolboys cohere with the institutional habitus of school to shape their identification as potential globe-trotting professionals and global citizens. This chapter illustrates the situated and localised nature of habitus by exploring how the taken-for-granted advantages, values and beliefs embedded in these boys' everyday practice of place is situated in localised debates on schooling and education. Examining the practice, or the boys' lived

72 Chin Ee Loh

experiences of habitus, allows for critical insight into how the "invisible knapsack" (McIntosh, 1988) of privilege, dominated by the twin discourses of meritocracy and cosmopolitanism, is played out in the Singapore context.

Theoretical Perspectives

I approach the study of elite students from a position of privilege as identity, thus foregrounding privilege as a form of self-understanding (Howard, 2010b). Elite students locate their privilege in relation to others, and within the field of practice that constitutes the sociocultural milieu, the school and home contexts in which individuals exist and live. They develop "ways of knowing" (Khan, 2012) about the world that are meaningful in schooling and high status occupational contexts, and these ways of knowing are evidenced in their "saying(writing)-doing-being-valuing-believing" (Gee, 1996, p. 127), everyday taken-for-granted dispositions that may be perceived as natural to an elite student's identity. *Becoming* a particular kind of elite student is the result of the interplay between agency and structure, where dialogic interaction with the world and others in it shape individual notions of who they are and where they belong (Holland et al., 1998).

Bourdieu's concept of habitus is useful for examining the complexities involved in the shaping of the identity—the values, beliefs, worldviews and actions—of an elite student. The habitus is

> the durably installed generative principle of *regular improvisations* ... a system of lasting and transposable dispositions which, integrating past experiences, functions at every moment as a matrix of perceptions, appreciations and actions.
>
> (Bourdieu, 1977, pp. 80/95)

The habitus, or an individual's life position, is thus a set of predispositions acquired by individuals through early upbringing, and is embodied by being inscribed in "the body of the biological individual" (Reay, 2004, p. 433). While habitus is "an open system of dispositions" (Bourdieu & Wacquant, 1992, p. 133) that is constantly subjected to experiences that may reinforce or modify structures, the family backgrounds that individuals are born into are more likely than not to lead to social experiences that reinforce perceptions, beliefs and values about self and others ingrained from early childhood. Attention to habitus reminds us that individual worldviews and actions are shaped by the social and cultural networks that individuals are steeped in, and that the highly personal act of identity-making is infused with power play.

The concept of habitus is the explanatory device for how individuals come to possess certain social, cultural and symbolic capital that holds value within a particular field of practice. The field is the space within which individuals or groups struggle to gain dominance through acquisition of suitable capital in order to move up the ladder of social mobility. Injustice, however, occurs when individuals are conferred dominance by virtue of their race, gender or class (McIntosh, 1988) and come to see their privilege as deserved and earned as a result of personal talent and investment without recognition of the structural advantages to their position (Howard, 2010a). Real or imagined boundaries shape the individuals' actual and perceived spaces, and attending to the imagined field or "figured worlds" (Holland et al., 1998) of individuals, institutions, and nations allow us to unearth individual ways of thinking that reveal much about the varieties of habitus that shape the identity construction of these elite schoolboys. By focusing on the personal and institutional practice of habitus, that is, the beliefs and values of the student and school inscribed in daily conversations and curriculum, I identify the dominant and contradictory discourses that shape elite schoolboys' understandings of self, school, and society to better understand how the habitus of excellence and cosmopolitanism are reproduced at institutional and individual levels. Making visible the mechanics for reproducing inequity in specific contexts allows us to locate spaces for possible change.

Research Methods

The study takes an ethnographic approach in the case study of six elite schoolboys' identity practice. Data included observations of different classes and interviews with Deans, teachers, current students at different grade levels, and alumni, examination of official documents such as the school website and curriculum documents, and interviews with school administration, teachers and students conducted over the course of a year from September 2008 to September 2009. In order to "understand complex social phenomena" (Yin, 2003, p. 2), case studies of boys were conducted over the course of one year. At the time of the study, these boys were between 14 and 15 years of age, and I followed them from Year 2 to Year 3 (equivalent to Grades 8 and 9 in Australia). I observed these boys over 49 classroom observations, interviewed them individually or in groups at least three times each, collected bi-monthly reading logs from them via email, and compiled field notes on a weekly basis.

I acknowledge my role as both an insider and outsider. While I was not from an elite school myself, I attended a Methodist church that was populated with Ace Institution boys and students from other Methodist institutions. I taught for six years in three schools, out of which three were spent in Ace Institution. I returned to Ace Institution as a researcher, an outsider whose gaze had been informed by her work on literacy, class and schooling, but who also remained in many ways sensitive to the discourses circulated and enacted within the school.

74 Chin Ee Loh

Social Class and Schooling in the Singapore Context

The Social Context of Schooling in Singapore

Previously a British colony, Singapore is a multiracial state with a Chinese majority (74.1%) and a substantial percentage of Malays (13.4%), Indians (9.2%), and other ethnicities (3.3%) (Singapore Department of Statistics, 2011). Given the lack of hinterland and resources, the Singapore government's emphasis has been on people as "its own prime asset" (Olds & Thrift, 2005) to maintain its competitiveness as a world-class city in a global economy. Education takes on a "manufacturing" dimension (Koh & Chong, 2014) where individuals are perceived as human capital to be shaped according to the economic needs of the nation, in large part through a centralised and highly effective education system. In the national imagination of Singapore, there is a constant drive towards cosmopolitanism and excellence to maintain economic competitiveness, yet maintaining a sense of "belonging and emotional rootedness" (Ministry of Education, 2011) to the nation paradoxically.

One dominant national discourse that has shaped much of the political and the education landscape is the concept of meritocracy, understood as the provision of equal opportunity for social and economic advancement, based on merit rather than race, religion, or gender. However, there is inherent contradiction between egalitarianism and elitism in a meritocratic system that is designed to cultivate the best and brightest in the belief that there would be a trickle-down effect to society at large (K. P. Tan, 2010). Given the widening income disparities in Singapore's market-driven economy (Smith, 2015), there are increasing concerns that a "class-blind" version of meritocracy may lead to elitism and social stratification. Yet, official educational policies and research tend to sideline socioeconomic status as a factor for school success (J. Tan, 2010).

The terms 'cosmopolitans' and 'heartlanders' coined by former Prime Minister Goh Chok Tong (1999) to describe two kinds of Singaporeans may well capture the mindset that lingers in Singapore's differentiated educational policy and practices (see Ho, 2012; Lim, 2014). Cosmopolitans have an "international outlook that enable them to work and be comfortable anywhere in the world" whereas the heartlanders are the "conservative majority" who tend to be more rooted to the nation and concerned with their daily bread and butter than political issues. The cosmopolitan–heartlander terminology has strong social inflections and generated much controversy when first used because of its uncomplicated division of Singaporeans into two types with their specific traits and dispositions. Cosmopolitans are perceived as more likely to treat Singapore as a "hotel" rather than a "home" because of their global marketability, whereas heartlanders tend to see Singapore as home because of their attachment to home, or their lack of choice (Ho, 2006). At the same time, because cosmopolitans are able to generate wealth through their skills and connections, they must be persuaded to regard

Singapore as home and the world as their marketplace. Thus, while elite students are expected to become globe-trotting cosmopolitans with international outlooks and skills to extend their economic reach beyond Singapore, heartlanders are less mobile, and invariably tied to the nation by their absence of options.

Institutional Discourses of Excellence, Cosmopolitanism, and Service

The concepts of cosmopolitan and heartlander are played out in the different kinds of schools in Singapore. As with many post-colonial nations, Singapore has inherited the British educational legacy of training elite students for leadership (Kennedy, 2013), and Ace Institution is one such elite school with a long history of educational and extra-curricular achievement. Elite schools are perceived as educational sites for the intense grooming of talent—whether academic, sporting or artistic—and stand apart from generic "neighbourhood" schools catering to the majority of Singapore students with their long and unique institutional histories and identities. Michael, one of the participants in the study, remarked that he chose Ace Institution out of the many schools available to him after his Primary School Leaving Examination (PSLE) because of the confidence projected by Ace Institution boys.

The school's institutional habitus is important in preserving and reproducing the social positioning of elite schools as choice schools for the cultivation of particular sorts of dispositions and skills required for a global world (Forbes & Lingard, 2015). The institutional habitus (Reay, David & Ball, 2001), "understood as the impact of a cultural group or social class on an individual's behaviour as it is mediated through an organization" (McDonough, 1996 in Reay et al., 2001), consists of the ethos, values and expectations of the school. Institutional habitus plays an important role insofar as it structures individuals' perceptions and expectations of choice and contributes to students' understanding of the purpose of education (for them) and their role in the wider world. The institutional habitus is situated and specific to its location. Discourses of excellence and distinction, tradition and progressiveness, and rooted cosmopolitanism comprise Ace Institution's institutional habitus, and are reflected in the boys' demeanour and attitudes.

Founded in 1886 by British Methodist missionaries, it can be said that Ace Institution had always had its eye on the (English) world with its emphasis on the English language and culture, an asset even after Singapore gained independence as English was perceived as the language of business, and eventually adopted as the language of education and business (Gopinathan, 1980). The school was one of the first schools in Singapore to organise annual overseas learning trips for its students before it became fashionable, a reflection of the school's cosmopolitan outlook as well as relative wealth. The school, with its long history of educational excellence, was also one of the first schools in Singapore chosen to become an

76 Chin Ee Loh

Integrated Programme (IP) school, where academically able, university-bound students are allowed to skip a national high stakes examination, the GCE 'O' level examinations, and move on directly from secondary school (Years 1–4, equivalent to Grades 7–10 in the Australian system) to pre-tertiary education within the school. The aim towards internationalism, in line with the national discourse of globalisation, is evident in the school's adoption of the International Baccalaureate Diploma Programme (IBDP), an international schooling system, as the selected route for students who qualified, and opted to skip the GCE O levels. Through the World Literature focus of the IBDP curriculum, the school shapes the cosmopolitan sensibilities of the Ace student as well read and multicultural in his or her ease with texts from different parts of the world (Loh, 2012). The emphasis on literary study in the IBDP English curriculum is telling in that it marks the elite school boy as above the rest, since Literature is perceived as a subject reserved for the elite who have a flair for language.

In the hypercompetitive educational climate of Singapore, Ace Institution students were given many opportunities to perform academically and in their extracurricular activities. Trophies for sporting, artistic and uniformed groups lined the main foyer and the principal's office and contributed to a sense of history and excellence. Like the students in other studies of elite schools, Ace Institution students more often than not display a sense of assuredness (Forbes & Lingard, 2015) in the way they related to others and with regard to their possible futures. A long-time teacher at the school described the Ace Institution boy to me as "confident, sometimes to the extent of being cocky" and suggests that "part of the confidence comes from speaking and writing well". In my interviews and informal conversations with school staff, alumni, recent graduates and students, there was a strong sense of loyalty to the school's superior "brand" (Demerath, 2009) of education. Ace Institution's brand included being fluent in English, both spoken and written, self-confidence, and having a strong arts and sporting culture. This culture of achievement and confidence is evident in the illustrious alumni records of the school, boasting of alumni from top-tier universities all over the world including Oxford in the UK, Yale and Stanford in the USA, and successful professionals, businessmen, politicians, and thespians well known in Singapore and overseas for their success in their respective fields. Beyond these prestigious fields, Ace Institution could also lay claim to a number of alumni involved in missions or not-for-profit work, in line with its aims to develop citizens willing to serve both nation and world in less (monetarily) profitable ways.

Elite Schoolboys Becoming Global Citizens

It is within these dominant and overlapping discourses of nation and school that the elite students in the study constructed their identities as both global and Singapore citizens. Elite schoolboys constructing themselves as globe-trotting cosmopolitans is very much in line with both national and institutional desires, yet this desire to go global has to be mitigated within the local context, where issues of human capital and economic interests have to be balanced with the school's mission to contribute in visible ways to the community. Ostensibly, the international curriculum and *ethos* of the school strives towards the ideal of constructing global citizens ready to participate and contribute to an interconnected world. Yet, the overriding pragmatic reason for most parents to invest in Ace Institution's international education represented by the IBDP with its emphasis on critical thinking, innovation and problem-solving is that of their child's future economic prospects and global job mobility (Bunnell, 2010; Resnik, 2008). At the same time, it would be simplifying matters to say that all parents and students saw only the economic benefits of elite schooling without recognising the service aspect emphasised in the institutional habitus of Ace Institution. Rather, there remains an ambivalent tension between education for self-gain and education for others in the everyday practice of becoming elite.

Meritocracy and Hard Work as the Route to Becoming Elite

The boys in this study are generally unaware of their class position and relative privilege in the Singapore context, seeing themselves as 'average' Singaporeans, a comparison made possible by the considerable number of wealthy students within the school. Their relative home advantage can be inferred from a news report stating that 72% of the students from Ace Institution's parents had university degrees, compared to the paltry 5–13% in neighbourhood schools (Ramesh, 2011). Of the six case study students, all parents were university graduates, all either had both parents in professional jobs or had a stay-at-home mother looking after them, all lived in private property and all travelled widely with their family.

Students learn privilege and imbued their right to their class position as part of their identity, as illustrated in the following focus group conversation where the boys positioned themselves as equal players in a meritocratic system where the best (and most hardworking) man wins (Howard, 2010a; Koh, 2014). In the following focus group discussion, the boys themselves bring up and acknowledge the division of school types in Singapore, seeing the division into 'NSK' or 'neighbourhood school kids' and elite school students as part and parcel of the Singapore landscape of schooling.

Robert:[1] That's why we're here in the Ace Institution.

Roger: I think that's quite true you know. Cos that's the divide between NSK and us. NSK.

Joshua: Yeah.

Roger: That is the divide.

78 Chin Ee Loh

Chin Ee: NSK?

Joshua: Neighbourhood school kids.

Robert: The general populace … for those who rise above the propaganda.

Chin Ee: Is it so clear-cut as this? That it's neighbourhood school kids versus elite school.

Robert: Seriously. You see, we're just making a generalisation. Most people are just satisfied with their lot in life …

Roger: Like, look at them? So we have two classes of people. Those that are rather educated and those that are educated but …

Michael: *But that's quite untrue. As in generally you know …*

Sanjeev: Those people, they have no interest in being the best, being globally competitive, don't care. Cos it obviously doesn't make any difference.

Robert: They're only concerned with living their lives happily, being content … It's one of those comparisons between those who are satisfied with going to SIM [Singapore Institute of Management] and those who want to go overseas.

Chin Ee: But what if you can't financially?

Robert: Get a scholarship!

Chin: What if academically you can't?

Robert: It's the goal. Those who dream of studying overseas will study for it.
(Focus Group, 19 May 2009, *emphasis mine*)

In the above extract, the students position themselves as intelligent and hardworking individuals, thus locating themselves in a position of power, which is in their opinion, earned. Individual agency is strong, and even the choice of school is seen as deliberate individual effort to excel ("That's why we're here in Ace Institution"). Their identities are constructed by distinguishing themselves from the NSK or neighbourhood school kids, a term used in a derogatory manner by the boys to mark those who "have no interest in being the best" (Sanjeev) and who are "only concerned with living their lives happily" (Robert). Roger, Robert, Joshua and Sanjeev position themselves as "those that are rather educated" (Roger) and who will work hard to achieve excellence, evidenced in part by a desire for an overseas education, a sign of their cosmopolitan outlook. In contrast, NSK are rooted to Singapore because they are easily "content" (Robert) and are not interested in "being globally competitive" (Sanjeev). The desire to go global is thus linked with the desire to be excellent.

Identities are positional and relational (Holland et al., 1998), and it is in comparison with others that individuals develop a stable sense of where they are (Taylor, 1989). The unproblematic acceptance of NSK as those who do not try and elite school students as those who do reflects the boys' superficial understanding of meritocracy as an equal system that will benefit all who work hard. They position themselves on the top rung of the social ladder of success but do not recognise that their movement up the academic and credential ladder may be due to their privileged family backgrounds, which include access to print-rich backgrounds (Lareau, 2003; Loh, 2013) and investments in private tuition and out-of-school enrichment activities such as piano lessons and annual holidays to far-flung places. Instead, the dominant discourse is that of the ethics of hard work, which drives the conversation about ambition, success and education. Using what Howard (2010a) terms a "naturalization ideological strategy", the boys accord achievement patterns to personal choice and effort rather than economic background. By according the same agency to all students, they are able to argue that less successful students do not succeed because of their lack of will and effort. In the process, social class is downplayed and their ability to be the best is attributed to innate intelligence, talent and hard work.

This same misrecognition (Bourdieu & Passeron, 1990) is observed by Stuber (2010) in her study of middle-class college girls. She notes their propensity to be "blind" to their own privilege. Instead of comparing themselves to the less privileged, privileged girls tend to relativise their privilege against those who are more privileged than themselves. Growing up in relatively cloistered and uniform social worlds with others in the same life position, the boys do not see their relative advantage. Thus, Sanjeev, one of the case study students, remarks that because he does not live in Bukit Timah, a wealthy residential area, he is not "super-rich" even though he lives in a large bungalow, and expects to go to the USA for an Ivy League education on his parents' sponsorship, following his sister's footsteps.

Yet, the issue of constructing a global identity as an elite student is a complex issue lived out in the everyday experiences and practices of these boys, which differ across experiences and across the years. In the discussion, Michael attempts to interrupt the dominant discourse ("But that's quite untrue"), but is silenced by the force of the discussion positioning NSK as uncompetitive and lazy. In a follow-up interview, Michael tells me that he is a "heartlander" and explains

> Yeah, I'm a freaking *Hokkien-speaking Ah Beng*! I don't say in front of you or act like that in school. But when I go out with my friends, they're not like these school friends. They're like people from ITE [Institute of Technical Education], neighbourhood schools, all those *pie kiah* ones … It's not true that they are not educated.
>
> (Interview with Michael, 27 March 2009)

80 Chin Ee Loh

Michael's alternative viewpoint comes from the fact that his out-of-school social circle includes friends at church and at his neighbourhood playground from other walks of life. Michael positions himself as a 'heartlander' as opposed to the cosmopolitan Singaporean. However, he is, paradoxically, the epitome of cosmopolitanism, a confident English language speaker whose favourite subject is Literature, and who is proud to be Ace-sian. His life experiences interrupt the dominant discourse that governs his classmates' mindsets about the 'NSK Other', and provides him with an alternate way of imagining the world as a Singaporean student. He proffers an alternate version of elitism that includes an awareness of privilege, chiefly because of his own experiences beyond the typical social circle of his schoolmates. His interaction with the NSK others gives him insight into the social lives of others against which he measures his life position and expands his knowledge of the world.

The Institutional Habitus of Cosmopolitanism and Service Through Overseas Learning

In contrast to the boys' limited knowledge of different social worlds in Singapore, the school seeks to expand students' knowledge of the world through the organisation of compulsory Overseas Enrichment Programmes (OEPs) for its students. These annual trips to places such as Vietnam and Thailand, and resulting fund-raising activities are in line with the school's core purpose for students to be "equipped and willing to serve and lead in the family, nation and global community" (school website) through international outreach programmes. The school's commitment to the programme is evident in the amount of resources pumped into it and its commitment to return to the same locations to serve. The institutionalised practice of overseas community service, repeated annually, becomes part of the school habitus, and is etched into individual consciousness. These overseas trips ostensibly served two seemingly contradictory functions: it imbues a sense of social responsibility in the students while adding to the students' character portfolio by demonstrating their willingness to engage in service and distinguish themselves as truly global, multicultural and cosmopolitan citizens from parochial others.

The students themselves saw these trips as significant and influential learning experiences, and acknowledged that it contributed to their understanding of the world at large.

> We went to Ho Chi Minh and we saw the war museums and all. There were also cultural programmes and we went to an orphanage with children with special needs. We went there and ate curry with them. It was quite fun … I guess family trips are more for enjoyment and school trips are for education, cultural bridging and all that stuff.
>
> (Interview with Roger, 24 March 2009)

Elite Schoolboys Becoming Global Citizens **81**

> I think OEP helps us to see the world. Going out to see the world is better than sitting in class and reading a text which might not even be relevant … Like for OEP, you go to Vietnam and you see all the kids from messed up families. And what you experience there is something that cannot be read at home.
>
> (Interview with Michael, 27 March 2009)

These overseas trips provide a way for students to move out of their comfortable homes and holidays to experience another version of the world other than the tourist gaze so often applied on family holidays. The institutional habitus supports their personal habitus of travelling to see the world, enlarging the purpose of travel with its focus on service learning rather than tourism. Ironically, however, students' reflections typically reflect how these experiences teach them to be grateful for what they have rather than enlarging their perspective on social injustice in the world.

> It's … It just makes you realise how much you have. And shows you how to give back to the community if you have the privilege to go. For example, if you have a degree, like you're an architect, you could design flats for them. I don't know, it's a whole give back to society thing …
>
> (Interview with Robert, 31 March 2009)

There is a strong sense of the need to see the world differently, and to give back to society, for example in Robert's example of how an architect can give back to society through designing flats for the needy. Given the strong missionary ethos of the school, it is hardly surprising that students imbue this "gift economy" mentality to give back to society, whether they see it as self-interested philanthropy or public service (Kenway & Fahey, 2015). Kenway and Fahey have argued in their study of a Scottish girls' school that this expected benevolence in elite schools may underwrite students' status quo rather than challenge it, especially when these acts of giving are used to justify existing power relations. In this case, the implication here is that acts of charity justify students' ignorance of larger injustice.

Ironically, these acts of altruism are not disinterested in that they yield moral and educational profit. Students develop "cosmopolitan capital", defined as the development of predispositions and competencies resulting in a "propensity to engage in globalizing social arenas and succeed in the struggle for global positions of privilege" (Weenick, 2008, p. 1092 in Windle & Stratton, 2012, p. 205).

> So the programmes give you an impression of what the world is like so you can see what the needs of other countries are … At the same time, it's a good way for us to build up our portfolio when we have to apply to universities.
>
> (Interview with Joshua, 27 March 2009)

82 Chin Ee Loh

Students themselves recognise the pragmatic nature of their investment of time and effort in these overseas programmes. These overseas experiences allow them to acquire a knowledge of the Other and enhance their character portfolio with the inclusion of a superficial multiculturalism as part of their portfolio of global dispositions (Resnik, 2008). Given the intense competition for places in top universities overseas and in Singapore, these experiences will allow them to position themselves as global citizens, committed to community service. Whether the students absorb the institutional habitus of cosmopolitanism for self-gain or are committed to a national or transnational form of citizenship, whether they see themselves as building a marketable transnational portfolio for personal economic gain or whether they gain a sense of responsibility for nation and world is uncertain.

The dominant discourse of the institutional habitus is that students must learn to be cosmopolitan citizens, able and willing to engage with the world at large, committed to doing good *outside* the nation. This cosmopolitan identity posits an awareness of the world but also highlights the lack of awareness of more local issues of social justice, demonstrated in the conversation about NSK and success in schooling. Because the trips are made to less privileged, often third world nations, students tend to locate themselves as citizens of a privileged nation rather than as privileged individuals within the nation. Their inattention to their own privilege is amplified by the dominant discourses of meritocracy where each man's success is seen as the result of his or her hard work. The blindness to local issues is echoed in Sim's (2012) study within an elite all girls' school in Singapore where she noted that while the students were aware of their responsibilities as future leaders to lead through example, there was a troubling lack of discourse "around issues of polarization and inequality confronting the Singapore society" (p. 206). The institutional habitus towards cosmopolitanism, while noble in its twin aims of preparing students both to be socially-responsible and for the international world of business, may have the unintended effect of closing students' minds to inequitable social worlds within the nation. Given the expectations that these students are likely to serve as future business and political leaders (Goh, 2015; Sim, 2012), greater awareness and empathy for local issues should constitute the habitus of elite students.

Conclusion

The identification of dominant discourses that shape these elite students' everyday practices of being elite and cosmopolitan helps us to understand how particular mindsets and attitudes are reproduced and reinforced. Rather than seeing habitus as fixed space, understanding habitus as a space for negotiation helps us to identify how the boys' belief in hard work and charity are in line with one of many versions of meritocracy (K. P. Tan, 2010), a version that does not take into account the different starting points of individuals in the field of the nation. The boys' personal beliefs in their status as gifted and hardworking (thereby adhering to international standards of excellence) can only be sustained and legitimised through the powerful dominant ideology of meritocracy that pervades their self-worth and their view of others. The institutional habitus towards cosmopolitanism (which reflects national discourses) serves as a form of distinction (Bourdieu, 1984) in the credential race, reinforcing students' understanding of themselves as cosmopolitans in relation to the more parochial others within the nation.

What this study reveals are the tensions present in the way class, schooling, global and local imaginations intersect with institutional and individual habitus. In the race towards global competitiveness, the school and students in the school have to negotiate the ambivalent aims of programmes designed to cultivate cosmopolitan marketability and citizenry. Students accumulate dispositions and experiences from both home and school that go towards the creation of a global cosmopolitan portfolio to add to their credibility and competitiveness in a credential society that prizes academic and moral excellence. Ironically, the focus on the cosmopolitan in the form of overseas experiences that distinguish the students as knowledgeable of the world at large masks students' superficial understanding of local politics and their position as privileged students within the local community. Locating the dominant discourses inscribed unto students' identities evident in their everyday practice provides a starting point for making visible how elitist attitudes towards meritocracy and cosmopolitanism are reproduced in everyday practices. While the quandary between fulfilling the economic and ethical dimensions of schooling will remain, rethinking how to disrupt existing dominant discourses at the level of institutional habitus may encourage more critical and compassionate versions of meritocracy and cosmopolitanism in elite students' identification as both national *and* global citizens.

Acknowledgements

I would like to thank the staff and students at Ace Institution for generously allowing me to conduct the research at the school. I am also grateful to Jane Kenway, Aaron Koh and the two anonymous reviewers for their invaluable feedback on the earlier drafts of this chapter.

Note

1 Pseudonyms have been used throughout this chapter.

References

Bourdieu, P. (1977). *Outline of a theory of practice* (Richard Nice, Trans.). Cambridge: Cambridge University Press.

Bourdieu, P. (1984). *Distinction: A social critique of the judgement of taste* (Richard Nice, Trans.). Boston: Harvard University Press.

Bourdieu, P., & Passeron, J. (1990). *Reproduction in education, society and culture* (Richard Nice, Trans.). London: Sage Publications.

Bourdieu, P., & Wacquant, L. (1992). *An invitation to reflexive sociology*. Chicago, IL: University of Chicago Press.

Bowles, S., & Gintis, H. (1976). *Schooling in capitalist America*. New York, NY: Basic Books.

Bunnell, T. (2010). The International Baccalaureate and a framework for class consciousness: The potential outcomes of a 'class-for-itself'. *Discourse*, 31(3), 351–362.

Collins, R. (1979). *The credential society: An historical sociology of education and stratification*. New York, NY: Academic Press, Inc.

Courtois, A. (2015). 'Thousands waiting at our gates': Moral character, legitimacy and social justice in Irish elite schools. *British Journal of Sociology of Education*, 36(1), 53–70.

Demerath, P. (2009). *Producing success: The culture of personal achievement in an American High School*. Chicago and London: The University of Chicago Press.

Draelants, H., & Darchy-Koechlin, B. (2011). Flaunting one's academic pedigree?: Self-presentation of students from elite French schools. *British Journal of Sociology of Education*, 32, 17–34.

Epstein, D. (2014). Race-ing class ladies: Lineages of privilege in an elite South African school. *Globalisation, Societies and Education*, 12(2), 244–261.

Fahey, J. (2014). Privileged girls: The place of femininity and femininity in place. *Discourse*, 12(2), 228–243.

Forbes, J., & Lingard, B. (2015). Assured optimism in a Scottish girls' school: Habitus and the (re)production of global privilege. *British Journal of Sociology of Education*, 36(1), 116–136.

Gee, J. P. (1996). *Social linguistics and literacies* (2nd ed.). Oxford, UK: RoutledgeFalmer.

Goh, C. T. (1999). First-world economy, world-class home. *The Straits Times*. Retrieved 2 December 2015 from http://www.nas.gov.sg/archivesonline/speeches/view-html?filename=1999082202.htm

Goh, D. P. S. (2015). Elite schools, postcolonial Chineseness and hegemonic masculinities in Singapore. *British Journal of Sociology of Education*, 36(1), 137–155.

Gopinathan, S. (1980). Language policy in education: A Singapore perspective. In E. A. Afendras, A. Evangelos & E. L. Y. Kuo (Eds.), *Language and society in Singapore* (pp. 175–202). Singapore: Singapore University Press.

Hannerz, U. (1990). Cosmopolitans and locals in world culture. *Theory, Culture & Society*, 7, 237–251.

Ho, E. (2006). Negotiating belonging and perceptions of citizenship in a transnational world: Singapore, a cosmopolis? *Social and Cultural Geography*, 7(3), 385–401.

Ho, L-C. (2012). Sorting citizens: Differentiated citizenship education in Singapore. *Journal of Curriculum Studies*, 44(3), 403–428.

Holland, D., Lachicotte, W. Jr., Skinner, D., & Cain, C. (1998). *Identity and agency in cultural worlds*. Cambridge, MA: Harvard University Press.

Howard, A. (2010a). Elite visions: Privileged perceptions of self and others. *Teachers College Record*, 112(8), 1971–1992.

Howard, A. (2010b). Stepping outside class: Affluent students resisting privilege. In A. Howard & R. Gaztambide-Fernández (Eds.), *Educating elites: Class privilege and educational advantage* (pp. 79–95). Lanham, MD: Rowen & Littlefield.

Howard, A., & Gaztambide-Fernández, R. (2010). *Educating elites: Class privilege and educational advantage*. Lanham, MD: Rowen & Littlefield.

Kennedy, K. J. (2013). Singapore's school curriculum for the future beyond: Mational development? In Z. Deng, S. Gopinathan & C. Lee (Eds.), *Globalization and the Singapore curriculum* (pp. 205–224). Dordrecht: Springer.

Kenway, J., & Fahey, J. (2015). The gift economy of elite schooling: The changing contours and privileges of privileged benefaction. *Discourse: Studies in the Cultural Politics of Education*, 36(1), 95–115.

Kenway, J., & Koh, A. (2013). The elite school as 'cognitive machine' and 'social paradise': Developing transnational capitals for the national 'field of power'. *Journal of Sociology*, 49(2–3), 272–290.

Khan, S. R. (2012). *Privilege: the making of an adolescent elite at St. Paul's*. Princeton, NJ: Princeton University Press.

Koh, A. (2014). Doing class analysis in Singapore's elite education: Unravelling the smokescreen of 'meritocractic talk'. *Globalisation, Societies and Education*, 12(2), 196–210.

Koh, A., & Chong, T. (2014). Education in the global city: The manufacturing of education in Singapore. *Discourse: Studies in the Cultural Politics of Education*, 35(5), 625–636.

Koh, A., & Kenway, J. (2012). Cultivating national leaders in an elite school: Deploying the transnational in the national interest. *International Studies in Sociology of Education*, 22(4), 331–351.

Lareau, A. (2003). *Unequal childhoods: Class, race and family life*. Berkeley, CA: University of California Press.

Lim, L. (2014). Ideology, rationality and reproduction in education: A critical discourse analysis. *Discourse: Studies in the Cultural Politics of Education*, 35(1), 61–76.

Loh, C. E. (2012). Global and national imaginings: Deparochialising the IBDP English A1 curriculum. *Changing English*, 19(2), 221–235.

Loh, C. E. (2013). Singaporean boys constructing global literate selves through their reading practices in and out of school. *Anthropology and Education Quarterly*, 44(1), 38–57.

McIntosh, P. (1988). White privilege and male privilege: A personal account of coming to see correspondences through work in women's studies *working paper 189*. Wellesley, MA: Wellesley College Center for Research on Women.

Meadmore, D., & Meadmore, P. (2004). The boundlessness of performativity in elite Australian schools. *Discourse: Studies in the Cultural Politics of Education*, 25(3), 375–387.

Ministry of Education. (2011). *National Education*. Retrieved 7 November 2014 from http://ne.edu.sg/home.php

Olds, K., & Thrift, N. (2005). Cultures on the brink: Reengineering the soul of capitalism - on a global scale. In A. Ong & S. J. Collier (Eds.), *Global assemblages: Technology, politics, and ethics as anthropological problems* (pp. 270–290). Oxford: Blackwell Publishing.

Ong, A. (1999). *Flexible citizenship: The cultural logics of transnationality*. Durham & London: Duke University Press.

Ramesh, S. (2011, 24 January). MM Lee says students' background plays a role. *Channel News Asia*.

Reay, D. (2004). 'It's all becoming habitus': Beyond the habitual use of habitus in educational research. *British Journal of Sociology of Education*, 25(4), 431–444.

Reay, D., David, M., & Ball, S. J. (2001). Making a difference?: Institutional habituses and higher education choice. *Sociological Research Online*, 5(4).

Reich, R. B. (1991). *The work of nations.* New York: Vintage Books.

Resnik, J. (2008). The construction of the global worker through international education. In J. Resnik (Ed.), *The production of educational knowledge in the global era* (pp. 147–168). Rotterdam, The Netherlands: Sense Publishers.

Rizvi, F. (2014). Old elite schools, history and the construction of a new imaginary. *Globalisation, Societies and Education*, 12(2), 290–308.

Sim, J. B. Y. (2012). The burden of responsibility: Elite students' understandings of civic participation in Singapore. *Educational Review*, 64(2), 195–210.

Singapore Department of Statistics. (2011). *Census of population 2010 advanced census release, June. 7, 2010.* Singapore: Singapore Department of Statistics.

Smith, C. (2015). *A handbook on inequality, poverty and unmet social needs in Singapore.* Singapore: Lien Centre for Social Innovation.

Stuber, J. M. (2010). Class dismissed?: The social-class worldviews of privileged college students. In A. Howard & R. Gaztambide-Fernández (Eds.), *Educating elites: Class privilege and educational advantage* (pp. 131–151). Lanham, MD: Rowen & Littlefield.

Tan, J. (2010). Education in Singapore: Sorting them out? In T. Chong (Ed.), *Management of success: Singapore revisited* (pp. 288–308). Singapore: Institute of Southeast Asian Studies.

Tan, K. P. (2010). The transformation of meritocracy. In T. Chong (Ed.), *Management of success: Singapore revisited* (pp. 272–287). Singapore: Institute of Southeast Asian Studies.

Taylor, C. (1989). *Sources of the self: The making of the modern identity.* Harvard: Harvard University Press.

Waters, J. L. (2006). Geographies of cultural capital: Education, international migration and family strategies between Hong Kong and Canada. *Transactions of the Institute of British Geographers*, 31, 179–192.

Windle, J., & Stratton, G. (2012). Equity for sale: Ethical consumption in a school-choice regime. *Discourse: Studies in the Cultural Politics of Education*, *34*(2), 202–213.

Ye, R., & Nylander, E. (2015). The transnational track: State sponsorship and Singapore's Oxbridge elite. *British Journal of Sociology of Education*, 36(1), 11–33.

Yin, R. K. (2003). *Case study research: Design & methods* (3rd ed.). Thousand Oaks, CA: Sage Publications.

5

THE JOY OF PRIVILEGE

Elite Private School Online Promotions and the Promise of Happiness

Christopher Drew, Kristina Gottschall, Natasha Wardman, and Sue Saltmarsh

Introduction

Images of happy, successful students are ubiquitous in "the education landscape and the idealized childhoods it invites us to imagine" (Saltmarsh, 2011, p. 33). Through a broad range of texts, policies and everyday practices, cultural imaginaries that equate childhood with happiness as simultaneously an ideal, an entitlement and a natural state of being, furnish normative frames of reference for which cultural understandings of childhood and studenthood emerge (Saltmarsh, 2011; Chapman & Saltmarsh, 2013; Fisher, Harris & Jarvis, 2008; Youdell, 2006). In this chapter, we consider how the promotional texts of elite private schools in Australia draw upon and contribute to the discursive constitution of childhood happiness as a commodified feature of ideal studenthood. We argue that in elite school promotions, happiness functions alongside institutional narratives of gender, sexuality, race, and social class as a device that equates social status and privilege with idealised imaginaries of child/student subjectivities.

Australian education has, since the emergence and entrenchment of the neoliberal project in the late 1980s, been characterised by policies favouring choice and competition in schooling sectors (Symes, 1998; Whitty, Power & Halpin, 1998). As Kenway (2013) points out:

> market liberalism and school choice have been the dominant policy discourses which … have led to a disastrous school funding model which has supported an exodus from the public sector, serious funding inequities between public and private schools and heavy burdens on the state sector which takes a disproportionate number of students needing extra resources and care.
>
> (p. 287)

In such a climate, independent, Catholic, and public sector schools alike have been expected by successive governments to 'hold their own' in an education marketplace in which some have been better positioned than others for success. Placed in competition for students and funding, schools have become involved "in various commodification (promotion and recruitment) practices at home, overseas and virtually" in which "'branding' through school and system websites becomes crucial" (Kenway & Fahey, 2014, p. 181).

Within such a context, our previous work in this field has highlighted and challenged the ways that educational marketisation exacerbates competitiveness, elitism, and exclusionary educational practices (Saltmarsh, 2007; Youdell, 2004). In particular, we have been interested in how the promotions, marketing, and impression management practices of elite schools discursively constitute their students as winners in the competitive educational climate, and in so doing simultaneously reinscribe the status and prestige of such schools (Drew, 2013; Saltmarsh, 2007, 2008; Gottschall et al., 2010; Wardman et al., 2010; Wardman et al., 2013; Symes, 1998). This work overall has maintained a sustained focus on the ways that gender, race, geographic location, and socioeconomic privilege are invoked in school promotions in the service of competitive educational and social hierarchies.

Here we turn our attention to the ways that happiness is utilised in the semiotic elements and discursive practices of elite school promotional websites, in ways that position elite subjectivities as proximate to the happy, good and desirable life. Institutional narratives of happy elite educational institutions, we contend, constitute elite subjectivities as inherently good, while excluding the possibility of unhappiness as a consequence of the marginalisation and competitiveness that underpin elitist narratives. Thus we focus on the ways that happy narratives of elite school websites produce educational inclusions and exclusions, enabling and encouraging privileged student subjectivities within the space of the elite school while discursively marginalising and sidelining non-privileged subjectivities as unhappy performatives. Such rhetoric, we argue, is not simply representational and symbolic, but also has the performative effect of entrenching discourses of the happy, good life as an exclusionary social imaginary. By highlighting how these happiness narratives are also contingent on the unhappy practices of marginalisation and competition, this paper challenges the assumption of the promotional texts analysed that elite gendered, racialised, and socially classed subjectivities are necessarily and wholly happy, good, desirable, and superior.

The Promise of Happiness

In commonplace western thought, happiness is an emotion to which all should strive in their daily lives (Frey & Stutzer, 2002), or, as Ahmed (2008b) puts it, "Happiness is often described as what we aim for, as an end-point, or even an end-in-itself" (p. 11). Contemporary discourse positions happiness as an indisputably positive emotion, and its attainment is prized as a sign of success in life. This way of thinking has driven the contemporary "happiness industry" (Ahmed, 2010, p. 4) that includes positive psychology, consumable self-help books and courses, and statistics outlining how individual happiness might be achieved (Ahmed, 2010). Global happiness, too, is consistently measured and lauded as an ultimate social goal to be achieved through scales such as the Gross National Happiness (GNH) indicator and the Happy Planet Index. Happiness and goodness are frequently elided in such projects, which assume that to induce happiness is inherently good (Ahmed, 2010; Frey & Stutzer, 2002).

The happiness industry has been instrumental in the commodification of happiness as a good that can be acquired (Frey & Stutzer, 2002). In "the virtuous liaison of happiness and profit" (Rose, 1999, p. 86), economic capital and consumer choice enable people to make up their lives through goods, services, and "experiential commodities" (Kenway & Bullen, 2001, p. 126) equated with happiness. As Frey and Stutzer (2002) argue, "Economic activity—the production of goods and services—is certainly not an end in itself but only has value in so far as it contributes to human happiness" (p. 1). In this context, advertising promotes happiness within the terms of consumption and economic capital.

However, recent cultural studies approaches focus not on how happiness might be achieved, but on "what does happiness do?" (Ahmed, 2010, p. 1). This approach can be seen as part of the affective turn in cultural studies that has gained traction largely since the emergence in the 1990s and 2000s of Thrift's nonrepresentational theory, which focuses on "the excessive and transient aspects of living" (Lorimer, 2005, p. 83). Thrift (2007) points toward the limits of representation theories concerned only with semiotic indicators, and instead focuses on affective practices and actions. Following Thrift, Lorimer (2005) argues that "the tendency for cultural analyses to cleave towards a conservative, categorical politics of identity and textual meaning" (p. 83) has overlooked how peoples' emotions impact their behaviours, calling for increased attention to emotions within social interactions.

Sara Ahmed's (2004, 2010) concern with cultural politics asks how emotions such as happiness might be *constituted through* discourse. From this vantage point, we consider happiness as an emotion that does not exist outside of social and cultural assumptions about what constitutes a good, desirable, and successful life. This approach highlights how cultural discourses can position certain privileged subjectivities as comported towards happiness, while foreclosing other, non-normative subjectivities as unhappy and therefore undesirable. Rather than happiness being rendered a factual and inevitable outcome of certain ways of being, we consider it as a performative rhetorical device that constitutes subjectivities as worthy or otherwise within cultural discourse.

Ahmed argues that emotions are discursive, and rely on cultural and historical understandings of particular objects and subjects as necessitating particular emotional reactions. For Ahmed, emotional reactions such as happiness are

90 Christopher Drew, Kristina Gottschall et al.

learned and sustained through discourse. Ahmed suspends the assumption that things that are happy are necessarily good or worthy, and argues instead that happiness produces things as good and worthy: "to be happy about something makes something good" (Ahmed, 2010, p. 210). When happiness is discursively associated with some ways of being more than others, it emerges that happiness is something to be achieved by striving towards certain subjecthoods. As Ahmed (2010) argues, "some bodies more than others will bear the promise of happiness" (p. 45). Happiness, here, is "what you get for being a certain kind of being" (Ahmed, 2010, p. 12).

Ahmed's examinations of emotion in *The Cultural Politics of Emotion* (2004) involve readings of the ways texts generate emotive effects that influence the readings of represented subjects. The "emotionality of texts", she explains, is produced through framing strategies—such as "figures of speech" and "metonymy and metaphor" (2004, p. 12), in ways that mark some subjectivities as desirable through their proximity to happiness, and others as unhappy and therefore undesirable. Texts, she argues, can use discourses of happiness to produce some interactions and narratives as requiring particular emotive responses to certain subjectivities. From such a perspective, texts performatively reiterate the happiness and goodness or otherwise of certain bodies, thereby entrenching, sustaining, or challenging discursive understandings of the happy, good, and desirable subject.

Here, we utilise Ahmed's happiness theory to consider how happiness might be used in elite school websites to frame certain student subjectivities as desirable and worthy within the context of elite education, and to foreclose other subjectivities from happy, good, and elite subjecthoods. In considering the promotional, semiotic, and discursive features of these websites, we aim to challenge prevailing educational discourses within our region. We see the promotion of educational elitism as situated within a marketised educational policy context that encourages competition and stratification of schooling sectors. The elision of happiness with the consumption of elite education, we contend, contributes to inequitable discourses that privilege some schooled subjectivities over others.

Elite school websites were located using internet search engines, through which we searched for schools following Gaztambide-Fernández's (2009) criterion for identifying elite schools. This criterion search involved the identification of high-profile local schools that featured elite school identification markers including influential alumni, longevity of establishment, boarding options, elite geographical indicators such as sandstone buildings and large manicured lawns, and participation in elite interschool rugby and rowing competitions (Gaztambide-Fernández, 2009). We identified 12 schools that met Gaztambide-Fernández's (2009) definition of elite, which we de-identified and renamed as Schools A–L in no particular order. Three of these schools are co-educational, five are all-boys, and four all-girls. We collaborated on the synthesis and analysis of the data using discourse analytic (Fairclough, 2001; Foucault, 1972; Lee, 2000; Threadgold, 2000) and social semiotic (Kress & van

Leeuwen, 2006; O'Halloran, 2004; Yell, 2005) methods. We searched for semiotic and discursive representations of happy elite subjectivities, and critiqued the performative inclusions and exclusions within the images, videos, and written text in order to examine the ways happiness was used on the websites to produce particular subjectivities as good, worthy, and desirable within the elite school contexts. Semiotic indicators of happiness included, but were not limited to, smiling faces, physical proximity of the students, hugging, giggling, eye contact, harmony, soft and natural lighting, and words alluding to the school's and children's joy, excitement, and contentment. Discursive indicators included references to social and economic comfort, inclusion, access to exclusive and privileged lifestyles, and references to positive psychology discourse which might imply that happiness is an end goal of attending the institution.

Happy Schools are Happy Families

Images of happy children and teachers appear in every website studied. Generally found on banners both static and moving at the top of the homepage, smiling children welcome viewers to the site. These smiling faces work to set a tone for the cyber-visit, as do the well-manicured, uniformed students walking through serene grounds. Students smile toward the camera, offering a visual invitation into the school's online space. Happiness, as one of the most immediate messages being conveyed on the webpages, functions as a central ingredient to the production of the school as a good and desirable place to be. As Ahmed (2010) puts it, happiness is not just an effect of goodness, but also "participates in making things good" (p. 13).

Frequently, homepages and 'boarding school' pages on school websites allude to the notion of the school as a *happy family*.

> We care for our Boarders as if they were family members in a warm, supportive, safe, and nurturing community, and take the time to listen to each of their needs.
>
> (School I)

> Like any family, you have your ups and downs; however, we seem to have had many more ups than downs. The range of friendships, the care of the students, the respect, and the Christian values that our children, all four of them, have received as a result of being enrolled at [School G] has helped them become the happy and successful people they are today.
>
> (Parent testimonial, School G)

The repetition of the notion of family on most school websites analysed emphasises a proclaimed commitment to family and its associated discursive ideals—loyalty, safety, nurturance, and togetherness. Just as the family "promises happiness in return for loyalty" (Ahmed, 2008b, p. 13), constructing the school within these terms equates the school brand with happy ways of being.

The school 'family' is also conspicuously heteronormative, with gender norms and sexualities closely policed over the course of students' stay at the school. The all-girl School A, for example, introduces socials with boys in Grade 9, the same grade when they become mentors for the younger girls in the form of junior sport captaincy. Such a structure constructs proximity between the responsibility to mingle with the opposite sex and the requirement to mentor younger girls in how to appropriately conduct oneself when in proximity to boys and masculine public space. The legitimacy of femininity and female sexualities rests on its manageability within highly contrived, heteronormative scenes of romantic mingling with boys, with no place in frames of recognition for queer subjectivities. Older girls are often given the opportunity to socialise with boys of the same age under controlled circumstances, and younger girls are kept away from boys, sustaining a narrative of asexuality for younger children and heteronormative sexuality for older girls (Robinson, 2013).

Constructing the school as a family also anticipates a potential concern of future clients—that children who board will spend extended periods of time away from home. School websites anticipate and attempt to address these concerns by constructing school as a 'home away from home':

> Sending a child away to school is a significant decision for any family to make. At [School B] we appreciate the responsibility parents entrust in us, to nurture and guide their daughter through her formative years. Our goal is to provide a safe and happy 'home away from home'.
>
> (School B)

> The emphasis in boarding is on creating a home away from home atmosphere with extra touches such as flat screen TV, pool table, music and a large common area.
>
> (School C)

By invoking the idea of school as a home, the school is constructed as a private space, a personal sanctuary for the students (Christensen, James & Jenkins, 2000; Sibley, 1995; Valentine, 2004). The home is a refuge and source of comfort, whose symbolism takes its meaning for its direct contrast to the world beyond (Sibley, 1995). The home is exclusive: a space which others generally enter only on invitation. In this way, the home can come to be a location that is highly policed and made to match the ideals of the owner. Unwanted people, and indeed unwanted ideas, can be excluded more easily in this private space than in public realms beyond. In this way, home can become a sanitised (Walkerdine, 1999), child-friendly space for anxious parents hoping to preserve the 'innocence' and 'safety' of their children.

The Joy of Privilege **93**

This recurring 'happy family' motif implies that happiness comes from embracing family ideals and norms, through which a shared sense of identity and belonging is derived. Normative family discourses also have a disciplinary effect, constructing conformity as a means to personal and shared happiness:

> We know that if a girl feels 'liked' and happy within herself, she is more likely to be able to concentrate on her school work.
>
> (School I)

> boarder students need to have the ability to communicate positively with the school community and remain happy to learn!
>
> (School G)

Happiness and camaraderie in conformity is confirmed in images as well as written text, such as on the School J site, where gender conformity is reinforced. On one image, girls hold hands while skipping along in lines through the green manicured grounds, with trees and grass framing the image. Another image shows the girls covered in mud and hugging while smiling at the camera. They are enjoying nature together. We have highlighted elsewhere that the emphasis elite school promotions put on girls' connectedness to nature invokes the discursive ideal of nature as "a trope through which femininity is constructed" in order to sell the schools as producing "'proper' and 'respectable' upper-middle-class 'ladies'" (Wardman, et al., 2013, p. 292). This constructs nature, and attendance at the school, as inherently good for girls. It attests to the schools' production of 'well-rounded' *girls* who will gain mastery over potentially unruly bodies and minds through performatives of naturally feminine ideals.

Furthermore, the intertwined arms and smiling faces in these images threads the girls together and removes distance between them—a visual strategy implying closeness and connectedness. Images of happiness and physical interconnectedness confirm a sense of family, closeness, and indeed a shared destiny, constituting natural femininity as a happy, hence inherently good, performative within the exclusive sanctuary of the school grounds. Natural girls are good girls, whose posture, dress, behaviour, and dispositions are consistently depicted as appropriate for their gender and social status as elite schooling subjects.

The heteronormativity within the 'boarding school' pages of the websites also produces the school grounds as places where some people can walk freely, and others—queer girls, at-risk students, disabled students, rebellious students—are conspicuously absent. Here, it is clear that there exist within the spaces of these schools what Alexander and Knowles call "territorial notions of space" (2005, p. 6), wherein spaces can be owned and possessed by particular groups of people, and in which people can appear to belong or otherwise to specific spaces. As feminist geographers have recently argued, moral geographies or specific kinds of emotional and empathetic investments and morally infused identities are

94 Christopher Drew, Kristina Gottschall et al.

inextricably tied to specific spaces and places (Cresswell, 1996; Little, 2007; Pini, Mayes & Boyer, 2013). This is particularly evident in the 'private' and 'homely' space of the private school, wherein the school has ultimate control in regulating the make-up of the student body. In these spaces, subjectivities and conduct aligned to the social class, gender, and heterosexual order of the school are privileged, and at-risk, disabled, queer, poor, and working-class subjectivities are conspicuously excluded.

Images of homogeneous and happy gender normative bodies within the schools thus orient prospective parents and students toward notions of individual and collective happiness and harmony. Boarders who embrace these norms are situated as both good and happy, among their peers and the school community more broadly. As Ahmed notes, "groups cohere around a shared orientation towards some things as being good, treating some things and not others as the cause of happiness" (2008b, p. 11). Inclusion and happiness of the boarding student in these images is contingent on managing one's subjecthood in relation to the collective norms reiterated within the elite schooling context. Norms of gender and sexuality in these elite school settings bear the tacit promise of happiness; "if you do this, then happiness is what follows" (Ahmed, 2008a, p. 125).

Winning as a Happy Enterprise

Images of victorious students on sporting fields are emblazoned upon 10 of the 12 websites examined, with children depicted high-fiving, holding up trophies, and jumping in the air after victories. School C, for example, contains an embedded video showing boys in the foreground holding up a football trophy, which is superimposed over an image of boys high-fiving immediately after the victory. The dominance of boys within the images of sporting victory produces sporting achievement as a sign of masculine success. Predominantly these victories are related to rugby, the 'good' Anglo-Celtic tradition of all-boys' elite schools in Australia (Light & Kirk, 2000), with rowing and cricket also featured. What is particularly interesting about the rugby successes is the cultural meaning associated with rugby. To win at the 'elite school sport' of rugby is to be among the upper echelon of social class elites. Furthermore, rugby's hyper-physicality offers the ideal semiotic opportunity to promote masculinity, reproducing "a traditional, hegemonic form of masculinity" (Light & Kirk, 2000, p. 163) reliant on "the production of physical force [as] a prerequisite for success" (Light & Kirk, 2001, p. 85). The depiction of smiling faces celebrating rugby victories in the all-boys' and co-educational elite school websites, therefore, reinforces both a commitment to elitism and a particularly physical form of dominant masculinity, while also demarcating it as 'happy' vis-à-vis the inherent 'goodness' of success.

Consumers of these images of happy 'winning' students are invited to anticipate the sporting event in a certain way: to view the event expecting happiness to come from winning, not from playing. Winning, we suggest, is a far

The Joy of Privilege **95**

more exclusionary act than playing. Yet in these images, winning is foregrounded as the more socially desirable outcome than playing. This is underscored in a montage on the School F website which features a football team huddled together with celebratory smiles, as if they had just scored a goal or won a game. Winning and happiness have a relational impact in these images. The children are happy because they are *winners* not because they are players.

Other websites similarly depict fit, well-toned bodies executing tennis shots or lunging out of the water mid-stroke. These images, too, represent elite sporting bodies—as exemplified by the refined movements and toned bodies of schoolboys and girls. However, these bodies are not smiling, but rather are depicted in action shots (Caldwell, 2005) in which the dominant expression is *focus*. In one all-girls' school website, for example, a girl riding mid-hurdle on horseback is shown with an intensely focused face, eyes on the landing point and brow furrowed with determination. Rather than depicting happiness as *attained*, we suggest that these images of focus imply happiness as *ahead*. The emphasis, again, is on joy in winning, not playing: *when we win we can smile.*

Winning is a concept defined by its proximity to the top of social hierarchies (Light & Kirk, 2000). It is a concept entwined with neoliberalist notions of competitivism, winners-versus-losers, and outdoing others. While football may have the potential to generate 'happy diversity' through the provision of "a level playing field" (Ahmed, 2008a, p. 123) based on an aspiration and talent; elite school websites emphasise hyper-masculinity and winning as exclusionary middle-class ideals. Winning as an elite accomplishment sits in stark contrast to social democratic notions of collaboration and collectivism, and happiness associated with winning is framed as proximate to power. To have access to the cultural, social and economic capital of elite schooling enables and guarantees sporting wins, through which happiness is conferred to students. Whether in education or in sport, to be powerful and successful, hence superior, is to be happy.

This message continues elsewhere on the School F website, where a circuit montage of nine images on the homepage—four containing smiling students—have the accompanying headings 'Dare to achieve', 'Lead', 'Excel', and 'Grow'. Again, occupying a place at the pinnacle of social hierarchies is reinforced as furnishing the conditions for happiness. These children who have 'excelled' are smiling: they are happy elites. The image equates attendance at the school with the acquisition of winning, elite aptitudes that will orient students towards an ostensibly happy life. Happiness connotes winning, leading and excelling as desirable attributes, consistent with neoliberalist competitivist ideals and economic notions of success.

While the images of winners and leaders are produced as ideal, they are also explicitly tied to notions that collective happiness and worth are secured by participation in, and success in, sport. Above one image of a sporting success on the School F website is a caption:

> The great sense of team-spirit and unity that exists at the college can be seen at the many sporting events when the entire college community comes out to support the [School F] boys.
>
> (School F)

The children who have met the school's ideal of being 'winners' are rewarded through collective adulation. Their bodies are watched and lauded under the banner of 'support'. The sport is placed below the boys, so that the community comes to watch the home players, not the game itself; they are there to "support the … boys". Such a framing strategy, in which winners are the foremost image, constitutes the school as a place where sporting winners are placed first. Winning is the goal through which individual and collective happiness is attained.

We are reminded of Ahmed's contention that, "happiness is an orientation" (2008b, p. 10) insomuch as certain activities or objects are understood as good *because* they are happy. That is to say, by constructing winning as a happy enterprise, these schools frame winning as something that is individually and socially desirable. What are left outside of these images are notions of play, creativity, camaraderie, and physical wellbeing. Without inclusion of these notions within the images, a narrow and individualistic sporting narrative emerges: *our school produces winners, so join our school and become a winner.*

Conclusion

In this chapter, we have argued that elite school websites promote happiness as both a commodity and an entitlement that can be acquired by attendance at a particular school. As one of the first points of contact between parents and schools, one of the primary functions of school websites is to explain to prospective clients what they can expect to get for their money (Drew, 2013). It is thus important to read these websites as a form of marketing within the highly competitive schooling sectors in Australia. A key promise made by schools via this form of marketing is happiness. Over and again, the school websites we examined reiterate that happiness comes about as a result of attending the school, as is exemplified in this quote from the Principal's page on the School F website:

> We are here to help boys, entrusted to us by their parents, to find genuine fulfilment, happiness and security in their lives. Our support and encouragement goes far beyond the time students leave us at graduation. As a college community we take great joy and strength from our ongoing relationship with our Old Boys and their families. To be part of the Joeys family is truly a gift for life.
>
> (School F)

The Joy of Privilege **97**

This implies that students can attain the social class status and cultural capital that the school has accrued over time (Gaztambide-Fernández, 2009) and carry it with them throughout their lives. Attending such a school is not simply a matter of acquiring an education, but it also involves the acquisition of lifelong identities, social status, and networks. In such narratives, attendance at the school involves purchasing a way of life associated with happiness accrued through alignment to the gendered, sexed, and social class norms preferred, promoted, and preserved through school participation. Consumption of an elite education, in this sense, is not just to purchase a product, but to "assemble a way of life" (Rose, 1999/1990, p. 230) which both endorses and aspires towards images of privilege which, it is implied, will ultimately lead to happiness for the children and their parents.

We have also highlighted the ways in which discursive proximity to notions of happiness can frame exclusionary imaginaries as individually and socially desirable. The happiness of the gendered bodies in the websites constructs gender norms as happy norms. By being a normatively gendered body, happiness could follow. As Ahmed (2008b) puts it, "happiness means ... living a certain kind of life" (p. 12), or being a certain kind of person. It is thus our contention that the use of happiness in these texts is a rhetorical device that compels viewers to consider the exclusionary norms of the schools as being good and desirable, specifically because they can lead to personal happiness.

We concur with Ahmed's contention that happiness should be read as a discursive emotion, with texts informing viewers about ways of being that might lead to happiness even before those ways of being are materially encountered. According to Ahmed:

> the judgement that certain objects are 'happy' is already made, before they are even encountered. Certain objects are attributed as the conditions for happiness so that we arrive 'at' them with an expectation of how we will be affected by them ... happiness is an expectation of what follows.
>
> (2008b, p. 11)

The school promotional website, then, "inevitably 'produces' what it claims merely to represent" (Butler, 1990, p. 5)—through representation, the website constructs normatively gendered, heterosexual, winning, and elite subjectivities *as happy—and therefore good and desirable—subjectivities*. The happiness of being/ becoming an elite social subject, these websites imply, is what students will get for being a certain kind of student, and what parents can expect in exchange for their school fees. As Ahmed (2008b) states, happiness "is promised through proximity to certain objects" (p. 11). It "directs us to certain objects, as if they are the necessary ingredients for a good life" (p. 11). Yet these happiness narratives are implicated in demarcating the space of the elite private school as exclusionary— as schools that are *for* people who aspire to educational happiness in its commodified form, and *not for* others who fall outside its frames of reference. Analysis of these websites, we suggest, warrants a re-thinking of the notion of happiness. We read these texts as producing happiness narratives through which parents and students are invited to participate in forms of education associated with achievement, success, winning, and social status. We also read them as producing exclusionary ideals and significant limitations with respect to what is able to constitute happiness and happy subjectivities within these schools.

References

Ahmed, S. (2004). *The cultural politics of emotion*. Edinburgh, UK: Edinburgh University Press.

Ahmed, S. (2008a). Multiculturalism and the promise of happiness. *New Formations*, 63(1), 121–137.

Ahmed, S. (2008b). Sociable happiness. *Emotion, Space and Society*, 1(1), 10–13.

Ahmed, S. (2010). *The promise of happiness*. Durham, NC: Duke University Press.

Alexander, C., & Knowles, C. (2005). Introduction. In C. Alexander & C. Knowles (Eds.), *Making race matter: Bodies, space and identities* (pp. 1—15). London: Palgrave Macmillan.

Butler, J. (1990). *Gender trouble: Feminism and the subversion of identity*. New York, NY: Routledge.

Caldwell, T. (2005). *Film analysis handbook*. Victoria, Australia: Insight Publications.

Chapman, A., & Saltmarsh, S. (2013). The politics of normative childhoods and non-normative parenting: A response to Cristyn Davies and Kerry Robinson. *Contemporary Issues in Early Childhood*, 14(1), 60–65.

Christensen, P., James, A., & Jenks, C. (2000). Home and movement: Children constructing family time. In S. Holloway & G. Valentine (Eds.), *Children's geography: living, playing, learning* (pp. 135–149). London: Routledge.

Cresswell, T. (1996). *In place/out of place: Geography, ideology and transgression*. Minneapolis, MN: University of Minnesota.

Drew, C. (2013). Elitism for sale: Promoting the elite school online in the competitive educational marketplace. *Australian Journal of Education*, 57(2), 174–184.

Fairclough, N. (2001). The discourse of New Labour: Critical discourse analysis. In M. Wetherall, S. Taylor & S. Yates (Eds.), *Discourse as data: A guide for analysis* (pp. 229–266). London: Sage.

Fisher, R., Harris, A., & Jarvis, C. (2008). *Education in popular culture: Telling tales on teachers and learners*. London: Routledge.

Foucault, M. (1972). *Archaeology of knowledge* (A. M. Sheridan Smith, Trans.). New York, NY: Pantheon Books.

Frey, B., & Stutzer, A. (2002). The economics of happiness. *World Economics*, 3(1), 1–17.

Gaztambide-Fernández, R. (2009). What is an elite boarding school? *Review of Educational Research*, 79(3), 1090–1128.

Gottschall, K., Edgeworth, K., Hutchesson, R., Wardman, N., & Saltmarsh, S. (2010). Hard lines and soft scenes: constituting masculinities in the prospectuses of all-boys elite private schools. *Australian Journal of Education*, 54(1), 18–30.

Kenway, J. (2013). Challenging inequality in Australian schools: Gonski and beyond. *Discourse: Studies in the Cultural Politics of Education*, 34(2), 286–308.

Kenway, J., & Bullen, E. (2001). *Consuming children: Education, entertainment, advertising.* Milton Keynes, UK: Open University Press.

Kenway, J. & Fahey, J. (2014). Staying ahead of the game: The globalising practices of elite schools. *Globalisation, Societies and Education,* 12(2), 177–195.

Kress, G., & van Leeuwen, T. (2006). *Reading images: The grammar of visual design* (2nd ed.). London: Routledge.

Lee, A. (2000). Discourse analysis and cultural (re)writing, In A. Lee & C. Poynton (Eds.), *Culture & text: Discourse and methodology in social research and cultural studies* (pp. 188–202). St Leonards, NSW: Allen & Unwin.

Light, R., & Kirk, D. (2000). High school rugby, the body and the reproduction of hegemonic masculinity. *Sport, Education and Society,* 5(2), 163–176.

Light, R., & Kirk, D. (2001). Australian cultural capital – rugby's social meaning: Physical assets, social advantage and independent schools. *Sport in Society,* 4(3), 81–98.

Little, J. (2007). Constructing nature in the performance of rural heterosexualities. *Environment and Planning D: Society and Space,* 25(5), 851–866.

Lorimer, H. (2005). Cultural geography: The busyness of being 'more-than-representational'. *Progress in Human Geography,* 29(1), 83–94.

O'Halloran, K. L. (2004). Visual semiosis in film. In K. L. O'Halloran (Ed.), *Multimodal discourse analysis: Systemic functional perspectives* (pp. 109–130). London: Continuum.

Pini, B., Mayes, R., & Boyer, K. (2013). 'Scary' heterosexualities in a rural Australian mining town. *Journal of Rural Studies,* 32: 168–176.

Robinson, K. (2013). *Innocence, sexuality and the construction of childhood.* Milton Park: Routledge.

Rose, N. (1999). *Powers of freedom: Reframing political thought.* Cambridge: Cambridge University Press.

Rose, N. (1999/1990). *Governing the soul: The shaping of the private self* (2nd ed.). London: Free Association Books.

Saltmarsh, S. (2007). Cultural complicities: Elitism, heteronormativity and violence in the education marketplace. *International Journal of Qualitative Studies in Education,* 20(3), 335–354.

Saltmarsh, S. (2008). Disruptive events: Elite education and the discursive production of violence. *Critical Studies in Education,* 49(2), 113–125.

Saltmarsh, S. (2011). Bus ride to the future: Cultural imaginaries of Australian childhood in the education landscape. *Global Studies of Childhood,* 1(1), 26–35.

Sibley, D. (1995). *Geographies of exclusion.* London: Routledge.

Symes, C. (1998). Education for sale: A semiotic analysis of school prospectuses and other forms of educational marketing. *Australian Journal of Education,* 42(2), 133–152.

Threadgold, T. (2000). Post-structuralism and discourse analysis. In C. Poynton & A. Lee (Eds.), *Culture and text: Discourse and methodology in social research and cultural studies* (pp. 40–58). St. Leonards: Allen & Unwin.

Thrift, N. (2007). *Non-representational theory: Space, politics, affect.* London: Routledge.

Valentine, G. (2004). *Public space and the culture of childhood.* Aldershot, UK: Ashgate.

Walkerdine, V. (1999). Violent boys and precocious girls: Regulating childhood at the end of the millennium. *Contemporary Issues in Early Childhood,* 1(1), 3–23.

Wardman, N., Gottschall, K., Drew, C., Hutchesson, R., & Saltmarsh, S. (2013). Picturing natural girlhoods: Nature, space and femininity in girls' school promotions. *Gender and Education,* 25(3), 284–294.

Wardman, N., Hutchesson, R., Gottschall, K., Drew, C., & Saltmarsh, S. (2010). Starry eyes and subservient selves: Portraits of 'well-rounded' girlhood in the prospectuses of all-girl elite private schools. *Australian Journal of Education*, 54(3), 249–261.

Whitty, G., Power, S., & Halpin, D. (1998). *Devolution and choice in education: The school, the state and the market*. Milton Keynes, UK: Open University Press.

Yell, S. (2005). Critical discourse analysis and social semiotics: Rethinking text and discourse in media and communication research. In K. Kwansah-Aidoo (Ed.), *Topical issues in communications and media research* (pp. 9–23). New York: Nova Science.

Youdell, D. (2004). Engineering school markets, constituting schools and subjectivating students: The bureaucratic, institutional and classroom dimensions of educational triage. *Journal of Education Policy*, 19(4), 407–431.

Youdell, D. (2006). Diversity, inequality, and a post-structural politics for education. *Discourse: Studies in the Cultural Politics of Education*, 27(1), 33–42.

6

OLD BOY NETWORKS

The Relationship Between Elite Schooling, Social Capital, and Positions of Power in British Society

Shane Watters

Introduction

Scholars of social stratification have long suggested a relationship between elite schooling and obtaining high status positions in society. In Britain studies of elites have persistently cited an 'old boy's network' of social ties as a key mechanism for gaining employment in government and a number of key professions. However, documentary evidence of the existence of old boy's networks and how they relate to the elite public schools to which they are associated is in extremely short supply. More broadly, there have only been limited attempts to bring together and critically analyse data regarding the link between private schooling and esteemed employment destinations. This chapter offers a quantitative and theoretical analysis of the relationship between private schooling (in its various forms) and positions of power in British society, and utilises new web-based resources to provide evidence of the existence and structure of 'old boy's networks' in Britain. The chapter puts forward two primary arguments. Firstly, that there is sufficient existing data to identify a strong longitudinal correlation between private schooling and high status employment in Britain; and secondly, that 'old boy's networks' in Britain are structured in such a way as to assist their members to attain employment in particular high status professions and areas of business.

Career Benefits of Private Schooling

Established empirical research regarding the link between private schooling and esteemed employment destinations has tended to focus on sampling the educational backgrounds of high status professionals. Boyd (1973) examined the educational backgrounds of senior figures in the civil service, embassies, the army, the air force, the navy, the judiciary, the Church of England and clearing banks at four decadal stages in the period from 1939 to 1971. His findings clearly show, across all the afore-mentioned occupational areas, and at every stage sampled, that a consistent majority had attended elite 'public schools'.[1] Unfortunately, the contemporary strength of his findings are somewhat diminished by their age and the professions sampled. This said, the data can be reinforced by more recent investigations. For instance, the Sutton Trust's study (2007) of the "Education backgrounds of 500 leading figures" in British society comes to very similar conclusions. It also utilises a largely different, and arguably more up-to-date, range of professions and employment destinations. That is, law, politics, medicine, journalism and business, comparing data mainly gathered in the mid- to late 1980s to records from 2007. In all cases, with the exception of politics, the study reveals that 50% and above of the sampled "leading figures" were former "independent school"[2] (an interchangeable name for private school in Britain) pupils. That politics differs from other categories may be partly accounted for by the amount of public scrutiny the profession is subjected to, and the fact that politicians are meant to be representing the views of the majority. It can also be noted that there are significant disparities between political parties with, for example, 54% of Conservative MPs coming from private schools and only 15% of Labour MPs (Sutton Trust, 2010).

The strength of the correlations made in both studies is not fully apparent until placed in the context of the proportion of school aged students who attended private schools for the periods examined, some 5–7% (Walford, 1986; Sutton Trust, 2007). In sum, there is a stark disproportionality here between the number of students educated in private schools in Britain and the share of top positions these students obtain. According to the Sutton Trust's (2007) study even those leading figures sampled that did not attend private schools generally came from 'selective' rather than 'normal' state schools. In the most extreme example, out of the 100 high court judges sampled in 2007, 70% hailed from private schools, 30% from state schools and, out of this 30%, only 2% came from 'normal' state comprehensives. What is perhaps even more striking, in terms of trends in social mobility and stratification, is that between the sampling carried out by the Sutton Trust in the mid- to late 1980s and the more recent examination in 2007, there has only been a marginal decline in representation of those from private schools. This amounted to 58% in the mid- to late 1980s, reducing to 53% in 2007. Even this slight improvement in the progression of those stemming from state education is questionable as the business or 'CEO' category used may not be appropriate. Here, it should be recognized that there has been internationalisation of those at the top of UK companies (Held et al., 1999), and this is likely to partly account for the decline in those educated at British private schools. Removing this category results in only a 1.75% decline in the representation of those from private schools in the top professions and areas of business over the last 20 or so years.

One of the key methodological concerns with both the studies reviewed above is that they rely on relatively small, subjectively determined occupational groupings. With regard to the size of the samples it would have improved credibility if figures were, where possible, set against the total in any given occupation. For example, by performing a somewhat crude analysis using Government websites (Parliamentary Website, 2012; Judiciary Website, 2012) it is possible to calculate that the hundred high court judges cited for the Sutton Trust's study (2007) accounted for over half of the total high court judges in the country. In another such case, the 100 members of parliament sampled constitute 15% of the total number in Britain. In this context the results from both samples are statistically significant. The Sutton Trust's study (2007) is also distinct in its methodology in that it focused only on the top representatives of each professional grouping. For instance, the hundred medics examined were selected from those serving "on the Councils of the medical royal colleges or other national representative bodies" (Sutton Trust, 2007, p. 3).

Problems regarding bias in occupational group selection can be mitigated by examining general economic and educational benefits of attending private schools. Here, Green et al. (2010) give a rare statistical insight into this phenomenon by utilising a range of extensive samples from the National Child Development Study (NCDS), the 1970 British Cohort Study (BCS70), and the British Household Panel Survey (BHPS) to arguably form a representative test group. The NCDS and BCS70 are used as the primary instruments to test the hypothesis that wages and educational attainment are increased by attending private schools. Green et al. (2010) employ two convenient variables; education, measured by degree acquisition of participants at the age of 23, and earnings, determined by participants' 'hourly rate' at the age of 33. They then set these against whether participants were state or privately educated in order to make inferences. There are two central characteristics that make this research pioneering and creditable. Firstly, the research combines two extensive samples to arguably form a representative test group. For instance, the samples for both the NCDS and BCS70 each account for over four and a half thousand participants, with the two cohorts selected from different time periods. Secondly, the study attempts to control for a range of factors not engaged with in the previously mentioned studies, such as the child's cognitive ability before entering education and their family background. The general conclusion reached after incorporating all controls is that in both differentials, education and earnings, performance of privately educated individuals has "risen significantly over time" in comparison to those who were state educated (Green et al., 2010, p. 18). Despite this study's merits, its narrow focus on income does not engage directly with access to prestigious professions. It would have also been useful if it detailed how the controls used for parental social class were determined (as it does with cognitive ability[3]). In respect to these shortcomings, it is important to recognise this is a discussion paper rather than a completed body of work.

One aspect which is inconsistent across all of the literature reviewed is the parameters used to define elite schools. For example, the Sutton Trust's study (2007) uses the term "Independent Schools", Boyd (1973) refers to "Public Schools" and Green et al. (2010) to "Private Schools". This is important as the name used can equate to a difference in the catchment of schools encompassed. For instance, the term 'Public Schools' generally refers to the most elite and distinguished private schools. This was once defined as any member of the Headmasters' Conference (HMC); however, this is no longer such a useful measure as the HMC has expanded dramatically to take in a large number of new schools (Walford, 1991). 'Independent' or 'Private schools' on the other hand can relate to any school which is not run/funded by the State (Ball, 1997). None of the studies above adequately explain these differences or account for them with regard to data gathering and findings. Failure to distinguish top-level schools from the rest of the independent or private sector is further problematized by the fact that many commentators (Bamford, 1967; Scott, 1982; Walford, 1984) attach unique advantageous qualities to these institutions. The foremost of these, known commonly as the 'Old Boy Network', is a particular type of social capital, which relates closely to career progression (Scott, 1982; Green et al., 2010; Walford, 1986). Defining and understanding the 'Old Boy Network' in Britain is explored through the following theoretical analysis and the primary research presented in this chapter.

Theoretical Considerations and Limitations of Current Research

Ostensibly the studies above converge to identify a strong longitudinal correlation between private schooling (in its various forms) and positions of power. The possible problems with this correlation are not apparent until placed under a theoretical microscope. Here, Bourdieu (1986, p. 248) and Lukes (2005, p. 29), in particular, suggest that there are a number of elements that may have been "disguised" or "covert" in terms of their power from earlier investigations, and that these should be disaggregated and considered. For example, application of Bourdieuian forms of capital suggest that children are receiving a transmission of "cultural capital" (that is, crudely put, the advantage an individual gains, with regard to social progression, from personal dispositions, knowledge, objects and habits) long before entering the school system. A child born into an upper-class family, for instance, almost immediately starts accruing characteristics such as a certain accent and vocabulary. These "embodied" elements are also supplemented throughout the individual's life by what Bourdieu coins "social capital" (Bourdieu, 1986, pp. 247–250). Social capital differs from cultural capital in that it refers to the benefits a person obtains through the social networks they are part of, or can access. Here, it is important to engage with the distinctions that exist between Bourdieu's and Putnam's concepts of social capital. While both are concerned with the existence of and operationalising of social networks, Bourdieu's orientation is towards critical examination of the mechanisms of social reproduction whereas Putnam (1995) sees social capital as a "good" to be identified and then developed and enhanced through social programmes.

One key criticism of Bourdieu's (1986) focus on capital influences could be seen as the limited weight he attributes to the innate cognitive ability of the individual. Here, applying findings from Feinstein's (2006) study of 2,457 pre-school children is instructive. On one hand it calls into question the weight Bourdieu (1986) attaches to innate ability by demonstrating that children display substantial differences in cognitive ability even as early as 22 months. On the other hand Feinstein's (2006) findings show that children displaying low-level cognitive abilities from high socio-economic status families overtake children showing high cognitive abilities from low socio-economic status families as early as 78 months. This latter finding to some extent corroborates Bourdieu's (1986) assertions with regard to the influence capital has from the 'outset' (p. 249) on educational achievement. Feinstein's (2006) study represents one of many important inroads that have started to be made into disaggregating non-curricular advantages. Other such works include Nash (2010) on the relationship between early cognitive development and class origin, Esping-Andersen (2004) on social inheritance and Horvat, Weininger, and Lareau (2003) on parental networks.

Despite these important steps forward, there is one non-pedagogical aspect that has lacked empirical scrutiny. That is, the relationship between access to elite schooling and entry to prestigious professions, specifically the role of public school alumni networks, and what is widely, if anachronistically, known as the 'Old Boy Network' (Scott, 1982; Walford, 1984, 1986). The basic premise here is that alumni from elite public schools can access an informal network of connections in top professions that enhance their career prospects. From a theoretical perspective, the constitution of this network may be seen as an example of what Lukes (2005) refers to as the third dimension of power. The third dimension is distinguished by Lukes from the first and second dimensions of power in that the former are concerned with processes of decision-making, whether overt as in the first dimension or overt or covert as in the second dimension. Within what Lukes has characterised as his third dimension of power, analysis shifts from the confines of decision-making to a wider perspective in which power is exercised through influencing the emergence of potential issues. As such, power operates through circumscribing the parameters of legitimate public discourse. In the present context, a dearth of research and public debate on the links between elite public and private schools and prestigious occupations may itself be seen as linked to the exercise of power.

What is perplexing is that a range of research both refers to, and attributes value to the 'Old Boy Network' (Scott, 1982; Walford, 1984, 1986; Green et al., 2010), and yet, there is almost no substantiated evidence of its existence or the core facets of how it is operationalised. The extremely limited research that has been conducted dates back to the 1950s (Heward, 1984). This consisted of using, *inter alia*, letter archives of correspondence between parents and a specific public school to chart how an alumni network helped facilitate occupational attainment. Unfortunately, the size of the sample catchment used, and the timing of execution

106 Shane Watters

(1930–50), makes the investigation's findings both antiquated and profoundly questionable in terms of their ability to represent wider trends.

The 'Old Boy Network'[4]

The following section offers an introduction to, and discussion of, new empirical research regarding elite public school alumni networks. This includes an outline of the methodology employed and the identification of seven salient network features.

Methodology

The units of analysis selected were principally derived[5] from a list of the most elite public schools established through Walford's (1984, 1986, and 1991) extensive research in the area. This list consists of some 28 schools divided into two sub-groups: The Eton Group and The Rugby Group. These informal groupings have been formed through mutual recognition amongst the schools themselves, the entry requirement literally being schools that are considered to be "something like Rugby" or Eton (Walford, 1986, p. 10). It is worth noting here that these schools have now, in public at least, integrated themselves into the much larger private school sector (Walford, 1991). Although the list offered by Walford is by no means definitive, it provides an undiluted snapshot of the majority of top public schools. This is achieved by incorporating the majority of Clarendon Commission schools (Clarendon, 1964),[6] and many of the original members of the HMC. In the content analysis undertaken seven specific questions were asked of each of 'unit of analysis' or school website. That is:

1. whether the school maintains a secure alumni network,
2. the number of alumni clubs and societies present,
3. whether networks are structured towards specific elite professions and career trajectories,
4. whether the school has its own registered Masonic lodge for alumni,
5. whether the school maintains a distinct international network which alumni can access,
6. whether a careers mentoring or advisory scheme is operated by the school and, finally,
7. whether the school connects with other selected schools in terms of both formal links through the HMC and informal meetings through sports fixtures and other inter-school competitions.

A number of these foci require some unpacking. For instance, the term "secure alumni network" refers to an alumni network that is only accessible through membership; the requirement of which being that you are a current or former

Old Boy Networks **107**

student of that particular public school. 'Alumni clubs and societies' are distinct subgroups of an 'old boy' or alumni network tailored towards a specific area of interest. These range from groupings formed around sports and hobbies to more formalised groupings focused on particular areas of business and commerce.

The research questions were emergent, in that they were determined through a process of cross comparison. Here, the first five units of analysis were juxtaposed to allow for a number of commonalities to be identified. The common elements identified were then tested for consistency against the remaining 23 units of analysis. The key purpose of this stage was to ascertain the extent to which the elements identified initially remained constant. Where new common elements emerged these were added to the search criteria, and the process was reset so that the new elements could be tested against previously investigated units of analysis. Any element that failed to return mutual content across 50% of the units of analysis sampled was then removed from the final matrix. The methodological approach used enabled networks to be refined to a succinct list of prevalent characteristics: testing, adapting, retesting and reducing the categorisations or coding stems from traditional 'content analysis' techniques (Krippendorff, 2004; Bernard & Ryan, 2010). The crucial methodological strength here is that peers and other researchers can use the table produced, and websites cited, to verify the frequency of the network characteristics.

The list of prevalent network characteristics then informed the extraction of qualitative citations from the units of analysis with the purpose of further detailing the structure of the networks and ways in which they are operationalised. Here it is worth highlighting that this research has clear limitations in terms of the range of sources used and the depth to which each network is able to be examined. Through the compilation of this data it is already evident that additional quantitative and qualitative investigation regarding the size of the individual networks, their interaction with each other, and the number of members who have benefited through initial position attainment and progression within a given field, would enrich the data and help to establish greater veracity in any inferences that are drawn. Future research in this area would also greatly benefit, in terms of validity, from corroboration from sources independent of the schools themselves. This is due to the schools having a perverse incentive to overstate the benefits of the networks as a means to justify their significant fees. Although it is important to recognise all of these limitations, the intention here is to create a preliminary platform to facilitate further discussion and research, rather than an attempt to present conclusive evidence.

Results and Analysis

The first striking characteristic of the data sets (Tables 6.1 and 6.2) is that all of the 28 schools sampled displayed significant evidence of operating 'Old Boys Networks'.

TABLE 6.1 The Eton Group

Public school	Secure alumni network	Number of alumni clubs and societies	Networks structured towards specific elite professions and career trajectories	School and 'old boy' lodge (freemasonry)	Distinct international network	Alumni careers mentoring or advisory scheme	Formal and informal connections with other listed schools
Eton	The Old Etonian Association	23	Yes	Yes	Yes	Yes	Yes
Dulwich College	The Old Alleynians Network	13	Yes	Yes	Yes	Not listed/accessible	Yes
Bryanston School	The Old Bryanstonians Network	Not listed/accessible	Yes	Not listed/accessible	Yes	Yes	Yes
Highgate School	The Old Cholmeleian Society	7 Not fully listed/accessible	Yes	Yes	Not listed/accessible	Not listed/accessible	Yes
King's School (Canterbury)	The Old King's Scholars Association	7 Not fully listed/accessible	Yes	Yes	Yes	Yes	Yes
Marlborough College	The Marlburian Club	12	Yes	Yes	Yes	Yes	Yes
St Paul's School	The Old Pauline Club	3 Listed, Area of the Site under development	Yes	Yes	Yes	Yes	Yes
Sherborne School	The Old Shirburnian Society	Not listed/accessible	Yes	Yes	Not listed/accessible	Not listed/accessible	Yes
Tonbridge School	The Old Tonbridgian Society	10	Yes	Yes	Yes	Not listed/accessible	Yes
University College School	The Old Gowers Club	7	Yes	Yes	Not listed/accessible	Not listed/accessible	Yes
Westminster School	The Old Westminsters Online	19	Yes	Yes	Yes	Yes	Yes

TABLE 6.2 The Rugby Group

Public school	Secure alumni network	Number of alumni clubs and societies	Networks structured towards specific elite professions and career trajectories	School and 'old boy' lodge (freemasonry)	Distinct international network	Alumni careers mentoring or advisory scheme	Formal and informal connections with other listed schools
Bradfield College	The Old Bradfieldians Online	11	Not listed/accessible	Yes	Yes	Not listed/accessible	Yes
Charterhouse	The Old Carthusian Club	35	Yes	Yes	Yes	Not listed/accessible	Yes
Cheltenham College	The Cheltonian Association	6	Not listed/accessible	Yes	Yes	Yes	Yes
Clifton College	The Old Cliftonian Society	8	Yes	Yes	Yes	Yes	Yes
Harrow School	The Harrow Association	16	Yes	Yes	Yes	Yes	Yes
Malvern College	The Old Malvernians	6	Not listed/accessible	Yes	Not listed/accessible	Not listed/accessible	Yes
Monkton Combe School	The Old Monktonians Club	Not listed/accessible	Not listed/accessible	Not listed/accessible	Not listed/accessible	Not listed/accessible	Not listed/accessible
Oundle School	The Old Oundelian Club	17	Yes	Yes	Yes	Yes	Not listed/accessible
Radley College	The Old Radleian Society	15	Yes	Yes	Not listed/accessible	Yes	Yes
Repton School	The Old Reptonian Society	5	Yes	Yes	Yes	Yes	Yes
Rugby School	Rugbeians On-line	14	Yes	Yes	Yes	Yes	Yes

TABLE 6.2 (continued)

Public school	Secure alumni network	Number of alumni clubs and societies	Networks structured towards specific elite professions and career trajectories	School and 'old boy' lodge (freemasonry)	Distinct international network	Alumni careers mentoring or advisory scheme	Formal and informal connections with other listed schools
St Edward's School	The Old St Edwardians Society	11	Not listed/ accessible	Yes	Yes	Yes	Yes
Shrewsbury School	The Old Salopian Club	9	Yes	Yes	Yes	Yes	Yes
Stowe School	The Old Stoic Society	8 Not fully listed/ accessible	Yes	Not listed/ accessible	Yes	Not listed/ accessible	Yes
Uppingham School	The Old Uppinghamians Association	6	Not listed/ accessible	Yes	Not listed/ accessible	Yes	Yes
Wellington College	The Old Wellingtonian Society	13	Not listed/ accessible	Yes	Yes	Not listed/ accessible	Yes
Winchester College	The Community of Old Wykehamists	12	Not listed/ accessible	Not listed/ accessible	Not listed/ accessible	Not listed/ accessible	Yes

Source: The data in Tables 6.1 and 6.2 were compiled using the official websites of some of Britain's leading public schools.

The vast majority entitle their network, and members of it, by combining the idiom 'Old' with a modification of the school's name using a belonging suffix. For instance, someone from Eton is part of the 'Old Etonian Association' and is referred to by the school as an 'Old Etonian'. This is not to say membership of the alumni network is always automatic; former students normally have to opt in or out after leaving the school, depending on the system operated. Branding former students in this way, and encouraging students to see themselves in this way, may foster an on-going connection between the school and former students and vice versa. Here, parallels can be drawn with Bourdieu's (1986) assertions regarding the creation of social capital by "application of a common name" (p. 251). Bourdieu's concept dictates that for the name to achieve benefits to its incumbents it would have to hold some resonance with proximal social structures. In the case of public school alumni networks, this could mean spheres outside of the schools, for instance professions having existing members who both recognise and attribute credit to the use of a particular 'Old Boy' title. According to Bourdieu (1986) the degree to which individuals can levy capital from such networks depends on two distinct factors: the size of the networks, and the ability of those in the network to bestow benefits on the individual members. Testing the research by the first of these principles is difficult because there is limited information available via non-secure areas of the school's websites regarding network size. The information that is accessible from eight schools varies considerably, suggesting networks ranging from as little as 800 members up to as many as 15,000. The validity of the network size data is also questionable as it relies on citations from the schools themselves, without corroboration from membership lists.

One of the most important research findings is that the exact size of the networks may not be as relevant as the way in which they are structured in terms of facilitating access to specific professions or areas of business. Here, the majority of schools sampled showed signs of structuring their networks towards particular employment destinations. The structuring takes two forms: the establishment of tailored occupational clubs or societies, and bespoke networking events focused on certain career trajectories. What follows is a précis of extracts from units of analysis demonstrating the common type of groups and events found.

Law
We are very grateful to commercial law firm Lewis Silkin for generously hosting this first meeting of Old Alleynians in the Law at its Chancery Lane offices. The firm has strong connections to the College dating from the time of its founder, Lewis Silkin, and his son, John, who was, like his two brothers, an Old Alleynian.

(Old Alleynians Law Professional Interest Group, 2013)

Medicine
The Medical Group sets up events between all Old Cholmeleians in the medical, dental and associated professions (including veterinarians,

physiotherapists, psychologists and psychiatrists) and Old Cholmeleians interested in entering those professions. The next event will be held at the Royal College of Surgeons.

(Old Cholmeleians Medical Group, 2012)

Arts and media

The inaugural Old Marlburians Film, TV & Theatre Event at the Only Running Footman in Mayfair was a great success ... some Old Marlburians arrived on the way to or from work, including Jack Whitehall, who managed to pop in just prior to his live performance nearby, and Carola Stewart who appeared with great style towards the end of the event having come directly from filming. We were delighted when Damian Jones, who produced the Oscar winning film The Iron Lady, made a surprise appearance too.

(Old Marlburians Film, TV & Theatre Group, 2013)

Finance

Old Harrovians who work in the financial industries held its inaugural meeting at the City of London Club on 1 October 2008 ... attendees included 130 Old Harrovians in financial services, financial consultancy and equity trading.

(Old Harrovians City Club Committee, 2012)

Property

The 6th Annual Rugbeian Society Real Estate Dinner took place on Thursday 8 November 2012 at the Army & Navy Club Pall Mall, London. Just over 40 Rugbeians and current and past parents who work in the property business and related professions attended.

(Old Rugbeian Society, 2012)

Notably, the groups and tailored events displayed consistently, although not exclusively, concerned five specific professions and areas of business: Law, Medicine, Arts and Media, Finance, and Property Management. Interestingly there are clear similarities between these and the professions identified by the Sutton Trust's study (2007) as being disproportionately represented by those deriving from private schools.

The units of analysis also give a variety of information regarding what services networks, and specific groups thereof, provide. These commonly include: tailored networking events by occupational area with established 'Old Boys' working in that particular profession, professional mentoring from established 'Old Boys', and internships and work experience placements offered to recent alumni from established 'Old Boys' in prestigious firms. Importantly the services provided indicate that being a member of an 'Old Boys Network' involves active participation as opposed to dormant membership. Indeed, the photographic and textual evidence from 24 of the sampled schools suggests a vibrant culture of well-attended networking events in extremely prestigious venues, and significantly interaction between a range of young and old members. Often this includes older, more established, network members arranging career orientated networking events at a venue connected to their current profession. Typical examples include events held at Inns of Court by 'Old Boys' in the legal profession, events held at City[7] investment firms by 'Old Boys' at the head of large stockbroking companies and events arranged by senior medical professionals at royal medical colleges. One purpose of the networks here is succinctly encapsulated by the Old Cliftonian Business Community (2014): "A specific network of Old Cliftonians with a commercial interest, providing access to and from Old Cliftonians and the school to leverage their combined knowledge to further each other's professional prospects."

The function and services of the networks towards aiding in members' professional development notably reconciles with Bourdieu's (1986) assertions identified above regarding acknowledgement and appreciation from proximal social structures, in that they suggest both recognition and favoured treatment from existing members of professions. The services provided also share the common characteristics of enabling new alumni to make personal contact with senior staff in a range of top professions. This is a potential key advantage as it allows members to single themselves out from formal application based routes. It is not suggested that 'Old Boys' will not have to go through a formal employment process, but rather that prospects for being offered positions can be enhanced through personal connections. This arguably represents what Lukes (2005) has described as a covert exercise of power. The job application process, to the extent to which it is observable, goes through a conventional procedure. Power is covert in the sense that power relations are at play in selecting candidates from a particular background while ostensibly presenting employment within a meritocratic system. The job application process alluded to above may also be illuminated by Bourdieu's (1979) work regarding classes and classifications that suggests a process of perception and recognition. When applied in this case, network membership may indicate a particular mix of characteristics and competences positively recognised by employers as signalling a certain social class suitable to specific occupations. Here, contemporary economic theorists argue that this is not so much a case of applying undue bias, but rather that 'old boy networks' constitute a valuable informal mechanism whereby employers can obtain 'hidden' information on prospective employees (Inci & Parker, 2012, p. 30), thereby allowing firms to make hiring decisions with greater assurity. In the case of public school old boys networks, it could be argued that employers presuppose membership entails minimum levels of both cultural capital (Bourdieu, 1986), in the form of accent, dress, manners and human capital (Halpern, 2005), in terms of knowledge and ability.

Green et al. (2010) above highlight the educational benefits of attending private schools. However, whether these lead to the development of distinct characteristics synonymous with those needed for high-status professions remains highly questionable. Furthermore, there is a significant problem with addressing issues of social reproduction if those arbitrating what constitutes required capital levels are largely members of the same network. Here, a combination of earlier data (Sutton Trust, 2007; Scott, 1982; Boyd, 1973), regarding the disproportionate representation in top professions for those hailing from private or public schools, and network data presented in this chapter certainly indicates this may be the case. If correct, this would signify maintenance of the status quo, effectively advantaging those inside the network, but restricting those outside of it. A further issue regards the networks as a mechanism in social reproduction, that is, that existing established members in a given profession may have a vested interest in employing staff who attended the same public school in an effort to make sure the value attributed to attending a given school is continued (Bourdieu, 1986; Curtis, 2000). In other words, by maintaining the presence of 'Old Boys' in particular professions and areas of business, established 'Old Boys' in these areas are able to reaffirm their own worth.

Although the effect of 'Old Boys' already in prestigious professions trying to preserve their status may be important to the enduring nature of an old boy's network, longitudinal network maintenance is also likely to require persistent and widespread "investment strategies" (Bourdieu, 1986, p. 252). Here, data drawn from the schools' websites illuminates some of the resources employed in this respect at the institutional level. For instance a number of schools have a whole office of professional staff dedicated to this very task. Marlborough College as a case in point has: a Club Secretary, an Alumni Relations Manger, a Development Officer, a Website & Publications Manager and an Information & Communications Officer working specifically to maintain the Marlburian Club (Marlborough School Development Team, 2012). Most networks are also headed by a President, who tends to be a distinguished old boy acting as a figurehead and champion. The type of structure identified here only represents one aspect of school level network maintenance and development. On top of this schools can mobilise an array of individuals with semi-formal roles within the network. For instance, St Paul's School's Old Pauline Club has 55 Vice Presidents, and 57 heads and members of various sub-committees (The Old Pauline Club Committee Membership List, 2013–14). However, the quantity here may not be as prevalent to bestowing advantages on network members as the quality of the individuals involved in terms of their prestige. In the example of the Old Pauline Club these include Knights (CBEs), admirals, judges, professors, Lords and the current Chancellor of the Exchequer, George Osborne, as one of its Vice Presidents (Cabinet Office, 2013).

One further facet of the networks is their international dimension. Here, 20 out of the 28 schools sampled, to a varying degree, displayed developed international networks. The remaining eight schools were not necessarily deficient in this respect, but rather that this data was not available in the non-secure area of the websites. The network information that is available tends to consist of an extensive list of international contacts willing to assist old boys wishing to establish themselves in a given country. For instance The Old King's Association (OKS) cites an impressive and characteristic list of contacts spanning much of the globe. When students or OKS click on a link for a given country they see a personal message from an alumnus who is now in a prominent position. The messages differ in content, but in general offer help with moving to/visiting the country and, pertinently, advice on employment in their given field (The Old Kings Association, Overseas Hon Secs, 2013). As with domestic branches of the networks, the affluence of the individuals cited and the social capital they represent is significant. If one excepts Bryanston School's careers and business networking group statements, such networks are able to provide a "rich source of useful contacts" that can offer "career pointers and friendly advice" from established alumni "working across a variety of industries around the globe" (Bryanston School, Careers and Business Networking Group, 2014). Moreover, the international networks on display transcend lists of useful potential social and business contacts. Instead the schools manage to provide dynamic international networks involving regular social and networking events. To achieve this, the schools continuously recruit representatives to facilitate and maintain these international parts or 'chapters' of their networks, assist with venues for meetings, and advertise events through their websites and distinct international newsletters. It is worth noting here that a significant number of international students now attend British public schools: these clearly provide a fertile recruiting ground for schools wishing to develop their international networks.

The development of the international dimension of the networks is significant in terms of discourses regarding the relationship between education and the global labour market. Here, Brown (2000), a prominent commentator in this area, poses the important question of "whether social elites are increasingly defining positional competition for credentials and jobs in international … terms" (p. 643). The research for this chapter certainly shows evidence that elite British public schools are aware of the threat presented by the globalisation of the labour market, and are actively involved in preserving their position in this context. The fact that these schools are mobilising their social capital in this way also challenges the concept (Lauder et al., 2006, p. 319) that a global labour market will result in increased meritocracy through the internationalisation of employment opportunities. The networks' abilities to cross domestic boundaries suggests that those children whose parents can afford this type of schooling will still possess an advantage in an international arena outside of their educational achievements. In a not unrelated point, 24 out of 28 schools sampled had strong connections with the Freemasons. This unanticipated finding is interesting for two notable reasons. Firstly, it shows a distinct link between the schools and one of the biggest

116 Shane Watters

gentlemen's organisations in the world (Ridley, 2011), and, secondly, it connects the sampled schools as their Lodges are all members of the Public School Lodges' Council. This is an umbrella organisation that arranges a variety of meetings and events between members of these Old Boy Lodges. Examples of the longevity of the link between Freemasonry and public schools, and their connections with each other through the Public School Lodges' Council, include Highgate School having the oldest Freemasons Lodge in the world (The Cholmeley Lodge, 2014) and the Old Etonian Lodge hosting "the 76th Public School Lodges' Council Festival" in 2009 (The Old Etonian Lodge, 2014). In addition to contact between the schools related to Freemasonry, there are also links through events arranged by the HMC and inter-school sports fixtures as indicated by a "Yes" in the final column of the results table above. These fixtures and events form an important part of the networks as they are not only for existing students, but also for alumni. For instance, there are distinct Old Boy teams and leagues in areas such as shooting, sailing and golf. This is significant as it shows the networks are interrelated and continue to interact long after decoupling from education-based contact.

Conclusion

The analysis of existing quantitative data brought together a range of sources not previously engaged with as a body of evidence. Although strengths and weaknesses of each source were exposed, collectively the data demonstrated a strong and recurrent link between private schooling and high status employment in Britain. Furthermore, both this and the subsequent theoretical analysis demonstrated that the category 'elite schools' requires unpacking both in terms of differentiation when approaching data gathering and findings, and in relation to the disaggregation of advantages that go beyond the curricular or co-curricular. Here, the chapter was able to break free of the confines of traditional ethnographical approaches and utilise contemporary content analysis techniques to examine a wealth of previously untapped data and information. Importantly, this enabled the research to transcend merely noting the role of elite schools in the 'social production of advantage' to actually beginning to evidence some of the mechanisms which facilitate this social production. The paucity of empirical evidence regarding non-curricular based advantages of attending elite schools highlights the significant problems of access associated with researching elite groups in society (Aguiar & Schneider, 2012), and the importance of adopting new methodological approaches. Employing content analysis techniques to elites not only demonstrated their benefits in terms of overcoming access problems, but also illustrated their potential with regard to directing qualitative research.

A research focus on Old Boy Networks substantiates the role of alumni groups and societies in penetrating prestigious professions. Not only were specific links uncovered in relation to law, medicine, arts and media, finance, and property management, but there were also clear parallels between these groupings and those identified in prior research as containing a disproportionate number of former private school pupils. In other words, networks are generated that enhance access to the higher tiers of the most socially esteemed and financially beneficial professions. Interestingly in terms of contributing to international research undertaken by Kenway and Koh (2013) networks were not bounded within national frameworks but rather gave former pupils access to global elite networks not necessarily connected to or serving any one nation state. Furthermore it was evident that British public schools are acutely aware of the importance of ensuring their sphere of influence extends beyond national borders and have established international networks to ensure alumni maximise their opportunities in global markets. The research also showed that the globalisation of British public schools extended beyond the domestic with regard to a number of schools having already established international satellite schools in locations such as Hong Kong, Shanghai, Tianjin, Iskandar, and Dubai, all including entry and access to associated British Old Boy Networks. A further dimension here is the extent to which the schools themselves recruit from global elites and enable students to develop valuable international social networks while undertaking studies in Britain.

Theoretically, Bourdieuian concepts of capital acted as a valuable mechanism to inform and direct the research undertaken. In particular these were able to illuminate possible causal factors not addressed in prior studies. Significantly this has included drawing attention to the capital accrued through social networks, and acting as an analytical tool in terms of: aiding an examination of how the Old Boy Networks in question interacted and maintained resonance with proximal social structures; how the networks could be operationalised to bestow benefits on their members; and whether necessary 'investment strategies' were in place to preserve and develop these networks. The research here confirms that the networks examined articulated all of these characteristics, and therefore, supports Bourdieu's foresight in these respects. Bourdieu's work also informed a value led examination of the resources network members had at their disposal. Here the research suggested that individuals, having attended the listed schools, were able to harness an impressive concentration of collective social and cultural capital. This took the form of a range of established and influential network members with official positions within the network structure. One symptomatic example, from St Paul's School, demonstrated both the capital value available in terms of the prestige of the agents listed, and the ease to which these resources were identifiable and accessible to new network members through the attribution of official positions.

Notes

1 The term 'public' stems from the schools' historical role in educating the poor rather than their current incarnation as the most elite private schools in Britain.

2 The terms 'independent schools' and 'private schools' refer to any school not run or funded by the State. The term 'independent' is preferred by the private school sector in Britain as it invokes more positive connotations.

3 That is vocabulary tests, Harris Figure Drawing Excises, standardised reading comprehension tests, and math scores (types of tests applied dependent on age).

4 This name should be considered somewhat anachronistic as the research for the present investigation suggests the schools' networks are equally accessible to both male and female alumni in cases where schools are co-educational.

5 The selected schools are intended to act as a representative sample rather than offering a complete list of the top public schools; however, it should be recognised that King's College, London is also part of the Eton group, and Haileybury school has been added to the Rugby Group since the time of Walford's research.

6 The Clarendon Commission was a Royal Commission set up in 1861 "to inquire into the Revenue and Management of Certain Colleges and Schools and the studies pursued and instruction given there" (Clarendon, 1964, p. 1). Importantly the commission report identified nine Great Public Schools.

7 City is a term that refers to the "City of London" or the banking and finance district

8 As an authenticity measure, only the official school sites, and formal links from the official school sites, have been used in the compilation of the research (2012–2015). Whilst web-based sources have the disadvantage of information not being static, the range of schools examined means it is unlikely that scholars will not be able to access similar information evidencing the central themes and information for this chapter regarding the presence and operation of old boys' networks.

References

Aguiar, L., & Schneider, C. (Eds.) (2012). *Researching amongst elites: Challenges and opportunities in studying up*. Farnham: Ashgate.

Ball, S. (1997). On the cusp: Parents choosing between state and private schools in the UK: Action within an economy of symbolic goods. *International Journal of Inclusive Education*, 1(1), 1–17.

Bamford, T. (1967). *The rise of the public schools: A study of boys' public boarding schools in England and wales from 1837 to the present day*. London: Nelson.

Bernard, R., & Ryan, G. (2010). *Analysing qualitative data: Systematic approaches*. London: Sage Publications.

Bourdieu, P. (1979). *Distinction: A social critique of the judgement of taste*. London: Routledge.

Bourdieu, P. (1986). The forms of capital. In J. G. Richardson (Eds.), *Handbook for theory and research for the sociology of education* (pp. 241–258). New York: Greenwood.

Boyd, D. (1973). *Elites and their education: The educational and social background of eight elite groups*. Windsor: NFER Publishing.

Brown, P. (2000). The globalisation of positional competition? *British Sociological Association*, 34(4), 633–653.

Cabinet Office. (2013). *List of Ministers' Interests*. Retrieved October 2015 from https://www.gov.uk/government/publications/list-of-ministers-interests

Clarendon, G. (1964). *The Clarendon report*. London: Eyre and Spottiswoode.

Curtis, R. (2000). The old-boy network and the young-gun effect. *International Economic Review*, 41(4), 871–891.

Esping-Andersen, G. (2004). Untying the Gordian knot of social inheritance. *Research in Social Stratification and Mobility*, 21, 115–138.

Feinstein, L. (2006). Social class and cognitive development in childhood in the UK. In H. Lauder, P. Brown, J. Dillabough & A. Halsey (Eds.), *Education, globalisation & social change* (pp. 409–419). Oxford: Oxford University Press.

Green, F., Machin, S., Murphy, R., & Zhu, Y. (2010). *The changing economic advantage from private school*. IZA Discussion Chapter No. 5018.

Halpern, D. (2005). *Social capital*. Cambridge: Polity Press.

Held, D., McGrew, A., Goldblatt, D., & Perraton, J. (1999). *Global transformations, politics, economics and culture*. Stanford, CA: Stanford University Press.

Heward, C. (1984). Parents, sons and their careers: A case study of a public school, 1930-50. In G. Walford (Ed.), *British public schools, policy and practice*. Lewis, UK: Falmer Press.

Horvat, E., Weininger, E., & Lareau, A. (2003). From social ties to social capital: Class differences in the relations between schools and parent networks. *American Educational Research Journal*, 40(2), 319–351.

Inci, E., & Parker, S. (2012) *Financing entrepreneurship and the old-boy network*. IZA Discussion Chapter No. 6288.

Judiciary Website. (2012, Official UK Government Site). Retrieved October 2015 from http://www.judiciary.gov.uk/about-the-judiciary/judges-magistrates-and-tribunal-judges/list-of-members-of-the-judiciary/senior-judiciary-list#headingAnchor1

Kenway, J., & Koh, A. (2013). The elite school as a 'cognitive machine' and 'social paradise'?: Developing transnational capitals for the national 'field of power.' In T. Bennett, J. Frow, G. Hage & G. Noble, (Eds.), Working with Bourdieu: Antipodean Cultural Fields. *Journal of Sociology* (Special Issue), 49(2–3), 272–290.

Krippendorff, K. (2004). *Content analysis: An introduction to its methodology* (2nd edn). London: Sage Publications.

Lauder, H., Brown, P., Dillabough, J., & Halsey, A. (Eds.) (2006). *Education, globalisation & social change*. Oxford: Oxford University Press.

Lukes, S. (2005). *Power: A radical view* (2nd edn). Basingstoke, UK: Palgrave Macmillan.

Marlborough School Development Team. (2012) *Staff resources*. Retrieved October 2015 from http://www.marlburianclub.org/club-pages/club-about-us/club---about-us-meet-the-team-2014

Nash, R. (2010). *Explaining inequalities in school achievement: A realist analysis*. Farnham, UK: Ashgate.

Old Alleynians Law Professional Interest Group. (2013). *Law reception*. Retrieved October 2015 from http://www.dulwich.org.uk/oas-development/news/2012/10/30/oas-in-the-law-reception

Old Cholmeleians Medical Group. (2012). Retrieved October 2015 from http://highgateoc.org.uk/page.aspx?pid=520

Old Harrovians City Club Committee. (2012). *Inaugural Meeting*. Retrieved October 2015 from http://www.harrowassociation.com/netcommunity/page.aspx?pid=400

Old Marlburians Film, TV & Theatre Group. (2013). *Inaugural Meeting*. Retrieved October 2015 from http://www.marlburianclub.org/affiliates/OMFTT

Old Rugbeian Society. (2012). *Real Estate Dinner*. Retrieved October 2015 from http://rugbeians.rugbyschool.net/page.aspx?pid=1889

Parliamentary Website. (2012, Official UK Government Site). Retrieved October 2014 from http://www.parliament.uk/about/how/elections-and-voting/constituencies/

120 Shane Watters

Putnam, R. (1995). Bowling alone: America's declining social capital. *Journal of Democracy*, 6(1), 65–78.

Ridley, J. (2011). *The freemasons: A history of the world's most powerful secret society*. New York, NY: Arcade Publishing.

Scott, J. (1982). *The upper classes: Property and privilege in Britain*. London: Macmillan Press.

Sutton Trust. (2007). *Education backgrounds of 500 leading figures*. London: Sutton Trust.

Sutton Trust. (2010). *The educational backgrounds of members of parliament in 2010*. London: Sutton Trust.

The Cholmeley Lodge. (2014). Retrieved October 2015 from http://www.highgateschool.org.uk/oc/oc-societies

The Old Etonian Lodge (2014). Retrieved October 2015 from http://www.oldetonianlodge.org/

The Old King's Association, Overseas Hon Secs. (2013). Retrieved October 2015 from http://www.oks.org.uk/?pid=39&level=2

The Old Pauline Club Committee Membership List, 2013–14. (2013). Retrieved October 2015 from http://old.stpaulsschool.org.uk/about-opc/committee-list

Walford, G. (Ed.) (1984). *British public schools: Policy and practice*. Lewis, UK: Falmer Press.

Walford, G. (1986). *Life in public schools*. London: Methuen & Co.

Walford, G. (1991). *Private schooling: Tradition, change and diversity*. London: Paul Chapman Publishing.

Websites Examined[8]

Eton. (2013). *Old boys network information*. Retrieved from http://www.etoncollege.com/TheOEA.aspx?nid=2799133b-bcd4–4946–856e-254dd7273967

Dulwich College. (2013). *Old Boys Network Information*. Retrieved from http://www.dulwich.org.uk/old-alleynians

Bryanston School. (2013). *Old Boys Network Information*. Retrieved from https://www.bryanston.co.uk/podium/default.aspx?t=108781&rc=1

Bryanston School, Careers and Business Networking Group. (2014). Retrieved October 2014 from http://www.bryanston.co.uk/networking?rc=0

Highgate School. (2013). *Old Boys Network Information*. Retrieved from http://highgateoc.org.uk/

King's School (Canterbury). (2013). *Old Boys Network Information*. Retrieved from http://www.kings-school.co.uk/document_1.aspx?id=1:32044&id=1:31637

Marlborough College. (2013). *Old Boys Network Information*. Retrieved from http://www.marlburianclub.org/page.aspx?pid=388

St Paul's School. (2013). *Old Boys Network Information*. Retrieved from http://www.opclub.org.uk/

Sherborne School. (2013). *Old Boys Network Information*. Retrieved from http://www.oldshirburnian.org.uk/

Tonbridge School. (2013). *Old Boys Network Information*. Retrieved from http://www.tonbridge-school.co.uk/tonbridge-society/

University College School. (2013). *Old Boys Network Information*. Retrieved from: http://www.ucs.org.uk/Welcome-to-the-Gowers

Westminster School. (2013). *Old Boys Network Information*. Retrieved from http://www.oldwestminster.org.uk/

Bradfield College. (2013). *Old Boys Network Information*. Retrieved from http://www. bradfieldcommunity.org.uk/OBSoc/bradfieldiansonline/Pages/default.aspx

Charterhouse. (2013). *Old Boys Network Information*. Retrieved from http://www. charterhouse.org.uk/ocs

Cheltenham College. (2013). *Old Boys Network Information*. Retrieved from http://www. cheltonianassociation.com/

Clifton College. (2013). *Old Boys Network Information*. Retrieved from http://www. oc-online.co.uk/

Harrow School. (2013). *Old Boys Network Information*. Retrieved from http://www. harrowassociation.com/Netcommunity/

Malvern College. (2013). *Old Boys Network Information*. Retrieved from http://www. malcol.org/old-malvernians/

Monkton Combe School. (2013). *Old Boys Network Information*. Retrieved from http:// www.monktoncombeschool.com/index.php?id=130

Old Cliftonian Business Community. (2015). Retrieved 6 December 2015 from http:// oc-online.co.uk/#businesscommunity

Oundle School. (2013). *Old Boys Network Information*. Retrieved from http://society. oundleschool.org.uk/OOclub/index.php

Radley College. (2013). *Old Boys Network Information*. Retrieved from: http://www. radley.org.uk/RadleianSociety.aspx

Repton School. (2013). *Old Boys Network Information*. Retrieved from http://www. repton.org.uk/old-reptonian-society

Rugby School. (2013). *Old Boys Network Information*. Retrieved from http://rugbeians. rugbyschool.net/

St Edward's School. (2013). *Old Boys Network Information*. Retrieved from http://www. stedwards.oxon.sch.uk/ose-friends.html

Shrewsbury School. (2013). *Old Boys Network Information*. Retrieved from http://www. shrewsbury.org.uk/page/old-salopians

Stowe School. (2013). *Old Boys Network Information*. Retrieved from http://www.stowe. co.uk/old-stoics/

Uppingham School. (2013). *Old Boys Network Information*. Retrieved from http://www. olduppinghamian.co.uk/

Wellington College. (2013). *Old Boys Network Information*. Retrieved from http://www. wellingtoncollege.org.uk/old-wellingtonians

7

EXCLUSIVE CONSUMERS

The Discourse of Privilege in Elite Indian School Websites

Radha Iyer

Introduction

India, a country of contrasts particularly in education, has a large variety of schools available to children. Post-independence India has a diverse education system that ranges from government schools, Ekal Vidyalaya, Madrassa schools[1] to government-aided private schools, un-aided private and elite private schools, and, more recently, private, elite international schools that offer the International Baccalaureate (IB). Private unaided schools are a heterogeneous group that range from schools funded by private corporations, family trusts, day and boarding institutions run by religious and non-denominational organisations to the more recent, low end, low fee schools for the poor. Elite schools are institutions that offer exclusive learning experiences with a selective faculty and highly controlled, intensive academic and extracurricular activities designed to promote individual productivity and competitiveness (Bourdieu, 1996/1989, pp. 81–85).

While scholarly focus has been on documenting the colonial and neoliberal agenda of select elite schools (Rizvi, 2014; Srivastava, 1998) little attention has been paid to the particular discourses and textual means employed by Indian elite school websites to promote their education programmes. In this chapter, 21 school websites are studied through a Foucauldian discourse analysis to examine how, through typological, demographic, historical, scholastic, and geographic dimensions (Gaztambide-Fernández, 2009b) as illustrated through texts and discourses online, elite schools create entities of scholastic and social distinction. The analysis demonstrates how Indian elite schools have a similar ideology and mode of operation to other elite schools worldwide (Kenway & Fahey, 2014; Kenway, Fahey & Koh, 2013; Khan, 2012) in that these largely promote tradition

Exclusive Consumers   **123**

and modernity, consumerism and meritocracy. This focus requires an explanation of the historical links of modern elite schools, which is outlined below.

Colonialism and the Modern Indian School

In 1835, the *Macaulay Minute on Indian Education* by Lord Macaulay, Chairman, *Committee of Public Instruction* in British India promoted English as the medium of instruction which became the means of novel forms of governance as it sought to create a "class of persons Indian in blood and colour, but English in tastes, in opinions, in morals and in intellect".[2] With English as the language of administration in 1837, Sir Charles Wood's despatch in 1854[3] deemed that western knowledge was the most suitable, a trend that was rigorously followed when the Crown took over in 1839. By the 1890s the school system was firmly characterised by the perceived superiority of the colonial system where western education in English was provided to the children of colonisers and economically affluent natives.

As scholars (Majumdar & Mooij, 2011; Bhattacharya, 2002, p. 6) note, "the valorisation of English education" led to forms of cultural, social capital and a means to mark the elites. The Indian elites readily accepted the colonial rule as a "pedagogic enterprise for the improvement of India" (Seth, 2007, p. 159) that led to the consolidation of an elite discourse that was based not on caste or class but on exclusion and inclusion in terms of western education. Elites and the upper middle class had such a desire for such education that there was an outcry against the new reforms that advocated the vernacular, as introduced by Lord Curzon, the Viceroy of India in the 1890s; these reforms were seen to limit India's "access to western education and to assert dictatorial government control" (Seth, 2007, p. 160). Western education was perceived to bring in "a whole series of adjustments" (Seth, 2007, p. 27), and be "an instrument for the control of minds" (Annamalai, 2004, p. 181).

A post-colonial standpoint illustrates how such knowledge became legitimate forms that overtook local knowledge and supports Spivak's (1988, p. 287) comment that the colonial attempt was to erase the voice of the colonised as "in the context of colonial production, the subaltern ... cannot speak". Post-independence, although the Indian elites were only 6% of the total population, they were, nevertheless, decision makers in the government (Annamalai, 2004, p. 179) and as Little (2010, p. 7) observes, "the education of the elite" received as much priority as mass education. English as the medium of instruction being preferred by the affluent class, the legacy of colonial education persists with schools set by the colonisers continuing the colonial discourse through rhetoric and through the adoption of a historically instituted education system.

As Prasad (2003) notes, within the Indian education system there is a heavy dependence on western forms of knowledge that inculcate western hegemony socially, culturally, economically and in their ideological content. The Cambridge

124 Radha Iyer

IGCSE (International General Certificate of Secondary Education),[4] an international school-leaving exam required by exiting secondary students in some elite schools in India, is an example of how educational philosophies of the UK and the west are still preferred. Similar to elite schools in the USA, UK, Australia, and Canada (Brooks & Waters, 2014; Kenway & Fahey, 2007; Lynch & Moran, 2006; Maxwell & Maxwell, 1995; Waters & Brooks, 2015; Weis & Cipollone, 2013), Indian elite schools are exclusive learning centres that illustrate Anglophone forms of knowledge and target Anglophone countries, primarily the UK and USA, as favoured future destinations for higher education for their pupils. A brief discussion on elite schools in India follows to highlight how, along with this historical legacy, market- and consumer-oriented, neoliberal discourses are scripted within websites.

The Indian Elite School: Local/Global Influence

Exclusive in terms of creating a space for various formal and informal forms of social capital, elite schools craft an agentive position for students (Forbes & Lingard, 2013) where through "a rite of institution" and through "pedagogic action ... a separate, sacred group" (Bourdieu, 1996/1989, p. 73) is created, one that has the current and potential symbolic capital to succeed. These schools have a stringent condition of entry and performance based on a meritocratic system (see Koh, 2014), one that "guarantee[s] students already endowed" and only those capable of undertaking the learning are eligible to apply (Bourdieu, 1996/1989, p. 73). A primary reason for this fundamental requirement is the elite niche carved out for the elite alumni in high-level bureaucratic positions and to preserve the upper-class ideals that perceive a future beyond local contexts (see Mullen, 2009). Subsequently, the overarching colonial and neo-colonial tradition endures with modes of teaching and learning widely adopted in the west being implemented that permits a "mental colonialist to continue and neo-colonialism to triumph" (Nguyen et al., 2009, p. 112).

As Rizvi (2014) and Srivastava (1998) argue, the changing political landscape after independence with greater focus on secularism, social equity, and equality of opportunity has meant that elite schools have had to adopt a new philosophy where nationalist sentiments, a scientific, rational approach, and principles of civil society (Srivastava, 1998) are emphasised. The colonial discourse of the supremacy of English medium for instruction and western oriented education continues but is distanced by a new national discourse that emphasises leadership, community activities and sustainability (see Rizvi, 2014). A post-colonial reading illustrates how, with very minimal internal difference in structure and ideology, these schools largely support western knowledge and their progress is often marked by their associations with the global (read western) elite groups.

Rizvi (2014) identifies two types of elite Indian schools, the old ones established during the colonial period and the new ones that cater to the growing, wealthy middle class. During British rule, these schools represented the superior status of a Eurocentric worldview and retained their elite status through mimicry and, as Srivastava (1998, p. 45), in a study of the elite Doon School observes, "display an Otherness of the past alongside symbolic markers of … a new age and future".

With economic liberalisation in the 1990s, the Indian economy has become market oriented and education, as elsewhere (Carnoy, 2014; Forsey, Davies & Walford, 2008, p. 15; see also Lingard, 2000), has become a means to achieve economic competitiveness and is a commodity where there is greater emphasis on excellence, performance and consumerism. Subsequently, to the two groups of elite schools identified by Rizvi (2014), a third type of elite school can be added, the transnational, elite institution that subscribes to a global curriculum and is oriented to serve a global clientele and children of expatriates. While this third group does not have a colonial heritage, these are elite due to their international curricula, a strong corporate focus and an explicit neoliberal agenda of being market oriented.

The neoliberal market oriented turn in education is exemplified in all the elite schools studied as these identify accountability, performance, academic and extracurricular achievement and global affiliations as central aims of schooling (Stromquist & Monkman, 2014). Transnational examinations such as IGCSE and schools being a member of the Round Square[5] are promoted to demonstrate the capacity of the school to have a global standard. Aligned with this agenda, elite schools offer greater parental choice, along with international and local learning competitions, the IB programme, and a suite of sophisticated extracurricular activities so that the venture is perceived as financially viable and as a truly global programme. The preference for a multiliteracies, multimodal approach to education, and global issues that draw on environmental, social, cultural, and political arenas, is aimed at building future leaders and turning students into transnational citizens who can compete in knowledge trading and knowledge discourses. Nowhere is this more prominently present than in the manner in which these schools project their education offerings on websites.

India's Elite School Websites

While the private elite schools continue to be sought after learning centres, the neoliberal agenda has driven these schools to advertise so that they retain their market domination. Scholars (Drew, 2013; Gottschall et al., 2010; Meadmore & Meadmore, 2004; Waters & Brooks, 2015) have depicted how prospectuses, marketing brochures, and websites promote institutional neoliberal agendas of elite schools as institutions of excellence. A study of Indian school websites depicts how the texts and images are market oriented to present an exclusive and elitist education system for wealthy parents who desire an exclusive, privileged education for their children.

Where, earlier, school brochures were the preferred mode of advertising for a school, with the public access to the Internet since 1991 there has been a steady move by Indian schools to incorporate a website. Websites are modes through which schools "reaffirm or reconstruct their existing institutional identities with varying levels of success" (Hesketh & Selwyn, 1999, p. 502). A job that was previously done through brochures with textual and visual representation is carried on through websites with colourful images of the school front, mission statement by the principal, representation of global alumni and international achievement news being presented with the added attraction of Blogs and Facebook links being provided. The recommendations and thereby word-of-mouth advertising that were provided by alumni, friends and family is now being conducted through websites that provide wider dissemination of learning programmes that are exclusive. Where school brochures would publish select information, websites operate in a more flexible space where the choice lies with the consumer as an active participant in the content (Hesketh & Selwyn, 1999). Websites are a means for elite schools to be economically and educationally productive as these share their resources with the viewing public to reaffirm their status and unique position within Indian education.

Methodology

Foucault's notion of discourse as constituting knowledge that permits certain statements to be uttered or presented became a useful methodology to study the school websites. Discursive formation for Foucault (1972/2010) enables an interrelated set of statements that "define a regularity" (p. 38), constitute all that defines the field, and are "subjected [to] rules of formation" (p. 38) that have coherence and meaning. For Foucault, discursive practices are historically, socially and culturally determined rules that assist in producing knowledge, here the knowledge of the type of discourses that successfully promote a school as elite. Discourses as a set of statements where ideas and language interweave to create "rules or forms to become manifest" (Foucault, 1972/2010, p. 88) become a means to recognise what is inclusive, nameable and what is exclusive which calls for the need to identify how particular statements and discourses are authenticated, the particular knowledge that constitute and sustain the field: in this study, how elite schools are discursively constructed in websites.

A Foucauldian discourse analysis takes a corpus of statements (Foucault, 1972/2010) and examines the continuity, discontinuities and the genealogical background of these statements to illustrate how discourses are problematic, and historically variable (Arribas-Ayllon & Walkerdine, 2007). Following from this, my attention is to examine the five dimensions of elite schools (Gaztambide-Fernández, 2009b) that are created through discursive practices. However, even where these elite dimensions are evident, the discourses adopted by websites are objective and factual. Subsequently, even though discursive practices that create the identity of the elite schools are palpably present, these are as a subtle presentation of facts and client desired information and mode of operation of elite schools.

Exclusive Consumers **127**

This study examined 21 websites selected from 100 private school websites that were initially searched on the web portal Google between December 2013–May 2014. Understandably, the small sample size is not designed to be representative of all elite schools but the modest aim is to describe the elite dimensions of such schools in some qualitative depth. Key words such as "private", "elite", "boarding", and "best private schools" were used to initially find schools. The web portal *Rediff.com* was searched for its survey of India's elite private schools. Although it is acknowledged that images contribute to the depth of meaning, to limit the study only the texts of the websites have been undertaken for discussion.

Three categories were identified: the boarding schools in hill stations established during the British rule; metropolitan day and boarding elite schools; and the IB international schools in small towns. The study was limited to schools that have a comprehensive website (see Table 7.1). Table 7.1 provides a list of identifiers in each category; for example, their history, affiliation, clientele and major discourses. The various hyperlinks on the school websites examined were: About this school; Overview; Principal's message; History and Future Vision; Admissions; Academics; Student life; Extracurricular; and Alumni. Twenty-one websites were chosen for the comprehensive information that is available on each and these are given the pseudonyms of ELS1 to ELS21 in no particular order to de-identify them. Although the websites are all publically accessible, issues of undertaking a study of these sites with the schools unlikely to have expected the websites to be closely scrutinised led to anonymising the schools. Each school being numbered ensures transparency concerning how frequently the sites are quoted and also to ensure accuracy of the quote.

A close reading of statements and discourses was undertaken to identify the five dimensions on which schools can be considered elite: typologically elite being identified as private and independent, and having a substantial endowment; scholastically elite with a distinguished learning programme that often includes expensive extracurricular activities and with a curriculum desired by the clientele; historically elite in terms of the networks and historical continuum schools have depicted; demographically elite based on the clientele that forms the community with careful selection of teachers and academically smart students national and international; and, geographically elite based in an exclusive environment with an idyllic location or a large space with all exclusive resources and material facilities.

Colonial Excellence

The discourse of historical continuity and preservation of traditions is clearly articulated but balanced with the nationalist, global standpoint that only serves to reiterate the sanctified position of these schools. Since their inception in the 1800s (for example, ELS7; ELS4) often as "believed to be the first co-educational boarding school in the world" (ELS4, Historical Foundations), "one of the oldest

TABLE 7.1 Distinguishing features of elite schools, India

School	History	Geographic location	Affiliation	Global/colonial leaning	Clientele	Primary discourse
Colonial excellence ELS 1–8	Since 1800s	Hill stations Large acreages Residential only	Established on the pattern of British Public School in the nineteenth century and continuing the traditions to date Offer IGCSE or ISC[1] exams	Colonial, often religious affiliation that is focused on the global in multiple ways: competitions, religious affiliations; exchange programmes Prefect system and school captains	Children of expatriates, of alumni, of royalty, of film and entertainment industry, senior government officials, children of Indian diplomats working abroad and a global clientele	Discourse of colonial heritage, historical continuity and tradition Spatial opulence Global links Streamlined discipline Academic excellence Individual attention Up-to-date infrastructure Expert faculty Internationalisation Sustainability Ecological awareness
Metropolitan excellence ELS 9–16	Since 1800s and some since 1970s	Metropolitan cities Day school/ residential	Established on the pattern of private school system drawing on the colonial public schools in India Offer CBSE, SAT/ IGCSE/ISC	Branches in cities and some in countries where there is a large Indian diaspora that depends heavily on Indian cultural heritage; Prefect system; school Houses; extra-curricular activities	Similar to the first category Children of politicians, industrialists, company executives, and upper middle class, or the business class	Present and future oriented Educational excellence Local and global competitiveness Holistic development Individual attention Up-to-date infrastructure Expert faculty Internationalisation
New excellence IB ELS 17–21	Since 1990 and 2000	Small cities or rural	Established as an International World College[2] or as an initiative of large industries	IB focused; goals and mission of International World Colleges	Children of different countries; children of upper middle/middle class, diplomats, international business people	International Baccalaureate Global and local engagement International faculty International clientele Up-to-date infrastructure

[1] The Indian School Certificate is conducted by the Council for the Indian School Certificate Examination and can be taken after completing the Indian Certificate of Secondary Education in Grade 10. The exam criteria are regulated by the University of Cambridge. This Certificate enables students to get admission without any bridging courses to universities in the U.K.

[2] An educational group that operates as an international organisation offering International Baccalaureate to students accepted based on merit.

boarding schools in Asia" (ELS5, Home) or being "a history of tradition and a heritage" (ELS7, Principal's Welcome) set especially "for the princes in 18xx" (ELS8, About Us) or set in 1850s to "strive to continue building this legacy and bring to fruition what was envisaged for posterity" (ELS3, Principal's Desk) these schools emphasise a symbolic association with traditions aimed at projecting robustness in learning. Recognising the need to be part of the modern nation state, contemporary relevance is stressed, for example, through "empowering men rooted in India's heritage" (ELS5, Vision). Often the "first of its kind in this part of the world to start the house system, organized games and the prefect system which were begun almost at the same time as they were developed in England" (ELS5, History), or the maharajah listed as the President of the General Council (ELS8, About Us), these are spaces of unquestioned exclusiveness being "presented with the King's Colours" (ELS4, Historical Foundations). The colonial aim of schools established with Christian Principles and values (ELS4; ELS1, Ethos & Aims) is balanced with "boys from different religious communities … living, working, eating … with boys from other nations" (ELS2, Welcome) where the history continues with these schools being "part of the Duke of Edinburgh Award Scheme" (ELS5, Curriculum).

Typological elitism is reiterated by these schools being self-managed with a Board of Directors or being in the exclusive Council of International Schools or belonging to the bandwagon of the Round Square (ELS4; ELS1). Key narrative tropes, for example, self-defined curriculum, self-selected faculty, self-governance, and small size (Gaztambide-Fernández, 2009a, p. 1100) emphasise the autonomous identities of these institutions. The presupposition that elite schools have the best provision is emphasised prominently, for example, "Eton of the East" (ELS8, About Us), "the syllabus is stipulated by the Council" (ELS5, Curriculum) and the system being affiliated to ISC (Indian School Certificate; ELS8; ELS5); these schools either have a "board of governors" (ELS5) or "affordable international education (drawn from a British tradition) based on sound Christian principles" (ELS6, Ethos & Aims). These tropes emphasise the independent character of these schools and by reference establish the indisputable reality of these schools being of very high excellence.

Scholastic elitism reaffirms the complementary aspects of achievement through learning that is rigorous, with "external examinations" along with "hands on experience" (ELS6, Academic Matters), "best of traditions with a modern approach to learning" (ELS1, Our History), "regular assessment of scholastic and co-scholastic areas of development" (ELS8, Reports), "in consonance with the latest changes and developments around the world" (ESL4, Academic Objectives). The provision of interactive smart boards for children being taught "formal education, social skills and manners and conversational skills in English" (ELS7, Introduction) depict how the modern state is envisioned as one that maintains the excellence in learning, for example "Admission to xxx is a privilege and not a right" (ELS7, Admission) and "all-round education" (ELS2, Curriculum). International presence and the need to engage in intensive academic activities or productivity higher than universities (see

Bourdieu, 1996/1989, pp. 85–87; also see Srivastava, 1998) is established as a necessary aspect of the historical continuity of elitist excellence.

The power of scholastic elitism is reiterated through the colonial and neoliberal ties that are subtly re-affirmed with the choice of Cambridge IGCSE and the Indian School Certificate Examination (ELS4, ELS7). Where schools have adopted the CBSE[6] exit mode (Central Board of Secondary Education), these emphasise their "school toppers" (read achievers) (ELS8, Awards) or become a means to retain links with England and to pave a way for students to gain access to universities overseas (see Kenway and Fahey, 2014). Extensive extracurricular activities from golf and polo (ELS8), outdoor learning through "student exchange programmes" through Round Square ideals and values (ELS1, ELS4, Extracurricular), a global reach in education that is innovative and future oriented support Rizvi's (2014) observation that old elite schools being aware of the immense competition from various newly formed private schools promote themselves in a strategic manner (p. 291). The demographic hegemony of the moneyed class is reflected in statements like, "to provide a resource for … business communities requiring an international education for their children" (ELS6, Ethos & Aims). The unquestioned truth portrayed on these websites is the ability of students to work together in a space that overrides the realities of race, class and caste distinctions. However, the discourse of exclusion operates as the student body is carefully selected by measuring affordability and merit based academic ability.

Often beginning as schools for the children of colonisers, these have changed over time to be ethnically diverse and "adapting to needs of families cross culturally" (ELS6, Life at xxx) thereby proudly aligned with the nation state, for example by stating that "the staff and the scholars are predominantly Indian" (ELS2, The School) while having a mix of internationals (ELS6, Life At xxx; ELS2, History).

The spatial discourse of affluence is created with location within exotic hill stations at 5,600 and 7,500 feet or at the foothills chosen for their cooler climate. All these schools possess huge acreage, sprawling fields, country views, lakes, valley and hills. Some promote their surroundings "forested with pine and evergreens" (ELS4, Campus); others their "ideal pastoral atmosphere conducive to a healthy learning environment" (ELS1, Our Campus) or the "advantage of living in surroundings not only of exceptional natural grandeur but also of cultivated beauty" (ELS2, Facilities). Where there is no access to a hill station these are on the foothills and promote their architecture as outstanding, for example "the Indo-Saracenic design that became a classic symbol" (ELS8, Main Building).

These discourses on the whole illustrate continuity and progressiveness that might be otherwise difficult to perceive in the post-independence schools in India. The elite discourse illustrates how exclusiveness is a successful venture and excludes those who do not fit the category of elite.

Metropolitan Excellence

Metropolitan elite schools illustrate typological elitism through the discourse of ascendancy by emphasising their independent status, being self-managing by either being part of a society (ELS10) or business, or being part of a diocese (ELS12; ELS11; ELS5; ELS16) or other religious organisations (ELS13). These schools reiterate autonomy through curriculum where "voyage of self-discovery" is emphasised (ELS14, About Us), or "self-reliance" (ELS12, School Profile) is supported by a faculty that is carefully selected. Their abundance in terms of financial independence, resources, and the carefully crafted programme sets them apart from other city-based private schools.

These schools are historically elite, established in the 1800s (ELS11; ELS16) or with 175/149 years of excellence (ELS16; ELS11; ELS15) or being set by societies of repute (ELS10; ELS9) or industries. This projects a discourse of stability that is balanced with progressiveness, with national and global identity being reinforced through exchange programmes like the Singapore Cultural Exchange or the Reach Cambridge programme (ELS12, Activities) or prestigious "membership to the IPSC" (Indian Public School Conference) that links the school with schools of "national standing" (ELS10, Mission). Progressiveness is also demonstrated through the social and educational networks that promote meritocratic education, for example Science Summer School, University of Melbourne, to enable students to "understand and appreciate cultural differences and make them productive citizens of the world" (ELS12, School Profile) or one that "shares a sister relationship with Billanook College, Australia" (ELS13, Profile).

The demographic discourse excludes by leaving unmentioned those who are not a part of such a system. The students are selected after applications are "scrutinised" after "interviews" and "entrance tests" (ELS15, Admission; ELS14, Admission). While affirmative action is endorsed with schools being "equally committed to ... gifted applicants" (ELS10, About Us), scholarships being afforded to "students from rural backgrounds" (ELS9, School Profile) or students with sports or academic excellence (ELS9, Learning), it is truly exclusive with fewer students being admitted with each student having a symbolic capital (Bourdieu, 1996/1989). These schools demand more of students and careful selection through exams and interviews leads to fewer students being admitted, but each being able to cope with the intense individual competitiveness that is demanded, the aim being to "develop a wholesome personality" and a "healthy, competitive spirit" (ELS11, School Profile). This is reiterated through their observation that their "illustrious alumni" (ELS12, Profile) "notable figures who have gone on to revolutionize the world" (ELS16, Alumni).

The exclusionary scholastic discourse operates through an emphasis on these being "a place where high marks have to be earned through sustained hard work" (ELS12, School Profile) or "the latent creative potential in every child" (ELS14, About Us). Progressiveness is indicated through "a unidirectional teaching method ... being increasingly substituted by a multidirectional group workshop method" where the teacher is "the co-ordinator" (ELS10, Academies), with the curriculum emphasising "hands-on learning experiences", "interconnected curriculum that is in tune with the real world of learning" (ELS13, Curriculum) or "preparing them for a world of tomorrow, full of challenges" (ELS11, School Profile). The rigour of being part of this discourse as Meadmore and Meadmore (2004, p. 377) observe, is elite school students are expected to have a vision, the ability to sit competitive or international exams such as ISC certificate or IGCSE, or international competitive exams such as SAT or Advanced Placement Programme for US colleges (ELS12, Accreditations). The extracurricular activities further illustrate who belongs by the activities offered such as a friendly cricket match with UK school students (ELS10, Mission), or the Reach Cambridge Summer School programme (ELS12, Activities), or Exchange Programme ... with Alexandra Infant School (ELS9, School Profile). That these schools endorse the neoliberal aim to "technicize knowledge" (Connell, 2013, p. 108) and be an exclusive "admired model" where there is an audit culture (p. 101), audited through their national and international enterprise, is not articulated.

The schools in the metropolitan cities promote their space either through the historical significance of their buildings or through landscapes and facilities. As entrepreneurial ventures that provide exclusive learning, for example, "in the portals of the [city], the school provides an invigorating and competitive atmosphere" (ELS10, About Us), "a sprawling green oasis of 20 acres" (ELS14, Ambience), "landscaped 20 acre campus that is a visual delight" (ELS9, School Profile), elite schools create a sumptuous, conducive atmosphere for learning. The sprawling campus, with facilities such as swimming pools, open air theatre, and auditorium with state-of-the art audio visual facilities, gymnasium and even a staff health centre, is often in stark contrast to the cramped spaces of public, government schools. As van Zanten (2013, p. 83) states, parents judge schools based on their own "respective locations in the class structure" and these schools readily cater to the symbolic capital of the middle and upper middle classes through exceptional facilities such as "a state of the art biotechnology laboratory" (ELS16, Welcome), range of activities, and an illustrious academic record.

The metropolitan schools focus on the discourse of exclusiveness through their scholastic offerings and facilities, some with their historical continuity and primarily through their nation building capabilities and background, to resist the spatial disadvantage of being in large, cramped cities or the merit based admission they offer.

International Excellence

Connell (2013, p. 100) notes that neoliberalism aims to expand markets with "companies selling services in a market". Therefore, it comes as no surprise that for-profit corporations and companies in India are commodifying education through various businesses having entered the education market by setting up International Baccalaureate schools in small towns. Schools that have the International Baccalaureate have sprung up in recent times and, unlike the above two categories, have no historical continuity. As transnationally elite, these schools are the result of globalisation's effect on the Indian education context. The transnational discourse of common forms of education, the branding through the IB model and the promotion of certain educational philosophies are leading to the forming of a "class-for-itself", one that is "keen to act as a class" (Bunnell, 2010, p. 356) being based on common aims, similar experiences and interests.

Being associated with the IB programme, these elite schools are typologically elite as these cater to in "international standard of education" (ELS17, About Us) or are a part of the "United World College movement" (ELS18, About Us), providing the same vision and mission as its different colleges worldwide successfully excluding a national curriculum and educational philosophy. Being "India's leading educational institution" (ELS20, About Us) or "one of India's most prestigious independent academic schools" (ELS21, Introduction) saves these schools from being foreign while "striving for Western Standards of what is described as universal" (Hughes, 2009, p. 139) promotes a transnational focus.

The lack of traditions and historicity is overcome by the association of these schools with IGCSE and IB and thereby to a larger global discourse on education. Schools claim to be providing "quality education over 30 years" (ELS20, Overview), some "the first IB school and first international school in India" (ELS21, Introduction) or as "one of 15 schools that are part of the UWC" (ELS18, Overview) and their links with "Council of International Schools" or by being "built on first-class British independent boarding school model" (ELS19, Know School). As new elites, these provide international education to the affluent middle class, once only possible for the Indian aristocracy or children of colonisers and, thereby, prepare students with skills necessary to succeed within a global context (Resnik, 2009).

Demographic elitism is designed to create future leaders, those who serve the capitalist economy, those who are "competent in assessing information and making critical decisions" (Bunnell, 2010, p. 357). These are sites where "students from 50 countries" (ELS18, About Us) or "with 26 nationalities" (ELS19, Admission) create "a beehive of international students from all across the globe" (ELS17, Overview) and learn and work together, disregarding a sizeable Indian population that cannot envisage international orientation in education. The purpose of "educating global citizens for over 100 years" (ELS21, Students) or where students are "agents of positive change" (ELS18, About Us) advocate how national boundaries have blurred and social class of a distinctive group is created based on market forces.

Stringent entry conditions of these schools create exclusiveness, for example "entrance test conducted wherever necessary" (ELS19, Admission), "age appropriate aptitude test/psychometric tests are administered to identify basic skills of a child" (ELS20, Admission) and children with special needs being "evaluated on a case by case basis" (ELS17, Admission), a privilege as only a "limited number of students with special needs" (ELS19, Admission Procedure) are admitted.

The aim to produce successful, responsible and creative global citizens who, in turn, will "strive for excellence and the progress of society" (ELS17, Vision & Mission) envisions these schools as scholastically elite. The global need of the middle and upper middle classes for high academic results (Tarc, 2009) is echoed through the provision of "education of the highest academic order" (ELS17, Mission), "a track record of internationally benchmarked IB results" (ELS21, IB at xxx) or being "consistently ranked among the top 10 international schools in the country", (ELS20, Know xxx) offering "a curriculum which stimulates intellectual curiosity, critical thinking and problem solving" (ELS19, Our School). Further, the IB narrative tropes of "transformative educational experience" where the aim is "to create agents of change for a more peaceful and sustainable future" (ELS18, Curriculum) indicate services that are sold as privilege to justify why only a selection of handpicked students get to experience an exclusive education (see Connell, 2013). There are "international exchanges with IB schools in Europe and Australia" (ELS20, International Exchanges) extracurricular activities to develop leadership, the arts, and volunteering so as "to produce the 'whole' child with market edge" (Meadmore & Meadmore, 2004, p. 375). IB, as the internationally branded product along with its symbolic values of intercultural understanding or multiculturalism (Resnik, 2012, p. 259), represents such leadership through "community interaction", with schools "striving to shape leaders of change in the world" (ELS18, Experiential Learning) and reaffirms the class-for-itself model of education.

The schools are set in idyllic small town locations such as the foothills of mountains or where "the climate benefits from altitude and is pleasant throughout" (ELS19, Our School). The sprawling campuses, with award winning architecture, for example, "Designshare Award from New York, USA" (ELS20, Know xxx) are fitted with swimming pools, amphitheatres and health care centres (ELS20, ELS18) or are within "the urban–rural belt within an InfoTech Park that benefits an expatriate community" (ELS19, Our School). Although not as rural and pastoral in landscape as the residential elite schools of the colonial era, nevertheless these have large, often unlimited space, for example, "180 acre biodiversity reserve" (ELS18, Our Campus) or "located at 2133m in the peaceful xx Hills of South India, a region known for its rugged beauty and cool temperate climate" (ELS21, Introduction to xxx) that allow students to find a space for themselves. In brief, the international schools have engaged in neoliberal denationalisation (Resnik, 2012) where through parent choice, school based management and the IB there is a takeover of the historically constructed national education (p. 256) to befit the forward looking nation state that wishes to be a global leader.

Conclusion

The narrative of the elite Indian school is created through the discourses of privilege and distinction and is illustrated through the five dimensions of elitism (Gaztambide-Fernández, 2009b). However, the level of conformity to the five dimensions depends on the historical, utilitarian purpose these serve the school in advertising their educational offerings. For example, in these websites, historical elitism is finely balanced with progressiveness or geographical elitism as a contextual phenomenon of spatiality distances the overcrowded city or creates an oasis within a cramped, overpopulated city. These dimensions are, therefore, applied differently to a degree to western elite schools such as the Weston School in Gaztambide-Fernández's study (2009b).

The discursive trends adopted by the school websites promote privilege, inclusion and exclusion as these are applicable to the Indian context. The discourse of exclusiveness is created through multiple means, for example, the supremacy of the English medium for instruction that, then, establishes regularity in discourse to signpost what has always been said about these schools. The exclusion of certain groups of students, for example the disadvantaged or the ones with special needs, or an emphasis that if these students are accepted they would be expected to fit in, are discourses as "practices that systematically form the objects of which they speak" (Foucault, 1972/2010, p. 49) and determine what constitutes elitism in these schools.

A sense of privilege, a market ideology of individual achievement and a global connection with elite schools worldwide promotes a discourse of elite ascendancy even where schools are presumably adopting a postcolonial ideology of promoting nation building. Similar to Ripon College (Rizvi, 2014), elite schools in this study embrace two cultures: that of being Indian and at the same time offering programmes that prepare students for western tertiary education. There is a discursive alignment with other Indian private schools without dismissing the social and cultural practices that define the private system instituted by the British, or more recently a global, international education. In a postcolonial manner, elite schools choose certain practices that align with other elite schools, and practices that situate them within the social and cultural aspects of India (see Srivastava, 1998). All the 21 websites reviewed project a similar agenda, that of being market oriented and an exclusive training ground for the affluent class. In conclusion, in India, the charm of the private, elite education system has not reduced since its inception during the colonial period and in a neoliberal, knowledge economy the private, meritocratic system continues to flourish.

Notes

1   There are a range of schools offered in India. There are public sector schools also known as government schools; then there are government-aided schools that are

partly private or managed by an association or a religious body. The curriculum, fees, teacher–student ratio and other procedures are mandated by the government, thus fees are also controlled. Private schools are owned by private bodies, and have the freedom to set fees structure, teacher–student ratio and also curriculum and entrance and exit exams. Ekal Vidyalaya is a non-profit organisation that aims at educating the village and tribal children through an indigenous mode of education that focuses on literacy, numeracy, healthcare, and environmental education. Madrassas are Islamic schools that focus on religious education and also offer mainstream subjects.

2 Minute by the Honourable T. B. Macaulay, dated the 2 February 1835. Retrieved from http: //www. columbia. Edu /itc / mealac / Pritchett /00generallinks / macaulay / txt_minute_education_1835.html (accessed 31 March 2014).

3 Sir Charles Wood was the President of the Board of Control of the East India Company and had an important role in the education system in India. In 1854 he sent a despatch to Lord Dalhousie, the Governor-General of India outlining various recommendations for a modern education system, most of which were implemented.

4 The popular international qualification is recognised by universities the world over and is a means for establishing high academic achievement.

5 Round Square is a network of schools in 40 countries and together these schools emphasise academic achievement and holistic development. The Round Square schools follow six ideals of democracy, service, adventure, internationalism, environmentalism and leadership.

6 India has two boards of education—the CBSE (Central Board of Secondary Education) and ICSE (Indian Certificate of Secondary Education). The CBSE syllabus is considered easier than other boards due to fewer subjects under common denominations and lesser emphasis on English. ICSE is more comprehensive, is recognised by all major universities worldwide and emphasises the importance of English.

References

Annamalai, E. (2004). Medium of power: The question of English in education in India. In J. W. Tollefson & A. B. M. Tsui (Eds.), *Medium of instruction policies: Which agenda? Whose agenda?* (pp. 177–194). Mahwah, NJ: L. Erlbaum Publishers.

Arribas-Ayllon, M., & Walkerdine, V. (2007). Foucauldian discourse analysis. In C. Willig & W. Stainton-Rogers (Eds.), *The Sage handbook of qualitative research in psychology* (pp. 91–108). London: Sage.

Bhattacharya, S. (2002). Introduction: An approach to education and inequality. In S. Bhattacharya (Ed.), *Education and the disprivileged: Nineteenth and twentieth century India* (pp. 1–32). New Delhi: Orient Longman.

Bourdieu, P. (1996/1989). *The state nobility: Elite schools in the field of power* (L.C. Clough, Trans.). Cambridge: Polity Press.

Brooks, R., & Waters, J. (2014). The hidden internationalism of elite English schools. *Sociology*, 49(2), 1–17.

Bunnell, T. (2010). The International Baccalaureate and a framework for class consciousness: The potential outcomes of a class-for-itself. *Discourse: Studies in the Cultural Politics of Education*, 31(3), 351–362.

Carnoy, M. (2014). Globalization, educational change and the nation state. In N. P. Stromquist & K. Monkman (Eds.), *Globalization and education: Integration and contestation across cultures* (pp. 21–38). Plymouth: Rowan & Littlefield Education.

Connell, R. (2013). The neoliberal cascade and education: An essay on the market agenda and its consequences. *Critical Studies in Education*, 54(2), 99–112.

Drew, C. (2013). Elitism for sale: Promoting the elite school online in the competitive educational marketplace. *Australian Journal of Education*, 57(2), 174–184.

Forbes, J., & Lingard, R. (2013). Elite school capitals and girls' schooling: Understanding the (Re) production of privilege through a habitus of 'assuredness'. In C. Maxwell & P. Aggleton (Eds.), *Privilege, agency and affect: Understanding the production and effects of action* (pp. 50–68). Basingstoke: Palgrave Macmillan.

Forsey, M., Davies, S., & Walford, G. (2008). The globalisation of school choice? An introduction to key issues and concerns. In M. Forsey, S. Davies, & G. Walford (Eds.), *The globalisation of school choice?* (pp. 9–25). Oxford: Symposium Books.

Foucault, M. (1972/2010). *The archaeology of knowledge and the discourse on language* (A. M. Sheridan Smith, Trans.). New York: Vintage Books.

Gaztambide-Fernández, R. (2009a). What is an elite boarding school? *Review of Educational Research*, 79(3), 1090–1128.

Gaztambide-Fernández, R. (2009b). *The best of the best: Becoming elite at an American boarding school*. Cambridge, MA: Harvard University Press.

Gottschall, K., Wardman, N., Edgeworth, K., Hutchesson, R., & Saltmarsh, S. (2010). Hard lines and soft scenes: Constituting masculinities in the prospectuses of all-boys elite private schools. *Australian Journal of Education*, 54 (1), 18–30.

Hesketh, A. J., & Selwyn, N. (1999). Surfing to school: The electronic reconstruction of institutional identities. *Oxford Review of Education*, 25(4), 501–520.

Hughes, C. (2009). International education and the International Baccalaureate Diploma Programme: A view from the perspective of postcolonial thought. *Journal of Research in International Education*, 8(2), 123–141.

India's best schools. (Sept. 2014). Retrieved 10 September 2014 from http://www.rediff. com/getahead/report/career-indias-best-schools-of-2014/20140922.htm

Kenway J., & Fahey, J. (2007). Policy incitements to mobility: Some speculations and provocations. In D. Epstein, R. Boden, R. Deem, F. Rizvi & S. Wright (Eds.), *World Yearbook of Education 2008: Geographies of knowledge, geometries of power: Framing the future of higher education* (pp. 161–80). New York: Routledge.

Kenway, J., & Fahey, J. (2014). Staying ahead of the game: The globalising practices of elite schools. *Globalisation, Societies and Education*, 12(2), 177–195.

Kenway, J., Fahey, J., & Koh, A. (2013). The libidinal economy of the globalising elite market. In C. Maxwell (Ed.), *Privilege, agency and affect: Understanding the production and effects of action* (pp. 15–30). New York: Palgrave Macmillan.

Khan, S. (2012). The sociology of elites. *Annual Review of Sociology*, 38, 361–377.

Koh, A. (2014). Doing class analysis in Singapore's elite education: Unravelling the smokescreen of 'meritocratic talk'. *Globalisation, Societies and Education*, 12(2), 196–210.

Lingard, B. (2000). It is and it isn't: Vernacular globalization, education policy and restructuring. In N. Burbules & C. Torres (Eds.), *Globalization and education: Critical perspectives* (pp. 79–108). New York: Routledge.

Little, A. W. (2010). *Access to elementary education in India: Politics, policies and progress* (CREATE monograph No. 44). Institute of Education, University of London, UK.

Lynch, K., & Moran, M. (2006). Markets, schools and the convertibility of economic capital: The complex dynamics of class choice. *British Journal of Sociology of Education*, 27(2), 221–235.

Majumdar, M., & Mooij, J. (2011). *Education and inequality in India: A classroom perspective*. Abingdon, Oxon: Routledge.

Maxwell, J. D., & Maxwell, M. P. (1995). The Reproduction of class in Canada's elite independent schools. *British Journal of Sociology of Education*, 16(3), 309–326.

Meadmore, D., & Meadmore, P. (2004). The boundlessness of performativity in elite Australian schools. *Discourse: Studies in the Cultural Practice of Education*, 25(3), 375–387.

Mullen, A. L. (2009). Elite destinations: Pathways to attending an ivy league university. *British Journal of Sociology of Education*, 30(1), 15–27.

Nguyen, P. M., Elliott, J. G., Terlouw, C., & Pilot A. (2009). Neocolonialism in education: Cooperative Learning in an Asian context. *Comparative Education*, 45(1), 109–130.

Prasad, A. (2003). The gaze of the other. In A. Prasad (Ed.), *Postcolonial theory and organizational analysis: A critical engagement* (pp. 3–46). New York: Palgrave Macmillan.

Resnik, J. (2009). Multicultural education—Good for business but not for the state? IB curriculum and the global capitalism. *British Journal of Educational Studies*, 57(3), 217–244.

Resnik, J. (2012). The denationalization of education and the expansion of the International Baccalaureate. *Comparative Education Review*, 56(2), 248–269.

Rizvi, R. (2014). Old elite schools, history and the construction of a new imaginary. *Globalisation, Societies and Education*, 12(2), 290–308.

Seth, S. (2007). *Subject lessons: The western education of colonial India*. Durham: Duke University Press.

Spivak, G. C. (1988). 'Can the Subaltern Speak?' In C. Nelson & L. Grossberg (Eds.), *Marxism and the interpretation of culture* (pp. 271–313). Champaign, IL: University of Illinois Press.

Srivastava, S. (1998). *Constructing post-colonial India: National character and the Doon School*. London: Routledge.

Stromquist, N. P., & Monkman, K. (2014). Defining globalization and assessing its implications for knowledge and education, revisited. In N. P. Stromquist & K. Monkman (Eds.), *Globalization and education: Integration and contestation across cultures* (2nd ed., pp. 1–19). Lanham: R & L Education.

Tarc, P. (2009). *Global dreams, enduring tensions: International Baccalaureate in a changing world*. New York: Lang.

Van Zanten, A. (2013). A good match: Appraising worth and estimating quality in school choice. In J. Beckett & C. Musselin (Eds.), *Constructing quality: The classification of goods in markets* (pp. 77–102). Oxford, UK: Oxford University Press.

Weis, L., & Cipollone, K. (2013). Class work: Producing privilege and social mobility in elite US secondary schools. *British Journal of Sociology of Education*, 34(5/6), 701–722.

Waters, J., & Brooks, R. (2015). The magical operations of separation: English elite schools' on-line geographies, internationalisation and functional isolation. *Geoforum*, 58, 86–94.

8

THE INSIDERS

Changing Forms of Reproduction in Education

Hugues Draelants

Introduction

Cultural capital is one of the concepts commonly used by sociologists of education to explain the role of schools in reproducing social inequalities. The now-classic explanation advanced by Bourdieu and Passeron ([1964], 1979; [1970], 1977) suggests that upper-class children inherit various cultural resources from their families (language, general knowledge, intellectual tools, body language and aesthetic predispositions, ways to stand and speak, refined tastes, etc.) and that these are accumulated and transformed into real benefits in the school context. Such a process is made possible because the curricula imposed on students, along with academic assessments, fall within a so-called 'legitimate' culture—in other words, a culture composed of socially valued symbolic products (arts, humanities, sciences) coming from the dominant social groups. Bourdieu and Passeron thus present school culture as an arbitrary culture, a class culture that favours upper-class children in the academic context.

In French-language sociology, the metaphor of the *inheritors*, taken from the title of Bourdieu and Passeron's first book, has come to be used to refer to students from the most privileged backgrounds whose familiarity with academic knowledge gives them a decisive advantage in school adjustment and learning processes. But is it still adequate for describing what is at stake today in the reproduction of social inequalities in school? Several societal and educational changes prompt us to take a new look at the theories and concepts used to explain and interpret the ways in which social inequalities are reproduced. I believe that the effect of cultural capital has to some extent taken new forms. What now matters, in my view, is less the familiarity with highbrow culture than knowing how to convert different types of resources into educational capital and social prospects, knowing which paths to follow in order to obtain diplomas which offer the most profitable opportunities and lead to elite social positions. Thus, in an attempt to sum up in an open-ended way what characterises the privileged student today, I will enlarge the metaphor of the 'insider' and consider what adaptations this new language suggests for the theory of social reproduction.

The Declining Profitability of Highbrow Culture

Cultural capital is well suited for explaining school inequalities insofar as there exists a distinctive 'legitimate culture' which is, on the one hand, clearly separate from ordinary culture and, on the other, adopted by school culture. In the present context, however, these two preconditions for the academic profitability of cultural capital would seem to be debatable.

First of all, can we say that there is still a dominant legitimate culture (in the sense of a relative social consensus about a cultural hierarchy) which is clearly separate from ordinary culture? The sociology of culture generally sees in the present period a weakening of the traditional split between high culture and popular culture(s), with fewer and fewer distinctions between the productions of elite status culture and those of popular or mass culture. The cultural hierarchies established by Bourdieu in *Distinction* ([1979], 1984) are unquestionably dated. The cleavage in question no longer opposes elites and masses but 'omnivores' and 'univores': the omnivores would be characterised by the eclecticism and exoticism of their cultural tastes and practices, whereas the cultural world of the univores would be much more limited and insular (Peterson, 1992; Donnat, 1994). That said, the argument that hierarchies and legitimacies are declining, as attested by the spread of a certain cultural eclecticism does not mean that we no longer observe a connection between social background and cultural preferences or a distinction phenomenon. As some researchers have shown, the way of relating to culture (reflexive and distanced) can be more important in the distinction process than the precise choice of cultural objects (Coulangeon, 2011; Prieur & Savage, 2013).

The relative decline of legitimate culture therefore does not mean that culture is no longer a marker of social class but does it still play a determinant role in the production of academic inequalities? We have every reason to think that the affinity between school culture and legitimate culture is not as clear as it used to be. We can see this through the transformation of disciplinary hierarchies and subject matter (Jacquet-Francillon, 2008). The 'literature' streams that used to dominate have now been supplanted by the scientific and technological streams. The kinds of academic knowledge and skills developed in the curricula are also changing: general knowledge or cultural knowledge as such, along with the most formal knowledge of languages and writings are losing their importance, whereas the ability to use and process information, solve problems and think logically receives increasing attention in educational programmes and school assessments. The school, moreover, is no longer a bastion erecting a rampart between itself and the teenage cultural world (Dubet, 2002). Apart from a few elite secondary institutions, it is no longer a space culturally removed from the rest of the society. The inheritors are submerged in the mass of students. Their marginalisation is expressed not only quantitatively but also in terms of culture and identity. Indeed, they have to suspend any pretension to high culture if they do not wish to be socially excluded by their peers and saddled with unflattering labels like 'brown-noser' or 'nerd'. In sum, the school has lost a large share of its ability to act as an authority of cultural legitimisation in favour of the cultural industries on the one hand and peer groups on the other (Pasquier, 2005). Teachers themselves have undergone a cultural evolution as the profession has moved away from its traditionally elitist social profile (Chapoulie, 1987), but also given the spread of a new model of professionalism. Today's teachers are expected to be good educators, or 'reflexive practitioners' (Schön, 1983), rather than 'learned masters' who are highly cultivated and knowledgeable in their subject area (Maroy, 2001). In this respect, we can observe their increasing openness to youth culture (Eloy, 2012) in line with a pedagogical concern for getting students involved. Teachers no longer hesitate to include in their courses material considered close to the students' culture, such as mainstream children's literature (*Twilight, Harry Potter*).

From Cultural Capital to Cognitive and Linguistic Capital: The Rejection of the Bourdieusian Cultural Arbitrary

In light of the decline of canonical culture, some researchers have attempted to understand in concrete terms what has become of the effect of cultural capital by comparing the impact of different accepted practices (De Graaf, De Graaf & Kraaykamp, 2000; Sullivan, 2001). By breaking cultural capital down into 'reading behaviour' and other kinds of activities such as 'participation in beaux-arts,' playing a musical instrument or listening to classical music, they show that what really counts is not cultural capital but reading, insofar as school culture remains above all a culture of writing. Diligent reading also permits the development of analytical, written, and language skills and these have more weight in the school context than the mastery of canonical culture, which occupies a very limited place in today's curricula. Otherwise stated, if culture counts for educational attainment, this is not only for an arbitrary reason (in keeping with Bourdieu's idea that the school would promote certain cultural contents corresponding more or less to the culture of the different social classes) but because they produce cognitive effects and predispositions.

Cultural Transmission: Not Only 'Osmotic' but Active

If current research no longer simply maintains, like Bourdieu, that the differences between family models and educational requirements are strictly arbitrary, it also distances itself from the Bourdieusian concept of family transmission of culture,

142 Hugues Draelants

which has been sharply contested in France because of its excessively mechanistic nature (see in particular Lahire, 1995; Henri-Panabière, 2010). Indeed, for Bourdieu, cultural transmission essentially occurs through osmosis: "all cultural goods—paintings, monuments, machines, and any objects shaped by man, particularly all those which belong to the childhood environment, exert an educative effect by their mere existence ..." (Bourdieu [1979], 1986, p. 255). In contrast to this idea of an "educative effect automatically exerted by the environment" (Bourdieu [1979], 1986, p. 256), recent studies demonstrate that having a fabulous library does not suffice to stimulate a child's intellectual development; an active transmission of the taste for reading is also necessary. And this presumes a considerable, time-consuming parental investment which entails, for example, the fact of reading stories to the child early on and providing guidance and accompaniment in his or her readings (Lahire, 1995). More generally, studies bearing on social class differences in family–school relationships and in parenting styles show that school reproduction strategies increasingly depend on an active transmission implying intensive family involvement, such as parental support with homework (Kakpo, 2012), participation in the life of the child's school and parent–teacher associations (Gombert & van Zanten, 2004) or, beyond day-to-day monitoring of schooling, a permanent 'educationalisation' of leisure activities (Daverne & Dutercq, 2013) and the use of educational toys (Vincent, 2000).

From Direct to Indirect Cultural Transmission

The active cultural transmission which occurs directly and vertically, from parents to children, is itself limited in its effectiveness, however. Not only does the acquisition of cultural capital call for an appropriation effort which is not self-evident, but recent studies show that cultural capital is modified in the transmission process: young people today are exposed to a variety of cultural influences and select what they inherit in light of what still seems useful and relevant to them. This explains why, in practice, some children do not benefit from their parents' cultural capital (Henri-Panabière, 2010). Such a "crisis of vertical cultural transmissions" (Pasquier, 2005) arises from changes in family educational styles, which are generally more democratic than before (Le Pape & van Zanten, 2009), but also from the parents' inability to control the socialisation of their children from start to finish. Indeed, family education is threatened by other factors of socialisation, especially the media and peer groups, which exercise a powerful cultural influence during adolescence.

For these reasons, even beyond the development of a strategic, reflexive relationship to the practices of cultural, cognitive, and linguistic socialisation, we observe the emergence of oblique or horizontal strategies of indirect cultural transmission. In some cases, indirect cultural transmission involves recourse to paid intermediaries who allow cultural capital to be transmitted obliquely or 'second hand' (Bourdieu [1979], 1986). Conscious of the difficulty of controlling the socialisation of their children in any effective way, some parents privilege professional intermediaries such as tutors (Glasman, 2001) or coaches (Oller, 2012). At the same time, they make every effort to limit potentially negative peer influences by seeing to it that the children's social environment is limited to 'their own kind' through the choice of schools and extracurricular activities (Felouzis & Perroton, 2010; van Zanten, 2009a). In this case, cultural transmission becomes horizontal, by virtue of informal peer socialisation. The fact that the children's leisure activities diverge from those of their parents with the onset of adolescence therefore does not automatically mean decreasing parental influence. Through the control of the company their children keep, the parents continue to shape their tastes and cultural habits indirectly. Although these reproduction strategies do not necessarily require cultural transmission, or at least not direct vertical transmission from parents to children, they do call for parental supervision and close attention to schooling, which implies a considerable investment, especially for the mothers (Vincent, 2010).

From Cognitive Skills to Behavioural Competences

Even though indirect strategies require constant parental attention and close control of the environment, their implementation seems easier than that of the direct strategies. Calling on professionals (tutors, coaches, etc.) or controlling the children's social circles (through the choice of schools and extracurricular activities) above all requires economic and social capital. On the other hand, making every effort to transmit the love of reading (the main cultural activity whose academic profitability remains unquestionable) requires time. But the time available for combining or reconciling private and professional life (and thus for taking care of children in the case of a family) is generally lacking, given the ever faster pace of life. Even among the middle and upper classes, dual-income families are the norm and this makes time a precious commodity. The lack of time helps to explain why, as we have seen, those who have the means delegate part of the educational effort to third parties. The limited availability and the fatigue occasioned by professional overdrive also lessen the ascetic tendencies characteristic of the traditional norm of cultural legitimacy and turns middle- and upper-class parents[1] away from private cultural consumption linked to information processing, notably reading, which they tend to replace by public cultural participation (attending plays, concerts, exhibitions, openings) that is linked to the communication of status (Ganzeboom, 1982; Coulangeon, 2011).

It is therefore not surprising to discover that a certain number of new social reproduction strategies used by middle- and upper-class families are aimed not so much at producing cognitive effects on their children as developing certain behavioural competences (Farkas, 2003). These refer to the 'soft skills' or interpersonal and communications competences sought by recruiters, in particular

144 Hugues Draelants

in the executive job market, where what is important for standing out from the crowd is less making a display of a cultural capital embedded over a long socialisation period than being able to present one's personality in a positive light by taking into account the behavioural criteria recognised and assessed in this context (involvement, dynamism, versatility, etc.) (Brown & Hesketh, 2004).

In a globalised world, developing aptitudes for mobility and multilingualism, for example, is perceived as a particularly useful, if not indispensable skill in order to qualify for certain professional posts which are now international and this has given rise to increasingly varied strategies for learning foreign languages at an early age as well as strategies for mobility or the internationalisation of educational trajectories (Murphy-Lejeune, 2002; Wagner, 2007; Ballatore, 2010).

Towards New Forms of Cultural Capital

For advocates of a broader understanding of the concept of cultural capital, these new strategies of educational reproduction simply come down to new forms of cultural capital. Some sociologists who accord an extended meaning to the concept thus include the parents' knowledge of the mysteries of the school system and of what it takes to prepare for elite paths (best schools, valued tracks and options, useful extracurricular activities, etc.). This idea is put forth notably by McDonough (1997), and van Zanten (2009a), who speak of an 'informational kind' of cultural capital. In the same way, it is possible to consider the behavioural competences permitting the development of social ease as cultural capital of an attitudinal or 'personal' kind (Brown, 2008), and those aimed at mobility as 'cultural capital of an international kind' (Prieur & Savage, 2013).

It must be noted here that two main kinds of definitions of the concept of cultural capital coexist in the literature (especially in the English-speaking orbit): a restricted one and a broad one (Lareau & Weininger, 2003; Goldthorpe, 2007). The restricted definition, which I have implicitly applied until now, assimilates cultural capital to highbrow culture, that of the high-status groups (which involve participation in art, classical music, and literature). It has been widely disseminated in the sociology of education, particularly in the Anglo-American world, following the influential article of DiMaggio (1982).[2] From the standpoint of Bourdieusian orthodoxy, this restricted definition can be perceived as simplistic. For Bourdieu, the relationship to culture is not merely the relationship to high culture; beyond the relationship with works of art or intellectual works, it includes bodily and aesthetic predispositions, ways of behaving and speaking, refined tastes which are expressed in all social activities—table manners, ways of dressing, and fitting out one's living space, and so on.

For partisans of the broader, more 'Bourdieu-compatible' definition of the concept, cultural capital refers to a variety of practices of parental education (Lareau & Weininger, 2003). This approach stresses the socially determined nature of cultural capital, which is associated with the educational standards of the social classes able to impose the assessment criteria most favourable to their children: "the critical aspect of cultural capital is that it allows culture to be used as a resource that provides access to scarce rewards, is subject to monopolization, and, under certain conditions, may be transmitted from one generation to the next" (Lareau & Weininger, 2003, p. 587).

Contrary to the restricted definition which focuses on the content of cultural capital and assimilates the latter to canonical culture (that of the high-status groups), the broad definition thus places greater emphasis on the effect of cultural capital, and notably its role in school and social reproduction. One of the merits of this alternative definition is therefore to make a distinction between the effect and content of cultural capital. In this way, it "gives serious thought to the relational dimension which Bourdieu assigns to his sociology of culture" (Fabiani, 2007). The content of cultural capital is secondary because it is arbitrary and unstable: any given skill or competence monopolised in a given time by elite groups can function as cultural capital.

If we accept this idea, it becomes clear that cultural capital is far from being obsolete. Beyond the modifications of its content, certain resources still permit access to scarce rewards and the new resources are thus the functional equivalents of the old ones. However, it is important to emphasise one essential difference between the classic and new forms of cultural capital: the latter are not autonomous; they depend on a conversion of the varieties of capital which are more dominant than ever, namely economic and social capital. In other words, the kind of cultural capital which is now acquiring growing weight is less and less independent of economic and social capital, as shown by the examples I present below. This situation implies that the segments of the middle and upper classes maximising the profitability of their cultural capital are not exactly the same as they were. The middle and upper classes with the most social and economic capital are the direct beneficiaries of this change, whereas the intellectual fractions of the middle and upper classes are challenged in their academic dominance.

In the remarks which follow, I examine one of these new strategies which seems particularly central: the choice of the school. By demonstrating that those whom I call the "insiders" are the most favoured, I will bring out the importance of this strategy for gaining access to an elite education in France.

School Choice: A Question of Information Which Favours the Insiders

In today's strategies of social reproduction, the choice of the school is an overriding concern of the families, not only for cultural reasons but because of the growing heterogeneity of the school settings. In the massified education systems, the value of an academic credential tends to depend on these contexts, which are now more heterogeneous than before, and in particular, on the reputation of the schools attended and the courses taken rather than the educational level attained (Duru-Bellat & Kieffer, 2008). Indeed, studies have shown that the advantage enjoyed by children from privileged backgrounds does not stem from a cultural inheritance but from the access to higher-quality settings (Duru-Bellat & Mingat, 1988). Far from marking the end of social inequalities in schooling, massification has led to the introduction of social-selection mechanisms within the school and the development of 'high roads' which, more or less signposted within the education system, grant access to elite pathways (Ball, Bowe & Gewirtz, 1995; Power, 2000; LeTendre, Gonzalez & Nomi, 2006). Well-informed parents are perfectly aware of this.

The difficulty parents encounter in making their ways through the twists and turns of the system is related above all to the quantity of available information. To some extent, we might speak of a lack of information: the diversification of contexts produced by massification has made the value of the educational provision uncertain, whereas classes and schools are relatively closed spaces and very little filters outside about how they work. That said, in our information-saturated society, the abundance of information complicates educational decisions just as much, given the difficulty of assessing the credibility of what is publicly available. And we then come up against the problem of information quality and interpretation.

In parallel to official information, users of the school system can turn to other information sources which are in principle accessible and available to all. These can include the specialised press or the mass media, as well as information coming directly from the schools or the bodies administering them (e.g., websites, descriptive brochures, information days, open house events). Ideally, however, the official sources can be complemented by, compared with or even replaced by the informal information mainly conveyed by the personal social networks (parents, friends, co-workers, neighbours). These sources provide 'hot' information (Ball & Vincent, 1998) which is customised rather than impersonal (van Zanten, 2009a). In addition, information coming from close relations, unlike official information, enjoys a high degree of credibility (van Zanten, 2009a). In principle, there is no reason for opportunism to come into play since the bonds are affective and in principle 'disinterested' (Bidart, Degenne & Grossetti, 2011).

I propose to use the term 'insiders' to characterise parents capable of mobilising such information, which allows them to personalise their school choices and draw the most profit from their educational capital. In other words, the insiders are those who possess the map and compass necessary for finding their way in the educational labyrinth. The insiders know how to read between the lines and decipher an institutional discourse which tends to place school programmes of unequal value on the same footing. In order to do so, they draw on the inside knowledge which their social capital brings them. Conversely, the non-insiders are those whose knowledge is limited to official information, which is public and impersonal, or informal information, which is scarcer and not always reliable.

Among the likely consequences, I would emphasise that the lack of information can feed false representations of certain educational pathways and encourage students to turn away from them in a kind of self-selection. Given the imperfection of the information and the fact that experience can only intervene after undertaking the studies in question, the non-insider also runs a greater risk of making errors in study options. To the extent that school choices have considerable impact on future socio-professional integration, any error of assessment and guidance can turn out to be extremely detrimental.

The Insiders: A Sociological Profile

When we ask who the insiders are, the first to come to mind are teachers. Their superiority, and therefore that of their children, in terms of knowledge about the system, the right programmes, the promising choices and so on, is clear. In a system characterised by a lack of transparency, those on the inside enjoy an advantage. On average, teachers are thus particularly astute 'school consumers' (Ballion, 1982). French research on the choice of a public or private institution from nursery school to *lycée* (upper secondary) has clearly shown that, as parents, teachers belong to the minority of families actually 'choosing' (about 25%), in the sense that they "develop genuine research strategies" calling for a considerable prospecting effort in order to collect relevant information (Héran, 1996, p. 21).

However, teachers are not the only parents endowed with a perfect mastery of the mysteries of the school system and what can be extremely subtle hierarchies between schools, pathways, and specialisations. In general, parents with higher education diplomas are probably competent to guide their children, at least towards the most prestigious pathways in educational terms (often the ones they have followed themselves as students). Within the 'choosing' minorities, another category which is quite active in prospecting and developing strategies in the area of study options is composed of the wealthy self-employed, with company heads and members of the professions in the forefront (Héran, 1996). According to Gombert and van Zanten (2004), moreover, those who deploy the most sophisticated educational strategies today are not the "middle classes of the public sector" (exemplified by teachers) but other categories closer to the "private sector of the middle classes", namely the professionals, engineers, and company executives.

It should also be noted that the insiders are not necessarily those who actually have the relevant information to make their way through the system but also those who can use this information by drawing on their social capital. The insiders have broad, diversified networks of family and friends liable to provide them with resources—especially information—at some time. But they also have to make use of these networks. Some social categories and occupations are predisposed more than others to cultivate personal relations and use them as resources (Bidart et al., 2011). Since teaching remains a very individual occupation (Barrère, 2002), we may suppose that teachers, unlike senior executives, are less accustomed to developing and handling their networks in a strategic way.

In addition, being able to choose presumes having access to a rich educational offer. In this respect, the spatial inequalities are flagrant. As Bourdieu and Passeron already indicated, "In fact, the geographical factor and the social factor in social inequality are never independent, since ... the chances of living in a city, where there is more likelihood of access to education and culture are greater, rise with position in the social hierarchy" (Bourdieu & Passeron [1964], 1979, pp. 42–43). In France, for example, the educational offer is considerably larger in Paris and the city centres than elsewhere in the regions. Overall, the greatest number of specialisations, rare languages, European and international sections, adapted class schedules, and qualified and older teachers is found in the most advantaged cities and towns (Oberti, 2007). In other words, the ability to choose the school best suited to one's child is not independent of economic capital insofar as the 'schools of excellence' are usually concentrated where the price per square metre is the highest.

Access to Elite Schools in France, an Empirical Illustration

The strategic role played by the school attended is particularly clear in the case of access to French preparatory classes and to the prestigious higher education institutions known as the Grandes Écoles. In France, it is widely believed that the students who manage to enter the best preparatory classes and then the best Grandes Écoles are high achievers who have been selected on the basis of a meritocratic competition. In reality, the observation of the academic and social profiles of France's school elites challenges the idea that academic performance is the only prerequisite for access to a top-notch education. My own research shows just how much those who gain access to these highly reputed institutions within the French education system, far from remaining passive, develop strategies early on for choosing pathways and specialisations, but also schools.[3] The phenomena of 'school-linking', statistically demonstrated elsewhere (Buisson-Fenet & Draelants, 2013), are indeed recognisable. The existence of paths facilitating access to the most prestigious programmes and schools is well known by those who are familiar with the functioning of the French system of elite education (Draelants, 2010):

> For ENS, you have to get started early. A friend of mine who lives in Paris told me a story about it. When she went to enrol her son in nursery school, the head teacher told her, "You know, a good pre-school, that means a good first year in primary school; a good first year, that means a good primary school, a good final year, and so a good start in middle school and a good middle school. A good middle school, that means a good *lycée*, and a good *lycée*, that means the *prépa*." In other words, that's how her son was

The Insiders **149**

going to wind up in the preparatory classes. She was shocked at the time, but it's really like that. When I talk to my own friends who're here, sometimes some of them tell me, "I've been wanting to go to ENS since I was 12 or 13 years old."

(Marc, an École Normale Supérieure student who entered by the so-called 'back door' of the 'second competitive exam' at university; lives with his mother, who does not have a *baccalauréat* [university entrance qualification] and is unable to work)

It is obviously not enough to know that the elite schools exist and recognise their social significance—it is also necessary to have the academic skills. That said, being an excellent student does not guarantee access to an elite preparatory class; it is a necessary but not sufficient condition and many excellent candidates are not accepted. My interviews with students at the elite schools are punctuated with references to the cases of outstanding students who, even in the opinion of these happy few, could have gotten into the same programmes if they were insiders:

The system's not at all transparent, y'know. I can really see it: in the final year before the *bac*, I was in a good school in the suburbs, well, "better than average". And in my class there was a kind of social diversity but everybody was still pretty good. I was in the best final-year class and there was a good level. And the ones who came from a certain social background, they all went on to a *prépa*. The day the application results were given out, the others asked themselves what was going on, y'know! They hadn't even heard of *prépas*. Even if some of them really could have taken a preparatory class and continued their studies that way.

(Adrien, student at Sciences Po; father graduated from the École Supérieure de Commerce, Paris, and Sciences Po, financial consultant; mother, five years of higher education, self-employed professional)

This interview excerpt brings out how many excellent students, for lack of guidance from either their parents or their teachers, suddenly discover after the fact a possible study option which, by the same token, escapes them. Unlike their better initiated fellow students, who have maintained a certain discretion about their intentions to apply for admission into the *prépas*.

Academic achievement thus has to be accompanied by the right information, but also specific penchants, such as the ability to make one's way with determination in study programmes with high value added, even if that means curbing less profitable tastes and desires. And the knowledge of the existence of the elite schools and the awareness of their social significance are powerful incentives for self-constraint. Possessing the information is one of the conditions of possibility: if students in the preparatory classes are willing to put their leisure activities and a large part of their social life on hold for two or three years without feeling that they've made a bad choice, this is, as they recognise themselves, "because they know they'll have many opportunities if they succeed".

As a result, information seems inseparable from ambition, and it is not entirely independent of performance. Contrary to the common perception, what I call excellence is not an immanent quality which would be present without being actively sought (even if this can be the case for certain candidates who are clearly heads and shoulders above the others). The insider who wants to enter an elite preparatory class undertakes the steps necessary for becoming excellent and signalling this excellence to others (e.g., by working harder or through private lessons and language study holidays):

> Some people know about the École Polytechnique in the last year of middle school and they work to get in. They have private math lessons at home, and that's what I call conditioning.
> (Denis, student at the École Polytechnique, comes from the École Polytechnique of Montréal, admitted through the university pathway for international candidates; father carpenter; mother social worker)

In other words, excellence is accessible to those who strive for it (Chambliss, 1989) and those who have sufficient economic and social resources to make this determination pay off. In order to do so, it is always beneficial to be initiated as soon as possible. Information provided early on increases the probability of not being eliminated, given the kind of academic record required for admission to the preparatory classes, or not eliminating oneself in anticipation of the difficulties to come.

In practice, the initiation process takes place in the family, but also in some schools which are known to the insiders. In the prestigious centre-city *lycées*, the tendency to opt for the most profitable, ambitious choices seems obvious, thus reflecting the power of local institutional standards. Studying in an elite school means finding oneself in a micro-environment which limits the space of possibilities. Indeed, some students speak of mental conditioning:

> In my mind, the French system is something I lived from the beginning of *lycée* (upper secondary school). Lycée Hoche is totally a part of the system, like Lycée Henri-IV, Louis-le-Grand, Ginette. When you go there, you're going into the machine. You're 15 years old and you're already future *prépas*. From that time on, they only talk to us about *prépas*, and about math.
> (Chloé, Masters student in Finance and Strategy at Sciences Po; father, head of a medium-size company; stay-at-home mother)

The elite *lycées*, as indicated in the foregoing excerpt, are worlds apart from the ordinary secondary schools and the fact of entering such an institution constitutes a major step towards the preparatory classes and then the Grandes Écoles. The difference between the elite schools and the others is less quantitative than qualitative: it does not simply involve doing more than elsewhere but rather, undergoing a specific socialisation. The initiation this kind of school offers its students is not only psychological, because of the local norms sharply influencing their aspirations, but also intellectual, inasmuch as their curricula generally provide much more advanced instruction which better prepares their students for confronting the academic demands of the preparatory classes. The rare students coming from small secondary schools in the regions who manage to enter an elite preparatory class are immediately struck by the distance separating them from the 'home-grown' students coming from the school offering the *prépas*.

> I went to secondary school in Épinal (northeastern France), in a *lycée* with a 70% success rate for the *bac*, but no one talked about what came after. I went on to a *prépa* at Henri-IV and there, it was a real shock for me to see just how many differences there were between the *lycées*. I had absolutely no idea of that (and incidentally, I'd say that it's still taboo). One very simple example: I'd done a Bac S (scientific) with a specialisation in math and when I got to my first math class at Henri-IV, I was completely lost. I had no idea of what was going on. The professor had students go up to the board and there, a student made a demonstration I couldn't understand about a theorem I absolutely didn't know, which is to say just how lost I was. And afterwards I learned that he was a literature student, but he'd come from Henri-IV.
>
> (Elise, student at the École Normale Supérieure; father, doctor, specialist in a public hospital; mother, hospital pharmacist)

This analysis, developed in greater detail elsewhere (Draelants, 2014), suggests that academic performance and information are inseparable and that, contrary to what is often thought, it is not necessarily performance which comes first, but information. The relationship traditionally assumed between these two elements consists of believing that performances condition study choices, and this is partly true if we observe the pathway at a point in time, which is to say, when the students are about to enter higher education. However, if we consider the school guidance process more broadly, we find that the choices made long before entry into higher education, during the entire educational path, themselves condition the performances.

Conclusion

Starting out from the question of whether the concept of cultural capital is still relevant for understanding social reproduction through schooling, I have shown that cultural capital, when it is assimilated to 'highbrow' culture, is a resource with diminishing profitability, limited effectiveness and far from automatic

152 Hugues Draelants

transmission. Indeed, given the widespread social decline of high culture, only reading practices remain effective for academic achievement. In this sense, the reason culture counts for academic success is not something arbitrary but the fact that it produces cognitive effects and predispositions which favour academic success. However, these are difficult to bring about, time-consuming and relatively uncertain. We do not inherit cultural capital like we inherit tangible goods or economic capital. This is why middle- and upper-class parents now develop active strategies of cultural transmission which entail daily monitoring of their children's schooling and the 'educationalisation' of their leisure activities, but which also leads them to call upon professionals (tutors, coaches) and pay greater attention to their children's social and cultural environments. Among the new strategies of school reproduction privileged by the middle and upper classes, I have also brought out the growing role of those aimed at the acquisition of behavioural rather than cognitive skills.

If the concept of the inheritor was useful for thinking about what defined the privilege of advantaged students in the meritocratic era, the concept of the insider, in my view, now allows us to think about the new forms of reproduction and determine what defines the privilege of advantaged students in a 'parentocratic' system (Brown, 1990), which is to say, a system where the parents' means and wishes play a key role in shaping their children's schooling. The parallel with the concept of parentocracy seems justified because initiated parents are essentially those who do not allow their children's outcomes or 'simple academic merit' to determine their future. The insiders tackle their children's schooling head on, as I have demonstrated through the example of access to France's elite schools. Entering a Grande École depends on academic skills and competences which are inseparable from temporal competence (Masy, 2013), insofar as the academic skills and competences are constituted over time, throughout the school career, and in particular, through the choice of schools. This temporal competence depends in turn on cultural capital of an informational kind which defines a world of possibilities in each person's representation of the future.

The shift from the metaphor of the inheritors to that of the insiders also reveals a real change in the role played by the different kinds of capital in social reproduction. The transition from the inheritors to the insiders marks a relative decline in the educational profitability of classic, highbrow cultural capital in favour of the new ones (informational, international, personal), which do not constitute autonomous forms of cultural capital but depend on a conversion of these ever-more dominant types of capital which are economic and social. The distinction between inheritor and insider thus has a heuristic value as well for describing the processes of internal educational competition between the different segments of the middle and upper classes according to the composition of their capital.

The Insiders **153**

Acknowledgement

Translated from French by Miriam Rosen.

Notes

1   I consider here upper-class but also middle-class groups, as a large part of the middle class is now competing with upper-class parents in the race for educational and social advantage (van Zanten, 2009b).
2   Paradoxically, the relevance of the highbrow culture is lower in that context than in the French one, where the academic culture is historically more rooted in the highbrow culture and focused on its mastery than is the case in the USA and even, but to a lesser extent, in the UK (van Zanten, 2009b).
3   My argument here is based on the analysis of some 200 semi-directive interviews carried out with students from four Grandes Écoles in Paris (École Normale Supérieure [ENS-Ulm], École Polytechnique, École des Hautes Études Commerciales [HEC] and Sciences Po) and two elite secondary schools offering preparatory classes (Lycée Henri-IV in Paris and the private Lycée Sainte-Geneviève in Versailles). The interviews were conducted between December 2005 and March 2009 within the framework of a collective research project under the direction of A. van Zanten. I participated in this project on the training of elites from secondary to higher education as a CNRS post-doctoral researcher.

References

Ball, S. J., Bowe, R., & Gewirtz, S. (1995). Circuits of schooling: A sociological exploration of parental choice of school in social class contexts. *The Sociological Review*, 43, 52–78.
Ball, S. J., & Vincent, C. (1998). I heard it on the grapevine: "Hot" knowledge and school choice. *British Journal of Sociology of Education*, 19(3), 377–400.
Ballatore, M. (2010). *Erasmus et la mobilité des jeunes européens*. Paris: PUF.
Ballion, R. (1982). *Les Consommateurs d'école*. Paris: Stock.
Barrère, A. (2002). Pourquoi les enseignants ne travaillent-ils pas en équipe? *Sociologie du travail*, 44, 481–497.
Bidart, C., Degenne, A., & Grossetti, M. (2011). *La vie en réseau: Dynamiques des relations sociales*. Paris: PUF.
Bourdieu, P. [1979] (1984). *Distinction: A social critique of the judgment of taste*. Cambridge, MA: Harvard University Press.
Bourdieu, P. [1979] (1986). The forms of capital (trans. Richard Nice). In J. Richardson (Ed.), *Handbook of theory and research for the sociology of education* (pp. 241–258). New York: Greenwood.
Bourdieu, P., & Passeron, J.-C. [1964] (1979). *The inheritors: French students and their relations to culture* (trans. Richard Nice). Chicago, IL: University of Chicago Press.
Bourdieu, P., & Passeron, J.-C. [1970] (1977). *Reproduction in education, society and culture* (trans. Richard Nice). London: Sage Publications.
Brown, P. (1990). The "third wave": Education and the ideology of parentocracy. *British Journal of Sociology of Education*, 11(1), 65–85.

154 Hugues Draelants

Brown, P. (2008). Elites (employabilité des). In A. van Zanten (Ed.), *Dictionnaire de l'éducation* (pp. 239–241). Paris: PUF.

Brown, P., & Hesketh, A. (2004). *The mismanagement of talent: Employability and jobs in the knowledge economy.* Oxford: Oxford University Press.

Buisson-Fenet, H., & Draelants, H. (2013). School-linking processes: Describing and explaining their role in the social closure of French elite education. *Higher Education,* 66(1), 39–57.

Chambliss, D. F. (1989). The mundanity of excellence: An ethnographic report on stratification and olympic swimmers. *Sociological Theory,* 7(1), 70–86.

Chapoulie, J.-M. (1987). *Les professeurs de l'enseignement secondaire: Un métier de classe moyenne.* Paris: Editions de la Maison des Sciences de l'Homme.

Coulangeon, P. (2011). *Les métamorphoses de la distinction: Inégalités culturelles dans la France d'aujourd'hui.* Paris: Grasset.

Daverne, C., & Dutercq, Y. (2013). *Les bons élèves: Expériences et cadres de formation.* Paris: PUF.

De Graaf N. D., De Graaf P. M., & Kraaykamp, G. (2000). Parental cultural capital and educational attainment in the Netherlands: A refinement of the cultural capital perspective. *Sociology of Education,* 73, 92–111.

DiMaggio, P. (1982). Cultural capital and school success: The impact of status culture participation on the grades of U.S. High School students. *American Sociological Review,* 52, 440–455.

Donnat, O. (1994). *Les français face à la culture: De l'exclusion à l'éclectisme.* Paris: La Découverte.

Draelants, H. (2010). Les effets d'attraction des grandes écoles: Excellence, prestige et rapport à l'institution. *Sociologie,* 1(3), 337–356.

Draelants, H. (2014). Des héritiers aux initiés? Note sur les nouvelles modalités de la reproduction sociale par l'école. *Social Science Information,* 53(3), 403–432.

Dubet, F. (2002). *Le Déclin de l'institution.* Paris: Editions du Seuil.

Duru-Bellat, M., & Kieffer, A. (2008). Du baccalauréat à l'enseignement supérieur en France: déplacement et recomposition des inégalités. *Population,* 63, 123–157.

Duru-Bellat, M., & Mingat, A. (1988). Le déroulement de la scolarité au collège: le contexte «fait des différences». *Revue française de sociologie,* 29, 649–666.

Eloy F. (2012). *Apprendre à écouter la musique: Culture légitime, culture scolaire et cultures juvéniles,* unpublished thesis. Paris, EHESS.

Fabiani J.-L. (2007). *Après la culture légitime: Objets, publics, autorités.* Paris: L'Harmattan.

Farkas G. (2003). Cognitive skills and non-cognitive traits and behaviors in stratification processes. *Annual Review of Sociology,* 29, 541–562.

Felouzis, G., & Perroton, J. (2010). Grandir entre pairs: Ségrégation ethnique et reproduction sociale dans le système éducatif français. *Actes de la recherche en sciences sociales,* 180, 92–100.

Ganzeboom, H. (1982). Explaining differential participation in high-cultural activities – A confrontation of information-processing and status-seeking theories. In W. Raub (Ed.), *Theoretical models and empirical analyses: Contributions to the explanation of individual actions and collective phenomena* (pp. 186–205). Utrecht: E.S. Publications.

Glasman D. (2001). *L'Accompagnement scolaire: Sociologie d'une marge de l'école.* Paris: PUF.

Goldthorpe, J. H. (2007). "Cultural capital": Some critical observations. *Sociologica,* 1(2), 1–23.

Gombert, P., & van Zanten, A. (2004). Le modèle éducatif du pôle "privé" des classes moyennes: Ancrage et traduction dans la banlieue parisienne. *Education et sociétés*, 14, 67–83.

Henri-Panabière, G. (2010). Élèves en difficultés de parents fortement diplômés: Une mise à l'épreuve empirique de la notion de transmission culturelle. *Sociologie*, 1(4), 457–478.

Héran, F. (1996). Ecole publique, école privée: qui peut choisir? *Economie et statistique*, 293, 17–39.

Jacquet-Francillon, F. (2008). Culture scolaire. In A. van Zanten (Ed.), *Dictionnaire de l'éducation* (pp. 98–102). Paris: PUF.

Kakpo, S. (2012). *Les devoirs à la maison: Mobilisation et désorientation des familles populaires.* Paris: PUF.

Lahire, B. (1995). *Tableaux de familles: Heurs et malheurs scolaires en milieux populaires.* Paris: Seuil/Gallimard.

Lareau A., & Weininger, E. B. (2003). Cultural capital in educational research: A critical assessment. *Theory and Society*, 32(5/6), 567–606.

Le Pape, M.-C., & van Zanten, A. (2009). Les pratiques éducatives des familles. In M. Duru-Bellat & A. van Zanten (Eds.), *Sociologie du système éducatif* (pp. 185–205). Paris: PUF.

LeTendre, G. K., Gonzalez, R. G., & Nomi, T. (2006). Feeding the elite: The evolution of elite pathways from star high schools to elite universities. *Higher Education Policy*, 19, 7–30.

Maroy, C. (2001). Le modèle du praticien réflexif à l'épreuve de l'enquête. *Les Cahiers de recherche du Girsef*, 12, 3–25.

Masy, J. (2013). La temporalité, une disposition sociale et culturelle de construction de l'avenir. *Sociologies*. Retrieved 14 November 2014 from http://sociologies.revues.org/4287.

McDonough, P. M. (1997). *Choosing colleges: How social class and schools structure opportunity.* Albany: State University of New York Press.

Murphy-Lejeune, E. (2002). *Student mobility and narrative in Europe: The new strangers.* London: Routledge.

Oberti, M. (2007). *L'école dans la ville: Ségrégation, mixité, carte scolaire.* Paris: Presses de Sciences Po.

Oller A.-C. (2012). Le coaching scolaire face aux nouvelles injonctions scolaires. *Sociologies pratiques*, 25, 85–97.

Pasquier, D. (2005). *Cultures lycéennes: Le tyrannie de la majorité.* Paris: Editions Autrement.

Peterson, R. A. (1992). Understanding audience segmentation: From elite and mass to omnivore and univore. *Poetics*, 21, 243–258.

Power, S. (2000). Educational pathways into the middle class(es). *British Journal of Sociology of Education*, 21, 133–145.

Prieur, A., & Savage, M. (2013). Emerging forms of cultural capital. *European Societies*, 15(2), 246–267.

Schön, D. (1983). *The reflective practitioner: How professionals think in action.* New York: Basic Books.

Sullivan, A. (2001). Cultural capital and educational attainment. *Sociology*, 35(4), 893–912.

Van Zanten, A. (2009a). *Choisir son école.* Paris: PUF.

Van Zanten, A. (2009b). The sociology of elite education. In M. Apple, S. Ball & L. A. Gandin (Eds.), *International handbook of the sociology of education* (pp. 329–339). London/ New York: Routledge.

Vincent, S. (2000). Le jouet au cœur des stratégies familiales d'éducation. *Sociétés Contemporaines*, 40, 165–182.

Vincent, C. (2010). The sociology of mothering. In M. Apple, S. Ball & L. A. Gandin (Eds.), *International handbook of the sociology of education* (pp. 109–120). London/New York: Routledge.

Wagner, A.-C. (2007). *Les classes sociales dans la mondialisation*. Paris: La Découverte.

9

CAN GEOGRAPHIES OF PRIVILEGE AND OPPRESSION COMBINE?

Elite Education in Northern Portugal

Eunice Macedo and Helena C. Araújo

Introduction

This chapter focuses on young adults in a private international school for economic elites, launched in the mid-1980s by a trust that aimed to develop education in the northern Portuguese region, in a period when the country joined the EEC (currently EU). The school curriculum has a strong emphasis on internationalisation and offers what it calls innovative, cooperative *hands on learning*, which is said to promote students' independence, autonomy and decision-making. The students of the study are privileged because they come from affluent backgrounds and they have access to a well-resourced school. We question, however, whether there is a price to pay for the privilege they live in.

In Portugal, high differentiation and specialisation can be associated with privatisation, liberalisation and modernisation (Afonso, 2013; Cotovio, 2004). There are increasing political, social and economic pressures on education, which include the growing vigilance over school life (Nóvoa, 2005) and high competitiveness. Moreover, the discussions on the quality of education have legitimated free school choice as an instrument and expression of the commodification of educational services (Ball, 2003). This has influenced educational policies, imposing 'rigour' and 'rationality' and the adoption of managerial models to education (Stoer, 2001), allegedly to meet people's needs and provide efficient and effective teaching.

Associated with processes such as the hierarchical organisation of classes in public schools that promote educational/social segregation (Cortesão, 1998), educational elitism has been particularly supported by the privatisation of education as a way to transfer government responsibilities to private entities (Carneiro, 2006). This has resulted in a tension between liberalisation and

158 Eunice Macedo and Helena C. Araújo

marketisation that assumes greater autonomy in the face of government rules and creates new markets that will provide other options, assuring the elite the *distinction* (Bourdieu, 1979) previously guaranteed by their exclusive access to education.

Keeping this context in mind, this chapter begins by presenting the philosophy, pedagogies, beliefs and assumptions of the school where the study was conducted followed by a description of the research methods and participants. Next, the chapter provides a historical overview of elite schooling in the last 80 years in Portugal to give a sense of how commodification, privatisation and liberalisation has affected the landscape of elite schooling in the present day. It explores the concepts of privilege and oppression and their manifestations in the elite school we studied, which we call the Park School. Building on the analysis of documents and young adults' narratives, we question *if* and *how* geographies of privilege and oppression combine, bringing to light intra-gender and inter-gender regularities and singularities, and 'class' hierarchies. Young adult narratives are brought to the fore to clarify how they see themselves in the world, and the ways in which they represent 'others'.

The Research Context: The Park School

The Park School advertised itself as an international school targeting local/ national and foreign students wishing to gain an education in English. The school promised a balanced, demanding and forward-looking education different from mainstream state education and other private schools, which offered the German, French, or English curricula and only until the 9th grade. The school's transnational curriculum matched up with the syllabi of the USA, the UK, and Portugal. A team of specialists, including a Portuguese national, worked on the three curricular proposals and adapted the non-national ones to the national curriculum by introducing environmental Portuguese studies and Portuguese language in junior school (grades 1–4) and Portuguese language and history in middle and upper school (grades 5–8 and 9–12, respectively). These varied Portuguese curricula were, however, adapted from the mainstream educational curriculum, and so was the system of junior, middle and upper school levels. The school's iteration of a transnational curriculum with a national/local flavour was endorsed by the state.

Currently, according to the principal, the school caters for around 800 students from a number of countries, including China, Spain, England, Sweden, Japan, Poland, and the Netherlands, to name but a few. The school's educational programme has continued to develop and expand, catering to learner diversity including those with learning disabilities. The school is considered now as one of the leading international schools in Iberia and has been evaluated by an international entity. The school is known for its exceptional curriculum that emphasises 'concept-based learning'. In this curriculum, students explore pressing problems in the world and seek sustainable solutions through various projects on topics such as hunger and global migration. These projects are implemented school wide. The aim is to prepare students to be principled citizens and lifelong learners, who will make a difference to those less fortunate than themselves.

The school was selected for the study discussed in this chapter due to its curriculum specificity and the fact that one of us worked there for more than 10 years before this research. This ethnographic incursion gave us the opportunity to immerse ourselves into the school *ethos*—a symbolic space of construction and assertion of a specific identity that highlights the school's cultural and educational uniqueness (Stoer & Araújo, 2000). The advantage of having insider knowledge of the school, however, meant also that there was a need for a critical reciprocation between proximity and distancing from the realities observed.

The data collected included school documents and focus group discussions. The study involved two gender-mixed groups in years 10 and 11, aged 16–18. Each group of 12 participants participated in four discussion sessions. Most participants were Portuguese; two young women were English, one young man was Japanese, and another Portuguese/Polish. We coded the discussion data and analysed it for emerging themes.

Elite Schooling in the Last 80 Years: A Short Historical Overview

The Portuguese educational system is a centralised one. In the so-called *Estado Novo* (New State) (1933–1974), Portugal was subject to an authoritarian, autocratic and corporatist political regime in which the monopolistic control of the state in relation to education and all public life prevailed (Abrantes & Quaresma, 2013; Araújo, 2000; Stoer, 1986). Most private schooling was subsidiary to the *Educator State* (Afonso, 1998). Bringing an end to the long period of dictatorship, the Portuguese Carnation[1] Revolution of 25 April, 1974, brought democratic political, social and economic change, including freedom of expression and the elimination of censorship. In this revolutionary and post-revolutionary period, private schooling was associated with the education of the bourgeois elite.

Like all policies, education policies have undergone advances and setbacks. Law No. 9/79 legitimised and enforced private education, along the lines of free choice among educational options and teaching conditions. This was reinforced by the Law of the Education System (1986) that strengthened the right of all to education and culture. The state lost the right to plan education and culture according to any philosophy, aesthetics, politics, ideology, or religion. Private schools and cooperatives guaranteed educational freedom and families' rights to guide the education of their children. The responsibility of the state to promote the democratisation of education was stressed, to assure equal opportunities of access and success in school.

If this legal framework was well regarded by the political far-right on the national political spectrum as it paved the way for privatisation, the left-wing criticised the provision of the law, arguing that it devalued public education and favoured elitist and socially selective schools for a strict group of a privileged population (Estêvão, 1998). In 1988, the education minister Roberto Carneiro stressed the value of private education, formulating the need to give it dignity and provide the means to assert its more specific vocation. In this line, the Ministry of Education made alliances with private education sectors to achieve the target of the national education project to provide education to a wider number of citizens in the vein of equal opportunities.

In the 1990s—and still in current times—the privatisation of education was a privileged aspect of neoliberal policies, which included the promotion of high-stakes testing and accountability directed at the competitive labour market under the argument that such reform was needed within the globalised economy, and would promote academic achievement and close the achievement gap. Privatisation profited from the lack of trust of the population in the political system and from a certain disenchantment regarding the expansion of equal opportunities that some authors have described as the crisis of the legitimacy of the state (Afonso, 1998; Estêvão, 1998). Given the state's inability to meet the needs of the population, privatisation was presented as a way to promote equal opportunities by means of fairer educational services (Estêvão, 2000). Hence, the implementation of elite education took place within the debate *for* and *against* private education. This still prevails in the current wider context of crisis. Unemployment, job scarcity and the general impoverishment of the population have led students to leave private institutions where they have had to pay for higher school fees.

The argument *for* private education is based on the right of parental choice of school and the improvement of schools' effectiveness in retaining students/clients through competitiveness (Carneiro, 2006). The argument *against* private elite education is that the inherent expansion of elite schools increases social inequalities. In terms of social justice, the private elite educational service contributes to segregation among social groups on the basis of families' economic levels (Belfield & Levin, 2004; Levin, 2003) and to reproducing intergenerational inequalities (Macedo, 2009), as some will have access to enriching pedagogies while others will be subject to poor, less stimulating mass education. Secondly, the impact on educational choice may increase the distance between the most vulnerable families and the school (Santiago et al., 2004), as the cultured elites have a closer understanding of the school culture. The attempt to divide education for the elite and the poor (Abrantes & Quaresma, 2013) veils the hierarchical nature of the educational system (Barroso, 2003) and its elitism.

Since 2001, when the first school rankings placed private education in the spotlight (Macedo, 2012a), the divide between state and private schooling has had a strong impact on educational elitism and hierarchism. The Portuguese education system encompasses several types of schools. Public schools are run by the state and are open to all. Among private schools sponsored by the state, some

Elite Education in Northern Portugal **161**

address the less favoured populations, including children with a low socio-economic status. Elite schools are very exclusive due to the very high fees and student selection. Within the wide spectrum of provision from the most deprived to the most privileged groups, educational privatisation includes the offerings by religious groups, private businesses, centres of solidarity[2] or parents, and the provision of state funding to private entities,[3] either directly (financial resources) or indirectly (student scholarships).

If 'most' students theoretically have access to private state-funded schools—a strategy that might reduce the elitist features of some private schools—many families, however, do not have the cultural strategic thinking to take advantage. This means that students from diverse socio-cultural groups are differentiated according to the ways in which they may (or may not) use their cultural capital in school (Bourdieu, 1986). Moreover, elite schools may select students among the upper classes who can pay for school fees, supplementary lessons, and other educational support, augmenting their possibility of entry to the most prestigious higher education institutions, with negative consequences on educational and social equity (Macedo, 2009). As is argued in other studies, the educational options of the "wealthy and highly educated families ... become normalized through the inculcated expectations of families, the explicit positioning of schools and the peer culture" (Mullen, 2009, p. 15).

Combined Geographies of Privilege and Oppression?

Located in the northern region of Portugal, the Park School was framed by educational privatisation, which resulted in the politics of 'class', educational choice, and the ability of upper-class parents to take advantage of educational choices. This type of situation is also widely documented in research in other contexts (see, for example, Arnot, 2009; Ball, 2003; Bernstein, 1996; Santiago et al., 2004; van Zanten, 2009; van Zanten, 2010). The school arose at a time of intense change in the game of power among nation-states within the global capitalist system, when political, social, and cultural transformation was increasingly subordinated to the economy. The school may be associated with a Westernisation or Americanisation movement; in particular, North American values, cultural artefacts, and symbolic universes such as individualism, political democracy, economic rationality, utilitarianism, and the rule of law (Santos, 2001) of dominant groups. Moreover, the school's concern about internationalisation shows that it moves from grooming national leaders (Koh & Kenway, 2012) to producing new elites who are able to perform well at the national and international levels (Cortesão et al., 2007; Macedo, 2009; Macedo & Araújo, 2014). Interestingly, the school invested in teaching Mandarin to prepare students for an anticipated imaginary future power of China and its influence in the global economy. Hence, the elite cultural and social power reproduction moves beyond the nation-state to the wider international, European, and global settings.

Privilege: 'Class' Resources, Action, and Cultural Strengthening

Educational sociologists have studied the 'glamour of elite schools', emphasising the ways in which they "reinforce the social, political, cultural, and economic privilege of dominant groups" (Koh & Kenway, 2012, p. 334). This is the case of the Park School. It is a school for the economic elites, indirectly sponsored by the state by means of an agreement between the municipal government and the trust that created the school, which is constituted by a new upper class comprised of professions such as engineers, doctors, lawyers, and so on. Whereas the state provided a building free of charge, the trust was to renovate and maintain it for a period of time.[4]

The school fits the trust's purpose to develop education and culture in the north of Portugal, and to strengthen and assure the educational/social privilege of the economic elites and of migrant students with economic capacity. In the same manner, the launch of the school seems to indicate the concern to assure *cultural inheritance* (Bourdieu, 1997; Perrenoud, 1982), resulting from a feeling of loss of educational exclusivity by the upper classes, due to the national effort to democratise public schools and the access of new groups to formal education, under the drive of Europe.

Our research data indicate the contrary belief of a 'social paradise' (Bourdieu, 1996; Kenway & Koh, 2013) where full mutual recognition boosts and confirms individual values within the group in the school. The view of the school as 'social paradise' risks generalisation that occludes tensions among adults and young adults, young men and women, richer and less rich students, and so forth. Hence, after referring to the ways in which privilege can be constructed and deconstructed (Howard, 2008) and the embodiment of privilege through elite schooling (Khan, 2011), we build on the discussion of oppression to question *if* and *how* privilege and oppression can combine.

Oppression: Positioning, Gender Invisibility, and the Naturalisation of Social Inequalities

The link between oppression and deprivation or poor access to goods is highlighted by Young (1990). This is not the case for the subjects in the study, as our analysis will show in the next section. As the author also underlines, oppression also involves aspects that do not fit into that logic, such as decision-making and the division of labour and culture, in conjunction with systemic constraints similar to the ones affecting the people in this study. Our data revealed that subtle dimensions of *systemic structural oppression* (ibidem) can combine with a geography of privilege to position them as 'others' within their 'own' group due to the slight presence of *symbolic violence* and *recontextualisation* (Bourdieu, 1992, 1997). In many cases, there is a coincidence between schooling and the individual's

Elite Education in Northern Portugal **163**

knowledge and repertoire that naturalises and maximises the power and effects of the school culture.

The identities of these elite students are politically and pedagogically shaped to be *high performing consumer citizens*, but the school culture indirectly reproduces gender stereotypes and the subordination of 'others' who do not belong to the dominant group. This is the form of structural oppression that is subtly embedded in the unchallenged rules, habits, symbols, and assumptions of the school (Bourdieu, 1992).

There are also other dimensions of *systemic structural oppression* that are not obvious. There is risk of the reversion of the emancipatory features of cooperative methodologies into tools for better competition. For example, peer and adult pressure combine for the completion of tasks and weaker students may be left behind. Another subtle form of oppression is the preoccupation of young adults with the accumulation of curricular and extra-curricular demands perceived to benefit their individual portfolio leaving no time for relaxation and unsupervised conviviality. Moreover, the vigilance over school breaks and student behaviour inside and outside the classroom and the strict regulation of lesson time follows very demanding and rigorous planning and daily routines, which most students cannot or will not follow. Upper secondary students are also subject to exam pressures with frequent tests conducted to ensure their success in national and international examinations and subsequent eligibility into universities, which is very competitive.

In what follows, we discus the various forms of oppression in greater detail, evidenced by the data collected through group discussion.

Positioning

Many youngsters verbalised the pressure for performativity and the ways in which it endangered their opportunity to 'be young'. Many also expressed that because of competing priorities from schoolwork, they are deprived of leisure time even to rest, let alone spending time with their parents. One representative student, for example, said that:

> I lack that freedom of ... "Oh this is cool ... now I'm here in bed, it is a joy, I'll take a shower, and then go out to lunch with my parents".
>
> (Young woman)

Students put in many hours of school and after-school work into the quest of getting the highest marks in order to get into the best national and European or American universities. The subtle lesson of competitiveness—useful for the future in the labour market—is present in the capacity to compete better. Many students are aware that there is no guarantee that, even with top grades, they are entitled to a place in the best universities. There is a next rung of competition where the best of the best compete and are chosen by the best universities. This view is reiterated by one student who observed that:

> Nowadays there is global competition and we need to take 'A' in all subjects to get to the top. Within the 'A' there are some who do not get in the best universities because they have to choose between these people.
>
> (Young man)

Putting at risk all other dimensions of being young and accepting competition as natural, their ultimate goal is to obtain the best jobs that will provide for a 'good life', associated with high consumption:

> If we do not enter a good university, we cannot get a good job, we may [not] be [able] to scrape the money [together] in the future ... We have to get very good marks so that we can go to a good university, then get a job in order to sustain us and our family ... When I talk about earning money to survive I mean for food, home life and for fun ... I do not want to have a luxury car, a big house ... I know perfectly well that in a few years, I'll think, 'Oh, I feel like having this', but at 19, 20 I do not want to have a Porsche.
>
> (Young man)

> What's the harm of wishing for that type of thing?
>
> (Another young man)

Consumption was seen as a way to assert status within class hierarchies, even if some could not care less, and girls in particular claimed the right to be happy:

> Money makes the most of our lives ... not all ... but if we only think of money we cannot search for happiness.
>
> (Young woman)

In terms of 'positioning', these data show how these young adults are under pressure to perform, to be *the* best, while accepting that some sacrifices are necessary such as giving up their freedom and time for families and friends. Investing in the future so that they may secure a good life is given priority above everything else. They therefore believe that their success is purely by merit (Bernstein, 1996).

Changing Gender Invisibility?

Unlike the males, who are represented as universal, fitting in a multiplicity of contexts and with the skills to handle them all (Arnot, 2009; Nogueira, 2001), women are represented in reference to the males. In the Park School, the education of young women for competitiveness, dominance, and success, linked to the expectation of prominence in the public sphere, points to the subtle dimensions of *systemic structural oppression* as well. As this investment is designed in accordance with male models, it despises other forms of labour that value women's experiences, giving visibility to the specificity of their pathways and expectations (Araújo, 2000, 2010). Because they are also expected to adhere to these same principles and models, young men are not allowed to break through male stereotypes by developing divergent thinking and identities.

This school (re)produces ideological and structural gender constraints through the curriculum and the daily politics. Gender is not taken into account in the assumptions and practices of the school and is subsumed to an elusive perspective of gender neutrality, which covers a universalistic male bias. Gender constructs do not allow the emergence of divergent masculinities and femininities (Macedo, 2012b). However, young adults' capacity to produce culture is expressed in the reaction against this. A small group envisages work as a way to become economically independent:

> At eighteen I will not be [at] home anymore and I then start to build my life. A person should not depend on parents for too long. We should not need their money ... we should try to live at our own expense.
>
> (Young woman)

Reinforced by the school, cultural and social inheritance are evident in the account provided by this dialogue during a focus group discussion:

> My mother works very hard! On Fridays her friends party or have dinner. Not my mother. 'So mom, what are you *gonna* do?' and my mother, 'Oh I have to work today.' She has her own catering business, alone. It was created by my grandmother. I will have my own enterprise.
>
> (Young woman)

Social inheritance is also reflected in this data:

> My father is the manager of his own metallurgical company. I think of studying business management because then I can take care of my father's company or follow along with him.
>
> (Young man)

> And you always have your job assured!
>
> (Young woman)

> Not really ... maybe ... you are right!
>
> (Young man)

166 Eunice Macedo and Helena C. Araújo

Work is associated with the possibility to learn how to manage money, fundamental for independence and the likelihood of high life standards:

> I'm not saying that I don't want to go to work. I want to get a living as I want. I want to have luxury cars. I admit that I want all those things ... but I want to earn it by myself ... of course I know that my parents will be there to help me.
>
> (Young man)

Even if young women in particular try to break through, competitiveness, dominance, and success are the key words in their socialisation, leaving little room for reflection and informed choice. Like young men, they are trained to compete in the labour market to fulfil the socially constructed *needs* they associate with the 'good life'.

The Naturalisation of Social Inequalities: Social and Cultural Autism

In a previous study (Macedo, 2009), *cultural and social autism* was described as a problem of incommunicability among groups based on the inability to acknowledge, understand, and embrace the richness of diversity. This perspective positions the 'other' (e.g., black people, homosexuals, uncultured, poor) as inferior, incompetent, or as failing to comply with the legitimate conditions of the dominant group, the elites in this case. Such a view can contribute to the construction of reality as a composite of naturalised facts. This paradigm is sustained in the myth of a common good in which the values of the group are alleged to be universal. However, only the group is reinforced by means of self-assertion and strategic individualism in the construction of its own pathway no matter what and who is left behind. The 'other' is made invisible or located in subordination. This dimension of *structural systemic oppression* may lead young adults to justify and accept inequalities as necessary for the 'proper' status quo. As a result, these elites often assume a charitable protectionist and well-intentioned 'social responsibility'. People who have money pay 'others' so they have the right to work to survive:

> A key thing for society to work well is that there are people with money to help others have a job.
>
> (Young man)

The 'social responsibility' ascribed to 'others' is to work for the comfort of those who can pay:

> Now I'm talking seriously. If there weren't people without studies who would be working for us? Who would do all the little things for us? Would you go and make your own snack? You're *gonna* tidy up your room?

Elite Education in Northern Portugal **167**

In these cases, the individualist personal view overlaps any form of recognition of the 'other'. The young adults who share this opinion see themselves as citizens whose rights are assured by the fact that they belong to the richest groups of the population, whereas others are unquestionably placed as dependent manual workers whose existence is justified by the possibility to assist in the low profile tasks the elites ought not to do.

Conclusion

The construction of citizenship *for* and *by* these young women and men of the economic elites took place within an institutional geography where privilege and subtle dimensions of oppression intersect. Over-stimulation and a hyper-demanding culture, gender invisibility and the naturalisation of social inequalities are some of the ways in which the price of privilege may be identified. The way the young adults construct their reality is conditioned by non-universal, specific structures and processes of cultural transmission *sensu lato* that (in)form their (apparent) subjectivity in the interpretation of the structures and principles governing practices, be they moral, aesthetic, and/or of social assertion. This leads to the construction of specific strategies and expectations regarding academic and social integration, and the later entrance into social and work realities.

Intra-gender and inter-gender regularities and singularities, 'class' hierarchies and (dis)similar views became clear, in particular in relation with 'others' and the meanings ascribed to 'having a good life'. In most cases, both the young women and men developed self-assertion, managerial, and communication skills, which will foster their high expectations of academic and professional practice at the top of the competitive national and international market. Within the institution, which often reinforced other social contexts of the subjects, most of the year 10 and 11 young women and men revealed the potential for participation and decision-making in the construction of their personal journeys, as part of the assertion and empowerment of the powerful side of their voice(s). Considering gender, some young women in this group intended to use their statutory and material power to shift away from naturalised forms of gender discrimination. To assure their right to an autonomous life, they have developed forms of strategic thinking that include postponing family life to study and build a career. Falling behind the young women's academic and professional expectations, most of the young men accepted family sponsorship and cultural and social inheritance, even if some asserted the will to shift away from it.

Highlighting the crucial role of this school on young adults' lives, its education policies and practices confirmed and empowered them within the particular culture and conception of life of the economic elite. However, as a form of *systemic structural oppression*, the construction of positions of power stands both on the induction to *consumer citizenship* and the strategic construction of pathways of individualisation centred on high performativity, as well as on the naturalisation of social inequalities. Youngsters' 'citizenship' can be seen as mitigated both by the obligation of high performativity, which requires the elimination of other dimensions of being young, and by the induction of *social and cultural autism*, where the subordination or annulment of the other emerges as natural. As a result, the preservation of hierarchies, 'class' and gender asymmetries, dependence, compulsion to consume, individualism, and lack of social commitment become legitimate. Giving rise to the (hopeful) perspective of a new elite culture that shifts away from this incommunicability, some people in this group expressed greater proximity to the different 'other' and proclaimed the need for a more balanced and fair society to which they want to contribute.

Acknowledgement

This work was supported in part by the Portuguese Foundation for Science and Technology (FCT – Fundação para a Ciência e a Tecnologia) [grant number PEst-OE/CED/UI0167/2014 – Strategic Project of the Centre for Research and Intervention in Education/CIIE-UP].

Notes

1 Nomination given to the Portuguese Revolution due to the total absence of violence and shutting out, even though it was performed by the army with the population's support; soldiers' guns were used as jars in which to place carnations.
2 Centres of solidarity are supported by the state to provide for people with low incomes. School fees are paid according to family income and the remaining part of the expense is covered by the state.
3 In 2013, 91 private schools had agreements with the Ministry of Education, a public expenditure of around 154.9 million EUR (State Budget, 2013). If state funding started as a means to guarantee education in areas where public schools were lacking or overcrowded (CNE, 2012), the current rules have eased the state's financing of students in private schools, independent of the public provision in the same area, a shift that puts at risk democratisation, as it fosters the most perverse effects of education marketisation (Stoer, 2001).
4 A researcher's inside knowledge as she was hired to start the school and worked there for several years as pedagogical director, teacher, and cultural coordinator.

References

Abrantes, P., & Quaresma, M. L. (2013). Schools for the elite, schools for the poor: The same educational system, contrasting socialization environments. *Italian Journal of Sociology of Education, 5*(2), 133–159.
Afonso, A. (1998). *Políticas educativas e avaliação educacional: Para uma análise sociológica da reforma educativa em Portugal 1985–1995.* Braga: UM.
Afonso, A. (2013). Um olhar sociológico sobre políticas para a educação, avaliação e accountability. *Revista Educação e Políticas em Debate, 2*(2), 286–296.

Araújo, H. C. (2000). Mothering and citizenship: Educational conflicts in Portugal. In M. Arnot & J. A. Dillabough (Eds.), *Challenging democracy: International perspectives on gender and citizenship* (pp. 105–121). London: Routledge/Falmer Press.

Araújo, H. C. (2010). Escola e construção da igualdade no trabalho e no emprego. In V. Ferreira (Ed.), *A igualdade de mulheres e homens no trabalho e no emprego em Portugal: Políticas e circunstâncias* (pp. 217–245). Lisbon: CITE.

Arnot, M. (2009). *Educating the gendered citizen: Sociological engagements with national and global agendas*. London: Routledge.

Ball, S. (2003). *Class strategies and the education market*. London: Routledge.

Barroso, J. (2003). A 'escolha da escola' como processo de regulação: integração ou selecção natural? In J. Barroso (Ed.), *A escola pública: Regulação, desregulação, privatização* (pp. 79–106). Porto: Asa.

Belfield, C. R., & Levin, H. M. (2004). *A privatização da educação, causas e implicações*. Porto: Asa.

Bernstein, B. (1996). *Pedagogy, symbolic control and identity: Theory, research, critique*. London: Taylor & Francis.

Bourdieu, P. (1979). *La distinction: Critique sociale du jugement*. Paris: Ed. de Minuit.

Bourdieu, P. (1986). The forms of capital. In J. Richardson (Ed.), *Handbook of theory and research for the sociology of education* (pp. 241–258). New York: Greenwood.

Bourdieu, P. (1992). *O poder simbólico*. Rio de Janeiro: Bertrand Brasil Press.

Bourdieu P. (1996). *The state nobility: Elite schools in the field of power*. Stanford, CA: Stanford University.

Bourdieu, P. (1997). *La misère du monde*. Paris: Seuil.

Carneiro, E. (2006). *A problemática da decisão: A opção dos pais pela escola privada*. Braga: Universidade do Minho.

Conselho Nacional de Educação (CNE) [National Education Council]. (2012). *Estado da Educação 2012. Autonomia e descentralização* [State of Education 2012. Autonomy and decentralisation]. Lisboa: CNE.

Cortesão, L. (1998). *O arco-íris na sala de aula? Processos de organização de turmas: Reflexões críticas*. Lisboa: IIE.

Cortesão, L., Stoer, S., Magalhães, A., Antunes, F., Nunes, R., Macedo, E., Costa, A. S., & Araújo, D. (2007). *Na girândola de significados: Polissemia de excelências em escolas portuguesas do século XXI*. Porto: Livpsic.

Cotovio, J. (2004). *Imagens organizacionais da escola*. Lisboa: Unive Católica Ed.

Estêvão, C. (1998). A privatização da qualidade na educação e as suas privatizações. *Sociologia—Problemas e Práticas, 27*, 117–127.

Estêvão, C. (2000). O público e o privado em educação: A providenciação pública do privado na educação portuguesa. In J. Pacheco (Ed.), *Políticas educativas: O neoliberalismo em educação* (pp. 137–157). Porto: Porto Editora.

Howard, A. (2008). *Learning privilege: Lessons of power and identity in affluent schooling*. London: Routledge.

Kenway, J., & Koh, A. (2013). The elite school as 'cognitive machine' and 'social paradise': Developing transnational capitals for the national 'field of power', *Journal of Sociology, 49*(2–3): 272–290, DOI:10.1177/1440783313481525 www.sagepublications.com

Kenway, J., & Koh, A. (2013). The elite school as a 'cognitive machine' and 'social paradise'?: Developing transnational capitals for the national 'field of power'. In Working with Bourdieu: Antipodean Cultural Fields. *Journal of Sociology* (Special Issue) 49(2–3), 272–290.

Khan, S. R. (2011). *Privilege: The making of an adolescent elite at St Paul's School*. Princeton: Princeton University Press.

Koh, A., & Kenway, J. (2012). Cultivating national leaders in an elite school: Deploying the transnational in the national interest. *International Studies in Sociology of Education*, 22(4), 333–351.

Levin, H. (2003). Os 'cheques-ensino': Um quadro global de referência para a sua avaliação. In J. Barroso (Ed.), *A escola pública: Regulação, desregulação, privatização* (pp. 111–146). Porto: Asa.

Macedo, E. (2009). *Cidadania em confronto: Educação de elites em tempo de globalização*. Porto: CIIE/Livpsic.

Macedo, E. (2012a). *School rankings on the other hand… Possibilities of young adult citizenship in the tension of educational and social change*. Porto: FPCEUP.

Macedo, E. (2012b). (Re)constructing femininities and masculinities: Northern Portuguese students speak about their lives, desires and dreams. *Educação, Sociedade & Culturas*, 35, 67–88.

Macedo, E., & Araújo, H. (2014). Young Portuguese construction of educational citizenship: Commitments and conflicts in semi-disadvantaged secondary schools. *Journal of Youth Studies*, 17(3), 343–359.

Mullen, A. L. (2009). Elite destinations: Pathways to attending an Ivy League university. *British Journal of Sociology of Education*, 30(1), 15–27.

Nogueira, C. (2001). Questões de género na orientação vocacional: (Re)construir novos discursos da prática. In AAVV (Ed.), *Reconstruir os nossos olhares* (pp. 19–36). Coimbra: ME/DREC.

Nóvoa, A. (2005). *Evidentemente*. Porto: ASA.

Perrenoud, P. (1982). A herança cultural. In S. Grácio et al., *Sociologia da Educação II* (pp. 33–39). Lisbon: Horizonte.

Presidência do Conselho de Ministros [Presidency of the Council of Ministers] (2013) [State Budget] [Orçamento de Estado], Proposta de Lei [bill] n° 103/XII, presented in 2012.10.10 http://app.parlamento.pt/OE2013/corpo.html

Santiago, R., Correia, F., Tavares, O., & Pimenta, C. (2004). *Um olhar sobre os rankings*. Coimbra/Matosinhos: CIPES/FUP.

Santos, B. S. (2001). Os processos da globalização. In B. S. Santos (Ed.), *Globalização: Fatalidade ou utopia?* (pp. 31–99). Porto: Afrontamento.

Stoer, S. (1986). *Educação e mudança social em Portugal, 1970–80: Uma década de transição*. Porto: Edições Afrontamento.

Stoer, S. (2001). Desocultando o voo das andorinhas: Educação inter/multicultural crítica como movimento social. In S. Stoer, L. Cortesão & J. A. Correia (Eds.), *Transnacionalização da educação: Da crise da educação à 'educação' da crise* (pp. 245–275). Porto: Afrontamento.

Stoer, S. R., & Araújo, H. C. (2000). *Escola e aprendizagem para o trabalho num país da (semi) periferia europeia*. Lisbon: Instituto de Inovação Educacional.

Van Zanten, A. (2009). *Choisir son école: Stratégies familiales et médiations locales*. Paris: Presses Universitaires de France.

Van Zanten, A. (2010). The sociology of elite education. In M. W. Apple, S. J. Ball & L. A. Gandin (Eds.), *The Routledge international handbook of the sociology of education* (pp. 329–339). London: Routledge.

Young, I. (1990). *Justice and the politics of difference*. Princeton: Princeton University Press.

10

"WE ARE NOT ELITE SCHOOLS"

Studying the Symbolic Capital of
Swiss Boarding Schools

Caroline Bertron

Introduction

"We are not, as they are sometimes called, elite schools."[1] This is how, during an interview, one headmaster described the secondary boarding school that his family has owned for 60 years. He then went on, opposing "academic intelligence that not everyone is good at" to "social intelligence that can be developed in every child", disregarding the former and praising the latter through examples of brilliant economic careers of academically mediocre former students.

"You need to understand that we are not a school" is what an admissions director from another school replied when I asked him about the curricula. He had no interest in talking about academics or the entrance selection processes. He talked instead about his career in luxury multinationals, and how the school mainly recruits students through the "people linked to" it, a more subtle way of discussing the type of "high society" networks the school relies on. During interviews, managers, and headmasters at "Swiss international boarding schools", as these schools are commonly referred to, frequently resorted to these explanations. The chapter aims at unfolding how such statements take part in the making of social distinction in elite schools. The production of symbolic statements around their uniqueness, implying specific definitions of eliteness and education, is central to the workings of elite schools' reputation. This chapter studies how within the context of an increasingly globalised space of education (Kenway & Fahey, 2014), the symbolic capital attached to 'Swiss boarding schools' is based on combining cosmopolitan and national categories of perception.

International boarding schools in Switzerland respond, although in very specific ways, to Gaztambide-Fernández's definition of elite schools (2009). They are *independent*; they provide a *sophisticated curriculum* that blends components of several national school systems; and they offer a wide range of extracurricular activities. They are *demographically* elite: their annual fees exceed 60,000 CHF (US$64,000) per student, and alumni have powerful careers. They are *historically* elite, recruiting abroad since the 19th century among Euro–North American aristocracies and bourgeoisies. As they were designed from their beginnings for a wealthy clientele living abroad, they have not contributed to the making of national elites in Switzerland. More recently, they have welcomed increasing numbers of children from Eastern Asia, South America, and post-socialist states. The last feature of Gaztambide-Fernández's definition is the starting point to the present study: these schools develop a specificity based on their geographical *location*. Campuses are based in isolated Alpine areas or along Lake Geneva, well known for having attracted wealthy foreigners since the aristocratic *Grand Tour* and as a result, for concentrating high standard services for the dominant class by developing banking, hotel, and leisure facilities.

Methods and Presentation of the Schools

The entire study (that I do not report here) relies on 70 interviews (2012–2014) with headmasters, staff members, teachers, students, and alumni of eight schools, complemented by the analysis of the schools' discursive and written productions over time, and a few observations. I restrict here the analysis to three schools, which present distinctive traits, such as size, range of price, ownership, international educational affiliations, and social capital (Bourdieu, 1980) as displayed by the level of cohesion among alumni and their families. Since schools' names are based on regional landscape attributes, I use pseudonyms that retain the imaginary they refer to (Table 10.1). This chapter relies specifically on interview situations with individuals in charge of shaping the images and reputations of the schools (headmasters, marketing directors, and admissions directors). In these three schools, I conducted interviews with four school representatives.

At Institut Les Alpes, the analysis is based on interviews with the headmaster and admissions director. Both insisted on the uniqueness of Institut Les Alpes, based on the aristocratic and Euro–North American social capital of the school. The school is owned by the headmaster's family and welcomes more than 300 boarders aged 8–18 years. It offers a full range of curricula (International Baccalaureate, British and American High school programmes, French Baccalauréat). It is also the most expensive of the three discussed. Several families have successively owned the school since the end of the 19th century.

In the second school, which I refer to as Lake Institute, the analysis relies on several interviews with the marketing director. There is no formal alumni association. The school welcomes more than 100 students and prepares the older ones for the Cambridge International Examinations, A-levels, and the American College Admission tests (PSAT, SAT). The same family has owned the school since the 19th century, and in the 1960s the school changed from being for girls only to co-educational. It is less expensive and smaller than Institut Les Alpes.

Symbolic Capital of Swiss Boarding Schools **173**

TABLE 10.1 Three boarding schools along Lake Geneva: Stylised properties and hierarchies (data 2012)

	Range of price (high school level)	Number of students	Age	Number of nationalities declared	Number of international curricula/sections offered	Alumni association	International standards and labels (CIS, ECIS, NEASC, etc.)
Institut Les Alpes	>US$90,000	>300	>8	>50	4	Very active	4 out of 6
Lake Institute	≈US$80,000	100–200	>11	30–40	2	None	4 out of 6
Rivage School	≈US$60,000	<100	>8	>10	2	None	1 out of 6

Note: In order to respect the anonymity of the schools and their actors, I only position these schools in relation to each other, without giving any figures.

In the third school, renamed Rivage School, I conducted a four-hour long interview with the headmaster. This school is also family-owned but claims to have no official membership in international networks of schools such as the Council of International Schools. It is the smallest (with fewer than 100 students) and the least expensive of the three schools. The school states that it was created at the end of the 19th century but has changed names, curricula, and owners several times since its inception.[2] Rivage School offers the same range of high school examinations as Lake Institute and has no alumni association.

These hierarchical elements were also reflected during fieldwork and in the level of public knowledge about these three schools, but they do not overshadow very specific common features. All three are family-owned English-speaking schools for a majority of students for whom English is not their mother tongue.[3] Learning French is also compulsory. They have never claimed any religious affiliation and were created during (or claim legitimacy from) the 19th century. The schools' longevity is embodied in their classic material wealth and patrimony (castle, villa, etc.). Finally, headmasters organise part of their marketing together.

Studying the Workings of "Symbolic Capital of Recognition"

Headmasters and managers extensively built their discourses around an image of 'Swiss private schools', all the more, perhaps, because I was perceived as a foreigner (as a French Korean PhD student). I will not address student and staff perspectives here, but I will draw on the role of these 'representatives' as actors promoting an educational model or a local commodity to be 'exported' as one of them put it, to attract students from abroad. The object of study thus becomes how the interviewees use the(ir) past to shape the uniqueness of their schools. Boarding school representatives indeed develop a sense of history: they emphasise

174 Caroline Bertron

past practices that seem to stand as immutable traditions (notably the *Grand Tour*) but whose meaning is embedded in the current transformations and global diffusions of international education models.[4]

The school 'representatives' that I interviewed are not only highly educated but they have upper-class backgrounds. On the one hand, their affiliation to the upper class is made visible by their aristocratic or bourgeois backgrounds and by their professional and long-time social networks of clienteles and families. On the other, they are servicing the upper class by taking care of their children. The privileged status of the interviewees also contributed to my being relegated to a generic outsider, who could nonetheless observe the workings of this symbolic production. To put it another way, the interviewees' intermediary position, as cultural producers and entrepreneurs at the service of the dominant class, is crucial to understanding the dynamics of the interviews.

The interviewees emphasised their status as regional economic actors. Boarding school headmasters have indeed manoeuvred as entrepreneurs in protecting and building a private educational sector on a par with other economic actors in Switzerland and through transnational circulations of pedagogies and social networks. Nevertheless, although their status as economic actors was made clear, the privilege of talking about the schools as companies was theirs only. Indeed, when I used economic lexical repertoires to refer to the schools' embeddedness in the economic world and to the standards of their educational model, I was reminded by the interviewees that my role was to praise the old cultural prestige of the schools. This interview dynamic of 'culture' and 'economics' first shows how their upper-class ethos is crucial for performing past values over the context of changes in national and old/new elite backgrounds of their students. Secondly, for several reasons that will be addressed here, it is highly questionable that these schools' reputation for attracting foreigners and their long-time cosmopolitanism (since headmasters purposely promoted their schools to foreign clients as an alternative to national schools and public schools) make them particularly responsive to international standards of education. I contend that the way headmasters and managers define the scope of education in their schools is situated in an interplay of national and international symbolism (Wagner, 1998). Building on the dynamics of the interviews discussed above, this interplay can be analysed as revolving around three topics: the schools' educational model, their economic history, and their spatiality. For each of these topics prevailed a discursive construction of their cosmopolitan image that rejected what is usually associated with globalisation of education, specifically the standardisation of curricula, economic globalisation logics in education, and spatial homogenisation.

Even though the interviewees take part in international networks of schools, they relegate the globalising phenomena in education to an imagined elsewhere and distinguish themselves through territorial identification. These expressions of social distinction can be considered as a symbolic construction of the "Swiss schools" image or their "symbolic capital of recognition" (Bourdieu, 1998). The chapter is thus building on Bourdieu's definition of symbolic capital as the object of strategies of "being perceived".

> Symbolic capital is attached to groups (or to the names of groups, families, clans, tribes) and is both the instrument and the stakes of collective strategies seeking to conserve or increase it as well as individual strategies to acquire or conserve it, by joining groups which possess it.
>
> (Bourdieu, 1998, p. 104)

Bourdieu referred to "symbolic capital of recognition" as a way of conceptualising Weber's charisma or Durkheimian school's *mana*. He states,

> Symbolic capital is an ordinary property (physical strength, wealth, warlike valor, etc.) which, perceived by social agents endowed with the categories of perception and appreciation permitting them to perceive, know and recognize it, becomes symbolically efficient, like a veritable magical power.
>
> (Bourdieu, 1998, p. 102)

Within the context of interviewing boarding school representatives, how does this symbolic capital work as an ambivalent construction? How is it produced by the struggles of the actors involved? This approach questions the (uncertain) effects of the use of *ancientness* or embodied long-time experience, as legitimation for the production and reproduction of elites.

Pedagogical Models: Building Private Education over National Narratives

In his recent ethnography of St. Paul's School (Concord, NH), Khan (2011) claimed that even though the upper-class profiles of its students have not changed, the ideals of meritocracy and openness have replaced old values of social heritage, namely establishment and entitlement, in the shaping of privilege. In a rereading of Bourdieu's work about high culture in France (Bourdieu, 1979), he concluded that these changes in values express contemporary transformations in the reproduction of elites and new logics of social distinction.

When considering the image promoted by boarding schools, my own observations along Lake Geneva are at odds with how Khan analysed openness and academic excellence to be central to socialisation in elite schools. During one interview, the headmaster at Institut Les Alpes expressed how they "educate heirs", insisting on the term, and that the school quite recently had to "commit to university". As he bluntly put it, "These heirs did not need higher education. Now, university has become part of their legitimacy." Furthermore, when I asked what had changed in the school since he arrived in the 1980s, he further commented on how "Here globalisation dates back to the 19th century, because

176 Caroline Bertron

the first eight pupils had eight nationalities." These statements suggest other symbolic and historical lines defining educational goals than those conveyed by nation-state bounded educational systems.

Alternative Pedagogies Versus Academic Excellence

The pedagogical vision that the headmaster of Rivage School conveyed merged his family trajectory with the history of alternative pedagogies. He elaborated on the local pedagogical filiation, quoting Swiss educators such as Pestalozzi.[5] He also pointed out his family's engagement in pedagogical research. His ancestors published a journal where scholars, psychologists, and pedagogues developed views on specialised education. This journal was also circulated in the public school system as an organ for educational sciences, but the interviewee repeatedly opposed the private school ethos of individualised pedagogy to the wider homogenising frame of public education. He raised private education as a national characteristic against the background of 19th-century Swiss figures of pedagogues. He made reference to an imagined European space of rising educational states, but he excluded Switzerland from it. In Switzerland, indeed, a unified school system did not emerge as such: education is still left to the local authorities (cantons), because of linguistic regionalism and separate traditions of schooling.[6] Federal unification initiatives were discussed throughout the 20th century but there remains wide discussion about how to define the historical importance of the Swiss federal state in educational matters (Hofstetter, 2012). Nevertheless, the historical line of Swiss pedagogues has also been used in Swiss state schools as a way of transmitting national values (Boltanski, 1966). This conjunction of public and private education around a national image embodied by great educators, raises the question of how boarding school owners appropriate this legacy for the sake of private education but also in order to produce a national image.

As in Rivage School, the headmaster of Institut Les Alpes described his school as a "Swiss product" that cannot be imitated. He praised the founder of the school as a visionary, who started a francophone school that would not be nationally contained and dominated by Germanic educational patterns. During the interview, he also quoted Swiss educators and mentioned his aim to "develop multiple intelligences" as opposed to what he described as the "French catholic education he received". He thus excluded both German and French influences referring to them as the neighbouring and bigger nation states exerting unwanted cultural domination, from Institut Les Alpes' specific genealogy. He spoke instead of the school's role as "educating a 21st-century *honnête homme*", among other oxymora, merging an old aristocratic conception of education within a future-oriented frame.

Institut Les Alpes is highly selective (400 applicants every year for 100 new places), but academic excellence does not define the selection. Applicants' practise of sports or arts at a higher level is praised as skills that will be valuable for the school community and for developing the student's personality. In a published essay that he wrote about his pedagogy and "vision",[7] the headmaster put forward that future students are "recognisable at first glance, in a flash that brings together the past, the present and the future". This strangely echoes Herzfeld's (2000) description of the "uncanny success" of elites or the mystique that elites usually develop to explain their perpetuation. The headmaster's disregard for academic skills and, more generally, his vision of academics as the surface of achievement were particularly prominent in the same document where he wrote on "not talking about technical questions connected to official curricula that do not present any originality". Similarly, for the Rivage School interviewee, disregard for matters other than the development and personality of the child was directly related to distancing himself from "globalisation".

> We are globalised enough. If you ask me if I have more boys or more girls, I could not tell you. I have students who look for education here, any religion, any nationality. I have no interest in knowing which. I accept these people as they are, and we do our best with the person.
>
> (Rivage School interviewee, April 2013)

International Pedagogies and the Dialectics of Business and Education

To headmasters, institutions producing assessments in international education are not primary sources of legitimacy. Quite to the contrary; even if they participate in these processes on various levels, they also oppose a bourgeois family education that would be innately cosmopolitan. Headmasters and senior managers develop alternative views on international pedagogy that show their actual anxiety for defining their internationality. "International" accreditations are relegated to the present time, an unenduring image or a global veneer of norms that schools want to give to parents. For instance, Institut Les Alpes was a pioneer in the making of the network of the Council of International Schools; the Rivage School headmaster studied pedagogy in the USA; and all three schools recruit teachers from IB schools and from public and private English-speaking schools around the world. To these managers, this did not make a difference in promoting the schools: "education" was opposed to "business", the latter being understood through the frame of education multinational firms, such as Nord Anglia,[8] that take over many boarding schools in Switzerland. Institut Les Alpes' headmaster named several of these companies, noting that "they don't come from education" and rejecting how financialisation shapes their goals. Similarly, in Lake Institute, the marketing director, who used to teach in the school, justified the existence of a separate marketing department, while dissociating herself from "people who take care of that" because, she said, they "come from the business world, they used to sell dairy products [meaning multinationals] or hotel rooms, but *I know*

178 Caroline Bertron

the house, and I know what I am talking about with parents. We don't have this commercial aspect that can frighten parents."

In a nutshell, during interviews, pedagogy was neither defined according to its adequacy in relation to international standards nor through academic excellence. Interviewees stressed the "magical power" of success, not by praising the best students at school but those who are economically successful professionals regardless of academic results. When interviewees talked about international standards of education, they either displayed their distance with multinationals in education and global educational organisations (even if they took part in shaping these networks) or they evoked the transformations in the local structure of the Swiss boarding schools market. In contradistinction, they defined themselves as family businesses.

Family Businesses: The Economic Logic of Education and its Negation

School owners and managers shifted from educational matters to economic matters rather naturally, using the analogy between family business and family education. More precisely, they insisted on an understanding of the family business as a way to present their pedagogy. Telling the story of their "company" can be considered as a strategy to differentiate themselves from the many and bigger international day schools that recruit among international managers living in Switzerland (although boarding schools do not directly compete with most of them). As a way to display their aristocratic distinction, they distinguished their own upper-class clientele from expatriates and mobile managers who attend international day schools (see for instance Wagner, 1998). But the interviewees also perceived the protection of local economic interests and networks of old families of entrepreneurs as threatened by newcomer international day schools. They clearly differentiated marketing and the common image of their schools as a "Swiss product to promote abroad" on a par with international day schools, from the long-standing connections and friendships with families owning boarding schools in Switzerland. They thus positioned themselves in a space of entrepreneurial discourses, and as such, I contend that their institutional images can be analysed as part of the sociology of companies' symbolic production (Boni-Le Goff & Laurens, 2013).

Symbolic Constructions: Equating Family Business with Family Education

The headmaster at Institut Les Alpes praised the irrational economic decisions and "mad projects" that the successive school owners with "entrepreneurial spirit" took over time in order to expand the campus and range of extracurricular activities. This narrative scheme relies on an economic discursive repertoire, as do the Lake Institute and Rivage School interviewees who use family education as another word for family business. School size, individualised education, and preceptorship, taken as remnants of domestic education, were commonly used for defining these schools' main features.

In Lake Institute, the head of marketing extensively relied upon the narrative of the family business. Lake Institute was presented as being handed down from mother to daughter and to sister since the end of the 19th century, changing from a French-speaking boarding school for girls (*finishing school*) to a co-educational English-speaking "international school". This institutional narrative can be understood with regard to the larger transformations of the local space of boarding schools. In the 1960s, as a result of family conflicts, the school buildings, which were then separated into two sections, became two distinct schools. One family branch took the finishing school for young women, while the other school, directed by another family branch, soon became co-educational and adopted internationally recognised curricula. At the end of the 1970s, the latter had acquired an academic reputation abroad. Their headmistresses, two sisters, were left without any successor, so their niece, the daughter of the heads of the all-girls branch, took over the two schools. She "brought back together the school and the family", the marketing director smilingly said, while giving up the finishing programmes that had made the school's reputation for families over the world, and that had contributed to further expanding a model of elite feminine education as European domestic and salon education.

The passage from an institution designed for educating elite young women to their future roles of housewives, to a co-educational English-speaking and self-labelled as "international" school has been turned into an institutional narrative. This gave rise to the institution cultivating two distinct types of legitimacy: a traditional upper-class education in a small-scale family school and a modern international instruction. Academics won over domestic education and "the family" overcame their inner division, at a time when the many girls' and finishing boarding schools in the region shut down, so that Lake Institute is also presented as the one girls' school having succeeded within an entire sector that collapsed.

In Rivage School, the headmaster took over the school after his father. He traced his genealogy from his grandfather to his own children, who were now about to be handed the same role. All the men in the family line have had either degrees in finance and careers as traders and bankers, or careers in psychology and education, before they took over one or several schools in the region, thus building what now resembles a family empire of schools. During the interview, this accumulation of economic and educational resources was performed in such a way as to highlight the interviewee's social position as an entrepreneur and regional leader. He explained:

> I could not have built this school myself were it not for my father and grandfather. I could not gather enough money. If you ever said *business* [said in English] for a school, my grandfather was really furious. Now, all

180 Caroline Bertron

of my colleagues speak about marketing. That is a threat, really. I can tell you that multinationals who take over schools here, they lost their soul; schools become like factories.

(Rivage School interviewee, April 2013)

The interviewee highly praised family continuity throughout the network of schools they run and if business and marketing are forbidden words to him, finance as a profession is omnipresent in his ancestors' careers; in this way, the economic dynasty endures. He equated family business to family education, pitting them against a background of changes in business situations and international curricula, processes from which he excluded himself. Dominated by these processes, the Lake Institute and Rivage School interviewees were both anxious to maintain an economically viable "small school" and put forward alternative narratives that associate past grandeur with local families, thus reinforcing their regional identification.

As mentioned earlier, the interviewees used and banned economic words at will, and I was reminded that it was not my place to equate the school with a company in any way. As I have discussed so far, calling anything "international" also proved a very sensitive area. To the interviewees, the common indisputable basis was "family" and "families", meaning at the same time the dynasty, the family enterprise, "family education" and their faraway clients. "Family" was the ideology that brought together "culture" and "economics", marrying international and local identification.

Family attributes can be analysed as the legal shape of ownership, the basis for social organisation, a sign of longevity and as a metaphor for education (see for instance, Marcus, 1988; Lenoir, 2003). However, as the privileged expression of elite exclusivity and succession (Herzfeld, 2000), "family" is also the marker for the interviewees' belonging to the upper class. As we saw in this section, their presentation as economic actors went through denying the use of economics to define their activity (education), meanwhile featuring the narrative of a successful family enterprise.

Presenting Schools as Local Economic Actors

School representatives performed their social status as entrepreneurs, by claiming their economic impact in the region, a role that they have promoted and been recognised for throughout the 20th century by the public authorities. Interviewees also considered themselves embedded in a local economy of luxury services, working on a par with other economic actors attracting foreign capital. As one interviewee put it:

Many alumni come back and buy an apartment or a cabin, since the 1950s. We have been invited by a group of Germans, they all had a villa in V***.

It was good to know. Students like the region and get attached very quickly. There is a high potential, like with an airline. I've been told that about Swiss Air. If you take an airline as a young man, you remain loyal, as with your bank. This is a real strategy actually. We work very well together; there is nothing to be said about them, airlines and banks. We treat our students, especially the older ones as "private banking". We pamper them and banks know that as well.

(Rivage School interviewee, April 2013)

While visiting the campus and its facilities, I asked the admissions director from Institut Les Alpes if students could come to the sauna and fitness centre whenever they wanted. He pointedly reminded me "We are not a hotel. They need to be accompanied." In Rivage School, after talking about academics for what was maybe a little too long for him, the headmaster switched topics: "We have one part that is about teaching, and you should not forget that, one hotel part." He was talking about how much the management in the school is organised the same way as hotels are.[10] At Lake Institute, as we saw earlier, domestic education is a difficult heritage: the "finishing school" for girls' past practices needed to be turned into formalised curricula. Nevertheless, the Lake Institute interviewee also emphasised the "hotel" and "family atmosphere" aspect, and talked about how the school has long been connected with touristic promoters in the region.

Lake Institute and Rivage School interviewees not only promoted a certain upper-class idea of comfort for sojourners and domestic education; they also pointed out the very high ratio of teachers and staff compared to students, which was almost 1:2, referring to an imagined world of "private lessons" and classes of fewer than 10 students. In Institut Les Alpes, the interviewees were at the same time prone to show the costly and unusual leisure campus facilities and to temper their recreational aspect by affirming academic rules of how students must use them. Drawing upon the memory of a common and local genealogy of boarding schools, hotels, and boarding houses,[11] these discourses can be better understood against the background of the rise of the "industry for foreigners" in the Lake Geneva region at the end of the 19th century (Figure 10.1) (Humair, Tissot & Lapointe Guigoz, 2011; Tissot, 2000).

Politics and Nature: The Symbolic Economy of Territorial Identification

During the interview, the Institut Les Alpes headmaster stated that "A true international school can only exist in Switzerland." Praising Switzerland's state educational model while at the same time restricting its scope of action, he added that "In France they call it *Education Nationale*; this is not accurate. In Switzerland, they call it *Instruction Publique*, and it is closer to reality." Affirming the school's territorial affinity, Rivage School headmaster explained that he had had "offers

FIGURE 10.1 Advertisements for all-girls boarding schools.

Source: Excerpts from *L'éducation en Suisse 1907–1908*, 1907 (4th edition), Paul-Ch. Stroehlin Editeur, Genève, p. 399 and p. 473. Bibliothèque de Genève, BGE Cc497.

from Saudi Arabia to create a school there", that officials invited him and he went, but finally refused: "I said that I could do it, but I would not have the mix of nationalities. If you come here [to Switzerland], you meet the world, and I cannot do that in another country." School owners and managers expressed local territorial identification, conveying both an idea of local cosmopolitanism and an affinity of the local landscape with a political model.

International Relations as a Worldview

Boarding schools' representatives introduced their roles and the historical evolution of their student body in the wider scope of world history and international relations.

> Three days after the collapse of the Berlin wall, we already had the first East Germans and the Russians. I asked them "Who talked to you about our schools?" And they said "Our grandfathers." They said "If you ever have the chance to send your children abroad, send them to Switzerland." These families want a personalised education, they want what we do here.
> (Rivage School interviewee, April 2013)

We once had Israeli parents who did not want their child to share his room with a student of Arabic origin, and that time, we refused. We refused that they change rooms. And at the end of the semester, the students had become real friends. Children accept things.

(Lake Institute interviewee, January 2013)

This view of the world order can be considered as a way for the interviewees to perform self-presentations as witnesses to such events as the fall of the Berlin wall. The Cold War, oil shocks, and exchange rates were also modes of interpretation for explaining changes in their student population. Calling on such great events, combined with their sometimes personal relationships with their protagonists, suggests two lines of interpretation. Firstly, it points to how these social actors produce mystique surrounding their role as the educators of children of the powerful. Secondly, these stories refer to a naturalised representation of the world order (according to which changes in recruits reflect those in the global society) and they refer to an imaginary of Switzerland's place in world history.

Landscape and Politics: The Building of a National Image

In a rather forgotten book entitled *Le Bonheur Suisse* (Swiss happiness), Boltanski (1966) provocatively discussed the construction of a national image and processes of identification asking "Why are the Swiss identifying with the picture that travellers and touristic books draw?"[12] Reversing the question, I examine how the use of the landscape takes part in the production of "*being perceived*" (Bourdieu, 1998). How do these schools' symbolic productions rely on the long-time association between landscape and national character?

Boarding school owners and managers emphasised environmental, sanitary, and aesthetic qualities that tend to convey a national image for foreigners.[13]

Here we are in the countryside [smiling before the castle and recent modern architecture building facing vast areas of green grass]. Before, there were cows in this meadow.

(Institut Les Alpes interviewee, December 2012)

Well-off families started to come to Switzerland to go to clinics and sanatoria, to have fresh air. [...] And they were enchanted by what they found: the beauty of the landscape, the quality of life here, also for people who like skiing and who like nature ... So people started to create schools.

(Lake Institute interviewee, March 2013)

184 Caroline Bertron

> Geographically speaking, you are in an area with a very healthy microclimate for our students, to which we pay much attention. I think it is one of the reasons why they built this building here.
>
> (Rivage School interviewee, April 2013)

This performance of the landscape refers to attributes usually associated with the Swiss national ethos. Interviewees easily presented themselves as observers of world history, seeing from a distance the coming and going of students from this or that nationality, calling attention to Switzerland's political advantages for foreigners and to local aesthetic attributes thus merging into the symbolism for neutrality and internationalism. The social and political discursive uses of the Swiss landscape are part of the *symbolic capital* attached to the schools, the long-time construction that the school representatives turn into a resource to promote their schools. We may then read the interviewee's abovementioned statement "An international school can only be in Switzerland" as the production of a nationally framed image. The production of stories, be they local or bigger narratives, converges in territorial identification. As a system of representation and of cultural categories, this identification is challenging sociological categories of analysis, such as 'international', 'elite', and 'excellence'. How the actors actually use it partakes in a struggle for the symbolic resources that elites may identify with.

Conclusion

From the perspective of painting a global picture of 'elite schools', the main specificity of 'Swiss boarding schools' is first that from their early years, these institutions were designed for foreigners. It follows that their location, along Lake Geneva and in the Alps, made them institutions contributing, from the margins of European systemic centres such as Paris and London, to the formation of a cosmopolitan ethos, which in return can be considered as a prerogative of the European elites (Cousin & Chauvin, 2014).

The space–time symbolic frame that the boarding school 'representatives' use to assert their long-time legitimacy in raising children of the elites expresses their position in a global space of elite schools. This claim reflects a tension between their current dominated economic and symbolic position among 'internationalist' and academic sources of legitimation for 'elite schools' on a global scale on the one side, and on the other side, the idea that glorification of the past and imagination of an aristocratic and territorial genealogy are longstanding resources central to the symbolic logics of elite reproduction.

Through promoting a sense of 'family' belonging and natural international environment, these actors indeed promote cosmopolitanism as a local tradition. These discursive arrangements contribute to keeping these 'Swiss boarding schools' out of the picture of nationally bounded elite schools. But, if they can historically be called 'cosmopolitan schools' because they partly reproduce the conditions of past practices and expectations of domestic education among European elites, they are also schools where the national scale is a major symbolic resource.

Acknowledgements

This PhD research benefits from funding granted by the Ecole Normale Supérieure (Paris) and Université Paris 1 Panthéon-Sorbonne. Thanks to Myrtille Picaud and Carse Remos for their careful readings of earlier versions of this chapter.

Notes

1 All the interview excerpts are translated from French.
2 This change of names actually allows analysing the school's foundation time as a claim for legitimacy. This raises discussion about how school owners seek legitimacy from older times, and the "invention of tradition" (Hobsbawm & Ranger, 1992) that the *Grand Tour* symbolic value gives rise to.
3 The younger students especially often go through intensive programmes of English as a second language.
4 For similar questions around longstanding elite schools using their historical legitimacy and positioning themselves into global dimensions of elite schooling in other areas, see Rizvi's study (2014) of Ripon College in Central India.
5 Johann Heinrich Pestalozzi (1746–1827), a pedagogue from Zürich, is well known, among other Swiss educational reformers of the 18th and 19th centuries, for having implemented his own pedagogy based on the understanding and autonomy of the child, in his institute in Yverdon-les-Bains. He also played a major role in the shaping of public educational systems in Switzerland, especially about educating lower classes. Influenced by Rousseau, he published many writings about his pedagogy that were read and followed abroad during his time, especially in France and Germany.
6 Switzerland is divided into 26 cantons. Each canton has its own educational system and related authorities. Educational coordination at the federal scale is limited and put under the authority of the Federal Department of Economic Affairs, lately renamed in 2013, Federal Department of Economic Affairs, Education and Research.
7 Full references of the essay (published 2012) have been shared with the editors of the volume. They remain confidential in order to preserve the anonymity of the interviewees. This also concurs with the changes of the school names in this paper.
8 Nord Anglia is a British multinational (1972) that was relocated in Hong Kong in the 2000s. It operates over 30 international day schools in 13 countries, notably British International Schools in the USA, Eastern Europe, China, and the Middle East (website, consulted 25 November 2014). Since the 2000s, it has bought out four old private schools in Switzerland. These are now the oldest schools of the group, and two of them are boarding schools.
9 Even though the programmes changed a great deal over the time, such schools as Lake Institute were designed in the first half of the 20th century to teach languages and arts,

186 Caroline Bertron

but also home economics, 'manners', or as documents from the school's archives show "how to become a good hostess".

10 Many managers are indeed recruited from the hotel sector.

11 As historians have suggested (Tissot, 1999), Swiss girls' boarding schools were sometimes indistinct in their structures and advertisements from boarding houses, clinics, and hotels that hosted European and especially British travellers. These businesses altogether contributed to the touristic development along Lake Geneva shores. Moreover, connections in the local economy between boarding schools and the hotel industry have constantly been reasserted throughout the 20th century. At the beginning of the 20th century, boarding school advertising brochures merged school, hotel, home and upper-class cosmopolitanism in their promotions.

12 Translated from French.

13 As historian François Walter put it (2005), the ideological and aesthetic system of the Swiss landscape is a system of production of metaphors.

References

Boltanski, L. (1966). *Le Bonheur Suisse*. Paris: Editions de Minuit.

Boni-Le Goff, I., & Laurens, S. (2013). Les entrepreneurs de la "nouvelle entreprise": Acteurs, pratiques et dispositifs d'une écriture institutionnelle. *Sociétés contemporaines*, 89(1), 5–16.

Bourdieu, P. (1979). *La distinction: Critique sociale du jugement*. Paris: Editions de Minuit.

Bourdieu, P. (1980). Le capital social. *Actes de la Recherche en Sciences Sociales*, 31 (1), 2–3.

Bourdieu, P. [1996] (1998). *Practical reason: On the theory of action*. Stanford: Stanford University Press.

Cousin, B., & Chauvin, S. (2014). Globalizing forms of elite sociability: Varieties of cosmopolitanism in Paris social clubs. *Ethnic and Racial Studies*, 37(12), 2209–2225.

Gaztambide-Fernández, R. (2009). *The best of the best: Becoming elite at an American boarding school*. Cambridge, MA: Harvard University Press.

Herzfeld, M. (2000). Uncanny success: Some closing remarks. In J. Pina-Cabral & A. Pedroso de Lima (Eds.), *Elites: Choice leadership and succession* (pp. 227–236). Oxford, UK: Berg.

Hobsbawm, E., & Ranger, T. O. (1992). *The invention of tradition*. Cambridge: Cambridge University Press.

Hofstetter, R. (2012). La Suisse et l'enseignement aux XIXe-XXe siècles: Le prototype d'une 'fédération d'États enseignants'? *Histoire de l'éducation*, 134, 59–80.

Humair, C., Tissot, L., & Lapointe Guigoz, J. (2011). *Le tourisme suisse et son rayonnement international, XIXe-XXe siècles*. Lausanne: Antipodes.

Kenway, J., & Fahey, J. (2014). Staying ahead of the game: The globalising practices of elite schools. *Globalisation, Societies and Education*, 12(2), 177–195.

Khan, S. R. (2011). *Privilege: The making of an adolescent elite at St. Paul's School*. Princeton: Princeton University Press.

Lenoir, R. (2003). *Généalogie de la morale familiale*. Paris: Seuil/Liber.

Marcus, G. E. (1988). The constructive uses of deconstruction in the ethnographic study of notable American families. *Anthropological Quarterly*, 61(1), 3–16.

Rizvi, F. (2014). Old elite schools, history and the construction of a new imaginary. *Globalisation, Societies and Education*, 12(2), 290–308.

Stroehlin, P.-C. (1907). *L'éducation en Suisse 1097–1908*. Geneva: Paul-Ch. Stroehlin Editeur.

Tissot, L. (1999). Hôtels, pensions, pensionnats et cliniques: Fondements pour une histoire de 'l'industrie des étrangers' à Lausanne. 1850–1920. In B. Studer & L. Tissot (Eds.), *Le passé du présent. Mélanges offerts à André Lasserre*. Lausanne: Payot Lausanne.

Tissot, L. (2000). *Naissance d'une industrie touristique: Les Anglais et la Suisse au XIXème siècle*. Lausanne: Payot Lausanne.

Wagner, A.-C. (1998). *Les nouvelles élites de la mondialisation: Une immigration dorée en France*. Paris: Presses Universitaires de France.

Walter, F. (2005). La montagne alpine: Un dispositif esthétique et idéologique à l'échelle de l'Europe. *Revue d'histoire moderne et contemporaine*, 52(2), 64–87.

11

TOURISM, EDUCATIONAL TRAVEL, AND TRANSNATIONAL CAPITAL

From the Grand Tour to the 'Year Abroad' among Sciences Po-Paris Students

Bertrand Réau

Introduction

Educational trips in the form of the circulation from one university to another, the *peregrinatio academica*, has existed since the Middle Ages and has since been a part of the cultural schooling of scholars and young elites in Europe. In the 17th century, the invention of the Grand Tour changed the functions of educational travel. The Grand Tour completed the education of young male aristocrats. These privileged youths had acquired their cultural exposure from the foreigners who were part of their family circle—a tutor or a servant who provided them with their first exposure to the social world. The Grand Tour further broadened their horizons. This journey lasting several months enabled them not only to meet with scholars and peers, but also to 'slum it' by living in physical conditions less comfortable than normal. Tourism (understood in this chapter as leisurely mobility which participates in socialisation) gets its name from the Grand Tour. This practice, at first reserved for aristocrats, then extended to the bourgeoisie, progressively expands to the middle and lower classes in the second half of the 20th century. In current times, educational travel is not exclusively reserved for an elite. Thus, the "European Region Action Schema for the Mobility of University Students" (ERASMUS) programme offers European students the opportunity to spend a year at a foreign university. Erasmus trips allow students to acquire and mobilise cultural resources such as knowledge of languages, 'openness' to other cultures and dispositions towards mobility. Elite French universities such as Sciences Po go even further by/in incorporating the year abroad in their curriculum: " in a world where borders are increasingly open, the training must be international" (Sciences Po website, 2011).

Sciences Po-Paris Students **189**

In keeping with Pierre Bourdieu's notion of capital, researchers are interested in the social effects of globalisation on the transformations of relations of power. The notions of "international capital" (Wagner & Réau, 2015), "cosmopolitan capital" (Weenink, 2007), or even "transnational capital" (Börjesson & Broady, 2007) allow us to reflect on transnational social spaces, on the relationships between national fields in a globalised world and seek to analyse the reinterpretations of power relationships involved.[1] Different social groups are mobile outside their country of origin and maintain relationships with individuals of other countries. The forms of mobility (labour migration versus authorised travel) and the types of relationships (cooperative versus elitist, private versus professional) vary socially and historically. But, in fact, mobility and an interpersonal network do not constitute, in and of themselves, a capital, which is to say a social relationship, at once a resource and a power struggle, in a field. Following the example of three types of cultural capital identified by Bourdieu (cultural, social and symbolic), international capital can be found in an institutionalised form (MBA degrees for example), an incorporated form (the cosmopolitan dispositions that constitute the mobility and interactions with the international as an integral part of the identity and social aspirations), and an objectivised form (the ownership of economic goods in several countries for example).

Using a summary of historical and sociological work as well as a survey of students from Sciences Po (interviews and analysis of their written reports concerning their study abroad year), this chapter questions the methods of transmission of international capital in its institutionalised and incorporated form. It is more precisely a question of putting into perspective the functions of tourism and educational travel (understood here as a measure explicitly oriented towards the transmission of cosmopolitan dispositions) in the development of a cosmopolitan habitus. The comparison between different types of mobility and of the acquisition of international 'attributes' (such as speaking several languages or travelling in various countries) emphasises the social conditions necessary in order for these 'attributes' to act as capital.

In which conditions, can students accumulate a transnational capital that reinforces their position in the national field of power (Dezalay & Garth, 2010; Kenway & Koh, 2013)? What are the functions of the educational trips and of tourism in the transmission of this capital? After having retraced the role of mobility in the schooling of elites, the analysis of Sciences Po will focus on the mechanisms of the transmission of cosmopolitan dispositions.

Aristocratic Mobilities in Europe (16th to 18th Centuries)

In *Humeurs Vagabondes*, Daniel Roche (2003) undertakes to "measure the effects of modernity, including the formation of modern states, on the mobility of people and their activities" (Pattieu, 2007, p. 111). Often presented as 'immobile' in relation to societies of the 19th century and the Industrial Revolution, the societies of the 16th and 17th centuries contained a different form of functional mobility that was not only limited to the aristocracy. However, successful mobility had to be prepared according to specific codes. For the aristocracy, several forms of mobility were involved in the education of youth. Without using the same means, the *peregrinatio academica* and the Grand Tour aimed at developing common rules for young male aristocrats. Between these two formulas, there were other practices that also contributed to educating young nobles, such as travelling with the army.

The *Peregrinatio Academica*[2]

Despite accounts to the contrary, the universities of the Middle Ages did not see staggering amounts of movement across their academic circles. In contrast, the universities of the Modern era (16th/17th century) witnessed a greater mobility among their students throughout Europe. Around 1400, less than 10% of students appeared to have attended more than one university. Thus, traffic between universities (*peregrinatio academica*) was a limited phenomenon. Students sought out both knowledge and social capital when studying in foreign cities such as Paris. Student mobility also varied by discipline. Students in law and medicine were more active internationally than those in theology and in the arts (with the exception of the Sorbonne and the University of Louvain for theology). Given that only a portion of the *peregrinatio academica* was concluded by obtaining a degree, what were the motives of these movements?

The quality of teaching was far from the sole criterion. Religious reasons or easy access to gaining a title were other motivations for pilgrimages. Mobility between universities facilitated students' exposure to other political and social systems and different lifestyles. It helped to expand family networks. In this sense, this circulation aimed to maintain and develop the international social capital of the family: the visits reinforced the connections between groups through the physical intermediary of an individual. This extra academic exposure derived from 'academic traffic' was regarded as just as important as the knowledge students acquired. For instance, between 1550 and 1600, Felix and Thomas Platter successively undertook their academic journeys in Switzerland, France and the Languedoc. During their travels, they were never truly alone: they belonged to a group of peers that shared the same classes, games, readings, parties and financial assistance. Aside from the scholarly-oriented academic journey (which continued until the 17th century), the Grand Tour provided another goal for the young nobility, to become 'civilly trained' according to the distinction made by the Secretary of State of Queen Elizabeth, Sir William Cecil.

The Grand Tour

Invented by the British aristocracy in the 17th century, the Tour was linked to renewed patterns of mobility. It represented the last step in the training of young male aristocrats. This practice applied to almost all European noblemen. The Tour had to take place at an age when a person was "not too young to be easily corrupted or too old to be able to change habits" (Pattieu, 2007, p. 112). The journey primarily taught a set of life skills that could not be learned at home. The travel books and guides that multiplied throughout the 18th century were both a form of literature in themselves and real guides that defined standards of travel and stabilised forms of travel writing. Knowledge of other countries could also serve as a reflection on the traveller's own society. Wealthy families supplemented their sons' education with a tutor who was expected to take on the role of guide, confidant and friend. Far from the family home, parental authority was relaxed. Pupils had a lot of freedom (Mead, 1914, pp. 103–139). The young Englishmen did not receive adequate preparation for their journey. In general, educational standards were low. If the young man had studied at Oxford or Cambridge, he would have learned the rudiments of Greek and Latin as well as some features of ancient Rome and other cities. However, he would be largely ignorant about the topography, history, government, art, architecture, and social conditions of the countries to be visited.

The journey took place in several specific stages. The first tour stop was the English coast. The second step brought tourists to Paris via Amiens, Chantilly, and the Abbey of Saint-Denis. Paris was a central destination in France and in Europe. While the city did not offer the antiques and art found in Rome and Florence, it was home to many important historical sites and a wide range of cultural and social activities in which tourists could participate. Those on the Grand Tour were not dependent on the recreation of the royal court as was the case in Vienna, Madrid, Berlin, or Dresden or more in the small German, Danish, and Polish courts. Luxury shops, especially for suits, were a major attraction. However, the most common route was one that led to Italy via Lyon and the Rhone Valley. In Italy, these 'grand tourists' took into account the climate, but also special events (like the opera in Reggio, Bologna, and Milan, the carnival in Naples and Venice, or religious ceremonies in Rome). From Milan to Venice, Italy offered a wide range of entertainment. The goal of many tourists was to reach Rome as a final destination. The city's economy depended more on tourists than that of Paris, notably through sale of paintings and antiques. Most roads in Europe were in poor condition and poorly managed, making access to many places difficult. For the most part, the young aristocrats chose the same roads (which did not necessarily mean they had the same experiences). They found a large variety of lodgings available to them (Black, 2003, pp. 14–76).

Grand tourists preferred big cities for several reasons: there could be found the greatest diversity of social and cultural activities, the largest variety of culinary experiences, standards of comfort best suited to their tastes, but also banks for withdrawing money. The young men travelled from one destination to another meeting men of state, and secretaries of embassies, attending the courts and churches, visiting the monuments, libraries, colleges, scholars, and processions, and even going to executions. While social pleasures often outweighed the rigours of scientific study, the young aristocrats retained elements of a pre-planned itinerary (Roche, 2003, p. 691). During their journey, they had to learn either French or Italian. French, in particular, represented an essential part of privileged young men's training. With knowledge of the French language, they could travel across France, Holland, Germany, Italy, Russia, and Sweden. In practice, the English rarely spoke French and often stayed together. Most had no other goal than to enjoy themselves in capitals like Paris, Berlin, Turin, Florence, and Rome. Finding visits to monuments boring, they played cards, walked through the countryside, and people watched. The moralists of the time denounced such behaviour as a kind of disease. Places to visit were largely predetermined before the trip. The Grand Tour was also an opportunity to live outside the constraints of one's family. Sociability with peers, dating, gambling, and alcohol were an integral part of socialisation of these young, healthy and poorly supervised men who found many opportunities for sexual adventures and/or love. However, very few explicitly wrote about this in their correspondence. Similarly, public opinion was largely hostile towards these adventures, for moral reasons as well as for practical reasons; many were concerned about the importation of venereal diseases into Britain. One major risk for families was a misalliance: if the young aristocrat eloped with a romantic conquest from a lower social class, it could ruin his family's hopes and the entire economy of marriage. In reality, most relationships were limited to one-night stands and many young aristocrats resorted to prostitution.

Gradually, as the 18th century progressed, increasing numbers of young men from the wealthy middle classes began participating in the Grand Tour, copying the vices and follies of young aristocrats, flaunting their wealth, and trying to become gentlemen. William Edward Mead defended the idea that by becoming a fashionable and 'conventional' practice in addition to a symbol of social status, the Tour had lost its educational function (Mead, 1914). Yet, it would be an oversimplification to say that the Grand Tour evolved linearly from an educational endeavour to a leisure activity. Jean Boutier proposed that diverse forms of travel co-existed (those with educational and mundane purposes) during the same époque (Boutier, 2007).[3] Finally, this system allowed families to avoid potential conflicts with young adults by tolerating abroad what they would not tolerate at home. Travel expenses and excessive indulgence of the young aristocrats remained a 'lesser evil' than their impatience in claiming political power and wealth within the family. In the end, "the Grand Tour was a prerequisite of social and cultural status bringing together diverse political and educational needs: it helped to train the statesman to be a man of the world, one with certain sensibilities" (Roche, 2003, pp. 694–695).

The *peregrinatio academica* and the Grand Tour were two forms of educational travel. Despite profound changes in the social structure since the late 18th century, the education of elites through travel continues today. The quality of educational travel remains a constant concern amongst teachers and thinkers who reflect upon the education of elites. However, with the spread of the practice of tourism and educational travel among the middle classes, how can education through travel continue to be socially distinctive? With the spread of international attributes, under what conditions do the different forms of travel participate in enhancing the transnational capital of upper classes (and thus, the reproduction of the dominant positions)? This can be explored through an examination of the practices of students from Sciences Po in the early 2000s.

Sciences Po: From the Opening to the International Integration

By the mid-1990s, the French elite school Sciences Po[4] had strengthened its worldwide network. With approximately 13,000 students, and a network of 410 universities worldwide, 14 taught languages, the *Institut d'Etudes Politiques de Paris* had mandated since 2000/2001 that the third year be spent abroad for internship training or university studies. Sciences Po also established specialised curricula (for example East European, Franco-German, Middle Eastern, Mediterranean, Latin American, Spanish, Portuguese, and Asian studies). "These programmes of studies aim to accommodate the same number of French and international students for a multilingual and comparative education. They aim to develop a generation of students familiar with the issues in different countries and different systems who are able to work in and with different cultures." (Sciences Po website, 2011). Sciences Po has introduced the possibility of enrolling in double degree programmes with prestigious universities (London School of Economics, for example). Among the 410 partner universities, a significant number belong to the top 100 Academic World Ranking of Shanghai (for instance, Berkeley, Columbia, Oxford). Sciences Po has agreements with prestigious universities on each continent. In 2002, 75% of students at Sciences Po found that "the internationalisation in the reform of Sciences Po" is "a very good thing". A large majority of students belong to the upper classes. In 2002, 32.5% had fathers who were senior executives, 19.1% had fathers who were professionals, and 15% of the students' fathers were teachers; 27.3% of mothers were teachers, 14.8% were employees or workers, and 14.5%, professionals. Of 100 students, 49 had a father and a mother who graduated with more than two years of education at the university or in an equivalent elite university (as Sciences Po). For 84% of students, their parents finance their studies (Catzaras et al., 2004).

International Attributes and Transnational Capital

Students must submit a report at the end of their time abroad. It is usually composed of three parts: one concerns the administrative steps taken to go to the university in question, the second deals with the administrative processes and course choices, the third provides practical advice and commentary about entertainment and travel. It is hardly surprising that an analysis of 239 student reports reflects the importance given to teaching, quality of life, and different forms of sociability. Sciences Po students are more often involved in clubs, and more 'politicised' than other students from universities (Catzaras et al., 2004); they also have regular cultural practices and celebrations (visits, outings with friends). Travel stories often occupy a large share of the reports: making explicit the expectations of study abroad. Given the social background of these students, we can assume that they have already had many opportunities to travel (Cousin & Réau, 2009). Similarly, they are more likely than other students to not live with their parents during their studies, thus experiencing a degree of autonomy.

Therefore, we find characteristics similar to those of Erasmus students: a more privileged social background, socialisation before travel, a first experience of independence, regular cultural leisure, and a diverse and quality education. But the difference between the Erasmus programme and that of Sciences Po is found in Sciences Po's agreements with prestigious universities and the diversity of universities offered for student exchange.[5] Still, the prestige and the variety of agreements offered at Sciences Po clearly distinguish them from other French university students. Thus, we can establish a scale of elite schools such as Sciences Po that offer agreements with various prestigious universities around the world— particularly in the USA—to universities in the provinces which only have agreements with less prestigious British and European universities. But even more importantly, this academic scale also intersects with the social stratification of the recruitment of students; students with parents belonging to upper middle classes and upper classes living outside of Paris compared to those with parents belonging to the Parisian bourgeoisie. On this scale, the functions of living abroad may be the same, but the results differ. As for the social benefits of a degree, the social, cultural, economic and family capital largely determine what students gain from their experiences abroad. Students from more modest backgrounds (Ballatore, 2007) than those of Sciences Po and that use the Erasmus programme can accumulate an institutionalised form of transnational capital (a degree), but on the other hand, they do not necessarily have cosmopolitan dispositions fitting with these practices (Réau, 2009). Similarly most often they do not have economic assets abroad at their disposal. Science Po students' year abroad fits into a set of international educational measures (specialised campuses, time spent with many foreign students in Paris, etc.) and dispositions towards the international passed down through their families (trips abroad, multilingualism, etc.). How does this experience abroad reinforce these dispositions and thus participate in enriching students' transnational capital?

Lifestyles and Socialisation During the Year Abroad

The lifestyle and social experience abroad of Sciences Po students is not characterised by excessive alcoholic consumption and partying as may be the case for students from prestigious universities in England (and perhaps students from schools like Central or ESSEC in France) (Masse, 2002). Rather, it appears that

Sciences Po-Paris Students **195**

there is a relative continuity between their lifestyles, their aspirations, their work and their 'ordinary' cultural practices. Studying abroad allows for the accumulation of transnational capital and personal development, including travelling, living with students of different nationalities, academic learning, and adaptation to different lifestyles. Even if their social origins were similar, meeting international students and brief encounters with various locals require the capacity for more openness and adaptation than in their own country. These 'soft' constraints imposed upon them are important and encourage their capacity to adapt. The dichotomy between rhetoric and practice is less obvious when one considers the differences between living at home and living abroad. These experiences ensure that the members of upper classes have an 'international' outlook. Education through travel is characterised by the relationship between 'ordinary' everyday practices and 'extraordinary' practices encountered abroad. The students are well supported by their host institutions. Additionally, their familiarity with travelling abroad provides a certain amount of know-how. However, their usual support network cannot be as easily accessed abroad as at home. They can count on moral and financial support from their family and friends, but this assistance is mostly 'help at a distance', although some may have relatives and friends to help them in their new host country. In this sense, they have to rebuild a network of friends locally.

This is largely made up of students of the same nationality or other nationalities, but not necessarily students of the host country (and to a lesser extent people from the local population). They constitute a group of international students with similar social backgrounds (Wagner, 2008). With this group, they gather for parties, and other leisure activities, which often includes exploring the host country. It is this temporary community that shapes the values of students abroad. Links can be maintained following the year abroad and provide networks such as sources of accommodation for future travels. Therefore, it is likely to be a good way to increase their international social capital. Support from parents and staff of the student travel programmes facilitates the lives of student travellers as opposed to working-class immigrants who have to manage their own administrative tasks such as visa and health insurance applications, opening bank accounts, and finding accommodations. However, students still have to do minimal tasks on their own even if the difficulty of these tasks is determined by the host country: for example, these tasks are easier in the USA and UK than in China. In their daily lives, they must communicate in a foreign language and adapt to the lifestyles of international students and the university system (courses, teaching methods, etc.). A supervised familiarisation of another culture increases one's ability to be cosmopolitan. Overall, this discovery takes place in a protected environment and with students from similar social backgrounds, which does not mean that students never encounter significant difficulties. Instead, these perhaps moral or financial barriers contribute significantly in shaping a student into 'someone with a worldly personality'. Likewise, meeting with students of other nationalities (from comparable social backgrounds) and occasionally with those that differ from them

196 Bertrand Réau

has the effect of cultural openness expected from such an encounter. As in certain leisure practices (e.g., bourgeois holiday clubs such as Club Med; Réau, 2011), the punctual attendance of other social groups and other nationalities provides coping skills useful to all those who aspire to one day occupy leadership positions. For those who have lived abroad, working knowledge of the elements of daily life in a foreign country differentiates their experience from that of people who have lived a sedentary or touristic lifestyle. Presumably, this difference is not so much a result of cultural knowledge of famous tourist places, but rather on the know-hows and 'insider tips' of those who experience living abroad. In this regard, the systematic review of the 'tips' in the reports of visits by students from Sciences Po is not trivial: there is a desire to maintain and share a form of practical knowledge gained through cultural integration practice during their time living abroad which is very different from the 'scholarly culture'. Through social trajectories and the representations of abroad by the students at Sciences Po (Box 11.1), one can identify the social conditions of the acquisition of transnational capital.

BOX 11.1 Trajectories of students from Sciences Po

MOHAMMED, MOROCCO, 22 YEARS OLD, FOURTH YEAR AT SCIENCES PO, LATIN AMERICAN STUDIES MAJOR WITH A MINOR IN FINANCE

His father is a banker and his mother works at Royal Air Morocco. After completing his studies at the highly selective French school in Casablanca, Mohammed passed the competitive entrance exam for business schools. He entered as a second year student at Sciences Po (major in Latin American studies). The members of his family speak Arabic, French and Spanish every day during his childhood. His sister attends an elite Spanish school in Casablanca. Mohammed has travelled extensively with his family and friends (visiting more than 20 countries, including Morocco), receiving free airline tickets. Several of his cousins and uncles live in the USA and Canada thus facilitating travel to these countries. He has a cousin at the Hautes Etudes Commerciales (the top elite Business School in France). He does not particularly wish to specialise in finance (despite his finance minor). The atmosphere of business schools, where "there is only partying and drinking", did not suit him and is the reason he changed to Sciences Po. Next year, he will enrol in a double degree programme at Bocconi University in Milan majoring in economics. For his year abroad, he has chosen Buenos Aires as the destination. Argentina, being a very European Latin American country, represents an excellent place to study. He found an apartment to share with two other roommates in Buenos Aires. One of them is a drug addict, which made the first six months difficult for him. At the university, he followed the advice given to him by students from Sciences Po to take courses that are not offered at Sciences Po such as psychology and art history. In addition to having extensive social and administrative support, foreign students like him also have more free time than local students. With only 12 hours of class per week instead of 24 at Sciences Po, academic work in Buenos Aires is rather light for him. He also travels around Argentina. He is able to easily arrange transportation and accommodation during his journey. He has never used travel agency services. The funding of his travels is not a problem. The cost of living in Buenos Aires is much less than in France, which allows him to visit the South American continent. In addition, he meets other students from Sciences Po in Brazil. His choice of Latin America is not part of a professional plan. It leaves all the doors open, figuratively speaking. He knows he can always work in the Moroccan Ministry of Foreign Affairs if he wishes to do so, after Sciences Po. He is planning to take up another Masters in economic anthropology: he wants to study economic development in different cultural areas. He has developed a cosmopolitan outlook and hopes to absorb the elements of various cultures during his career.

CAMILLE, 22 YEARS OLD, FOURTH YEAR AT SCIENCES PO, MAJOR IN FINANCE

With a father who is a project manager/business manager at France Télécom and a mother who is a primary school teacher, she does not benefit from the international network of some of the other students from more privileged backgrounds. She thus aspires all the more to upward mobility and to a symbolic recognition of her status. After completing a Baccalauréat Scientifique in a Parisian suburb and a year at a private business preparatory school, Camille entered Sciences Po as a second year student. Professionally, she hesitates between finance and consulting. During her year abroad, she chose to go to the University of Pennsylvania in Philadelphia (USA) (Wharton, "the best undergraduate business school"), where she discovered finance. She also took language and theology classes. All of her choices concern schools in the USA. Her mother is Mauritian. They have therefore been to the Republic of Mauritius and Reunion Island. They have also travelled to Germany, Spain, Great Britain and France. They have also been to Mexico during an all-inclusive trip (flight + hotel). They do not do organised tours. She has been to Italy and Spain with her boyfriend. She has also gone to Great Britain twice and the USA once to study English. During her stay in the USA, she travelled around, meeting up with students from Sciences Po in

New York and California as well as Montreal, Canada. She took out a loan to pay the 42,000 dollars in school fees. Her mother has travelled a lot. She has family in Australia and in South Africa that she has never seen.

ANNE, 22 YEARS OLD, FOURTH YEAR AT SCIENCES PO, JOURNALISM MAJOR

After a Baccalauréat in economics at Henri IV, Anne passed the competitive Sciences Po entry exam as early as her second year and she appreciates having more classes in the social sciences. Passionate about cinema, for her year abroad she looks for a structure that corresponds to her artistic ambitions. First she thinks about Prague, India and Australia. Eventually she discovers the system of American liberal arts colleges, which grant much importance to the personal development of each student within structures of modest size. As a result, she only mentions liberal arts colleges in her choices: she does not get her first choice. Assigned to Oberlin College in Ohio, she has classes in "cinema studies" and finds the "social and cultural" diversity that she was looking for in this type of establishment. She went to Venezuela when she was six years old. Otherwise, every year with her family she travelled for two weeks with the tour operator *Terres d'aventure*. Her father is a doctor, professor and researcher at the Université Paris V. Her mother worked in the marketing department at Hachette. She currently works for an association for the protection of children. One of her brothers went to the Université de Dauphine and then Sciences Po. He lives in Peru. Her other brother continued his studies at an American university in Illinois after going to Polytechnique. After having worked in Chicago he wishes to return to France. With *Terres d'aventure* they went backpacking in several countries. For her part, Anne has travelled alone in Greece, Germany, Slovakia and Great Britain. She goes to Germany every year to see a pen pal who lives near Cologne. In Greece, she went to babysit for a family that she met with her parents. She has also participated in an international Habitat for Humanity type programme. The first two months of her year in the USA were a little difficult emotionally. She was mostly with the other "international" students. She joined a vegetarian co-op (80 students who organise daily lunches and dinners together). Gradually she began to attend parties that take place off-campus in students' houses. She made a film for a microcredit fund in Nicaragua. Five students were selected for this project for a three-week trip: a week of travel, a week of work for the micro-credit organisation ("a lot of responsibility"), a week with a family.

Unlike upwardly mobile middle-class students or fractions of classes less endowed with capital, these students accumulate a high volume of economic, cultural, social, and more or less transnational capital. Each benefits from regular and varied previous tourist experiences, but also from club activities and/or professional activities abroad; they speak several languages, most often learned in a multilingual familial context and sometimes have lived abroad. These elements participate in the construction of a cosmopolitan habitus through the internalisation of dispositions towards mobility, of a familiarity with the world. In this context, the year abroad follows in the steps of previous practices. It is the length of the experience and its modalities/methods that contribute to reinforcing these cosmopolitan dispositions. The Sciences Po degree represents an institutionalised form of transnational capital. Finally, certain interviews mention the possession of economic assets abroad, which constitutes the objectivised form of this capital. The three types of transnational capital are present among these students. Nevertheless, we observe variations depending upon gender and the class to which their parents belong. Thus, the young women had experiences in community-based organisations and as baby-sitters abroad, while the man worked in companies. Likewise, Camille's professional aspirations and international attributes differ from those of Mohammed. The former, better endowed with economic capital than cultural capital, invested in a costly American education that she hopes to make profitable in the world of finance and consulting. As for Mohammed, he gives himself the time to think about his professional future and sees himself continuing his studies in anthropology. One also finds variations in the uses of the international experiences depending on the original endowments of capital, which determine the modalities of acquisition of institutionalised, incorporated and objectivised forms of transnational capital.

Conclusion

Without being assured of a certain set of results, the upper classes practised the common adage: "Travel broadens the mind." But travel alone is not enough. The travel environment determines the end result, which is to gain some specific abilities. The acquisition of these abilities is subject to a certain set of conditions. Unlike working-class immigration, which embodies "the illusion of a temporary stay" (Sayad, 1999) the upper-class travellers have the assurance of return to their home country: financial and social class of the family is a prerequisite for going abroad. Those who travel for educational purposes are in a position of 'double presence'; they are supported and waited for at home, but simultaneously hosted and supervised abroad. They are never abandoned, are able to find familiar people and landmarks on their journey and, most importantly, have the insurance to return home. Thus they have nothing to lose; if the journey fails they can always return home. Without the pressure to succeed, they are more open to learning, which makes it easier for them to adapt to other cultural contexts (and to some extent other social contexts). Thus, social backgrounds are central in explaining what people can gain from living abroad. The volume and the structure of the initial capital to a great extent determine the possibility of transforming international attributes into transnational capital: this clearly differentiates the students from Sciences Po from the Erasmus students. The transnational capital represents rather a multiplier of existing economic and social capital (Wagner, 2008).

Acknowledgement

I would like to thank Eileen Chen and Madeline Bedecarre for editing this text.

Notes

1 For a summary of these notions, see Wagner and Réau (2015).
2 All quotations and data in the following two paragraphs come from Roche (2003, pp. 569–734).
3 Norbert Elias advanced the idea that the decline of physical violence and the change of sensitivity to violence were partially responsible for the emergence of these pacified practices of distinction. It was no longer important to show one's physical strength, but rather one's cultured or civilised side and the social prestige associated with travel and high-society conversations (Elias, 1976; Dunning & Elias, 1986).
4 In France, a system of 'Grandes écoles' exists alongside universities. These 'Grandes écoles' (Sciences Po-Paris, Polytechnique, ENA, HEC, etc.) educate children predominately from the upper classes and therefore participate in the social reproduction of positions of power. Sciences Po represents, in this sense, a school of power, which produces many political leaders (like François Hollande), economic leaders and senior civil servants. See Bourdieu (1996).
5 For instance, Berkeley (USA), Cambridge (UK), Columbia (USA), Freie Universität Berlin (Germany), Fudan (China), Keio (Japan), London School of Economics (UK).

References

Ballatore, M. (2007). L'expérience de mobilité des étudiants ERAMUS: les usages inégalitaires d'un programme «d'échange». Une comparaison Angleterre/France/Italie. Thèse de doctorat en sociologie, Université Aix-Marseille 1 et dell'Università degli studi di Torino.
Black, J. (2003). *The British abroad: The grand tour in the eighteenth century*. Stroud, UK: Sutton Publishing.
Börjesson, M., & Broady, D. (2007). Nouvelles stratégies dans le marché transnational de l'enseignement supérieur. In A. Kouvouama, A. Gueye, A. Piriou & A.-C. Wagner (Eds.), *Figures croisées d'intellectuels: Trajectoires, modes d'action, productions* (pp. 387–397). Paris: Karthala.

Bourdieu, P. (1996). *State nobility: Elite schools in the field of power*. Stanford, CA: Stanford University Press.

Boutier, J. (2007). Le Grand Tour: une pratique d'éducation des noblesses européennes (XVIe-XVIIe siècles). In *Le voyage à l'époque moderne*, Bulletin de l'Association des Historiens modernistes des Universités, 27 (pp. 7–21). Paris: Presses de l'Université de Paris-Sorbonne.

Catzaras, N., Chiche, J., Maurer, S., Tiberj , V., & Muxel, A. (2004). *Les étudiants de Sciences po: leurs idées, leurs valeurs, leurs cultures politiques*. Paris: Presses de Sciences Po.

Cousin, S., & Réau, B. (2009). *Sociologie du tourisme*. Paris: La Découverte.

Dezalay, Y., & Garth, B. (2010). *Asian legals revival: Lawyers in the shadows of empire*. Chicago, IL: University of Chicago Press.

Dunning, É., & Elias, N. (1986). *The quest for excitement: Sport and leisure in the civilizing process*. Oxford, UK: Basil Blackwell.

Elias, N. (1976). *La dynamique de l'Occident*. Paris: Calmann-Lévy.

Kenway, J., & Koh, A. (2013). The elite school as a 'cognitive machine' and 'social paradise'?: Developing transnational capitals for the national 'field of power'. In T. Bennett, J. Frow, G. Hage, & G. Noble (Eds.), Working with Bourdieu: Antipodean Cultural Fields. *Journal of Sociology* (Special Issue), 49(2–3), 272–290.

Masse, B. (2002). Rites scolaires et rites festifs: les «manières de boire» dans les Grandes écoles. *Sociétés Contemporaines*, 47, 101–129.

Mead, W. E. (1914). *The grand tour in the eighteenth century*. Cambridge: The Riverside Press.

Pattieu, S. (2007). À propos de Daniel Roche, *Huàeurs vagabondes. De la circulation des hommes et de l'utilité des voyages*, Paris, Fayard, 2003. *Actes de la recherche en sciences sociales*, 170, 110–115.

Réau, B. (2009). Voyages et jeunesse «favorisée»: Usages éducatifs de la mobilité. *Agora*, 53(3), 73–84.

Réau, B. (2011). *Les Français et les vacances: Sociologie des pratiques et offres de loisirs*. Paris: Editions CNRS.

Roche, D. (2003). *Humeurs vagabondes: De la circulation des hommes et de l'utilité des voyages*. Paris: Fayard.

Sayad, A. (1999). *La double absence: Des illusions de l'émigré aux souffrances de l'immigré*. Paris: Seuil.

Wagner, A.-C. (2008). *Les classes sociales dans la mondialisation*. Repères, Paris: La Découverte.

Wagner, A.-C., & Réau, B. (2015). Le capital international: un outil d'analyse de la reconfiguration des rapports de domination. In J. Siméant, B. Réau, S. Roux, R. Lecler, A.-C., Wagner & C. Rabot (Eds.), *Enquêtes globales en sciences sociales* (pp. 33–46). Paris Éditions CNRS.

Weenink, D. (2007). Cosmopolitan and established resources of power in the education arena. *International Sociology*, 22, 492–516.

12

SCHOOLS AND FAMILIES

School Choice and Formation of Elites in Present-Day Argentina

Sandra Ziegler

Introduction

Examining the relationship between education and elites is a relatively new research area in Argentina. In the sociology of education this issue has become widespread and is linked to an interest in understanding how the more relevant groups in society are comprised (Howard & Gaztambide-Fernández, 2010; Khan, 2011; Kenway, Fahey & Koh, 2013; Maxwell & Aggleton, 2013 and others). Existing literature looks to explain the dynamics of inequality and the prevalence of poverty by focusing on disadvantaged groups; however, studies lack an approach centred on the groups that concentrate conditions of privilege. We agree with Howard and Gaztambide-Fernández (2010, p. 1) when they argue that "the lack of attention to privileged groups is not simply a gap in the existing research but a conceptual link missing in our understanding of inequality".

The persistence of inequality carries a distinct dimension in present-day Argentina. In contemporary Argentina, a social order restructuration is characterised by two important transformations: a period marked by new capital accumulation and concentration, and changes in integration and exclusion patterns. Such transformations lead to a rise in inequality characterised by high poverty and marginalisation rates. In fact, studies conducted suggest that a widening of the social gap is due to a shift away from a social composition with higher integration and cohesion levels (Svampa, 2005, 2001; Kessler, 2002; among others). This phenomenon, characterised as 'social fragmentation', drives our inquiry into how such dynamics manifest in the educational field. I argue that the structural changes modifying the social landscape of our country since the 1990s have also found their expression in the educational arena. Without necessarily establishing a direct relationship between both spheres, I believe that the educational field has undergone unprecedented transformations. Indeed, several studies reveal connections between social fragmentation phenomena and differentiation processes shaping educational institutions (Tiramonti, 2004; Kessler, 2002, 2014; Veleda, 2012; Tiramonti & Ziegler, 2008).

In Argentina, studies examining poverty conditions and their impact on the educational system emerged to explain these complex processes of impoverishment and social polarisation. In this context devoting resources to examining the education of the most privileged and advantageous groups would seem unjustifiable. However, from my point of view, inquiring into elite schooling is necessary for understanding the complexities of an interdependent society. Tilly (2000) highlights that inequality is a relational process; thus, in order to understand inequality in today's educational system it is fundamental to examine the dynamics of processes that tend to concentrate both advantageous and disadvantageous conditions. This follows Stich and Colyar (2013), who adopted a relational thinking model—as formulated by Bourdieu—and represents an approach that potentially enriches class and elite studies.

This chapter discusses the school selection process in Argentina, a country in which no institutionalised mechanisms of elite school selection exist, as opposed to other countries such as France or Brazil (Tiramonti & Ziegler, 2008; Ziegler & Gessaghi, 2012; Heredia, 2012). This investigation examines the role that school choice plays in guaranteeing socialisation with elite peers and, above all, acquiring the social and cultural capital necessary to informally compete for prestigious and powerful positions. Thus, one objective of this chapter is to understand how individuals who seek to have their children socialised in schools aimed at training youths to occupy the highest social, cultural, and/or economic positions inform themselves. Additionally, examined throughout is the role schooling plays for these groups, the general expectations that families hold concerning school, and finally, their specific expectations regarding future power positions.

This chapter presents results from a study conducted in secondary schools[1] located in Buenos Aires City and the northern part of the Conurbano Bonaerense, a suburban area surrounding Buenos Aires City.[2] Both are located in Buenos Aires, the largest province in the country with respect to both territory and population. The latter is an urban area with a high concentration of high-income individuals. The Conurbano Bonaerense is densely populated, housing more than 60% of Buenos Aires Province's inhabitants. According to the 2010 national census this region is home to nearly 25% of the national population and 24.6% of the student population. On the other hand, Buenos Aires City is one of the most affluent cities nationally. Although it holds only 7.2% of the total population, this is the city where political, cultural and economic power concentrate. Compared to Buenos Aires City, only 6.4% of the total national student population attends school here.

Furthermore, in Argentina education for the elite is offered primarily at private institutions. If we analyse students attending private schools relative to the total school population, the highest rates of privatisation are found in the most affluent and central conglomerates. During the late 2000s, the proportion of students attending private schools reached 48% in Buenos Aires City, and 30.5% in Buenos Aires Province, as opposed to a national average of 25%. In Buenos Aires Province, privatisation levels were higher in the more affluent municipalities. For example, Vicente López (62%) and San Isidro (58%) are the municipalities in Buenos Aires Province with the highest percentage of Basic Education (1st through 9th grade) students attending private institutions (Veleda, 2012). In addition to geographic concentration, the socio-economic composition of private enrolment leads to increased association with affluent groups. In 2011, 57% of secondary students pertaining to households in the top quintile of the Metropolitan Area (Buenos Aires City and suburban areas) attended private schools.[3] Public free secondary education oriented towards elite formation is provided only by a small group of schools that form part of a university.

In summary, in Argentina, elite formation at the secondary educational level tends to be concentrated in the most affluent urban areas, largely in private schools. Access to these schools is not granted initially on the basis of student academic competence. Rather, families' economic possibilities and a legitimisation criteria based on the schools they attended, the surnames of the families, the job positions and a personal interview (with the adults) are deciding factors. In the case of public university affiliated secondary schools oriented towards elite formation, access is granted according to a meritocratic criterion whereby applicants sit a difficult admission exam. These schools, however, do not charge fees.

This chapter integrates results from a qualitative study conducted in three secondary schools aimed at elite formation, located in the City and the Province of Buenos Aires. The investigation includes findings from in-depth interviews with three headmasters, 20 parents and 24 students, along with observations at relevant schools, and an analysis of secondary documents. Demographic information regarding students' families was collected during interviews and in the schools. These data made it possible to analyse school selection and examine this relationship with the groups that constitute the local elite.

The schools define themselves as "traditional" institutions "of academic excellence". The schools examined in this chapter include two private schools: one religious and the other secular. A public school was also selected because of its admission selection procedures and history of educating national leaders. This attests to its character as an institution that has formed elite groups, both political and intellectual. This study examines institutions explicitly designed to train their students to occupy powerful and privileged positions. Privileged positions are those that offer membership in economically, socially, and culturally advantaged groups. This chapter discusses the reasons informing parents' decisions to choose a particular school, examining the objectives motivating those families to make such choices.

Families and Traditions Underpinning School Choice

Scholars examining school choice have incorporated various approaches, in Argentina and in other countries. Some studies driven by policy debates aimed at "free educational choice" have produced literature that challenges the foundations of the alleged free rational choice: among them, important contributions from England (Whitty, Power & Halpin, 1998; Ball, 2003; Crozier et al., 2008), the USA (Weis, Cipollone & Jenkins, 2014), Australia (Windle, 2009), and France (van Zantén, 2009). Several commonalities are present in these studies, including an explanation of the distinct rationalities that converge when actors choose a school, differing interests across social classes and subclasses, and the relationship between making choices with the political, urban, and historical context where they are made. Additionally, these studies debate the assumption that choices take place independently from historical and social conditions, thus it is not the individual manifestation of human attributes that account for the dynamics present in the 'school market' sphere.

A number of studies conducted in recent years reveal the active role played by upper-middle- and upper-class groups regarding the school selection process. Jay (2002) in Switzerland, Aguiar (2012) in Belo Horizonte, Brazil, and Waters (2007) and Kenway et al. (2013) examined families in Hong Kong who send their children to Canada and the UK. This list of studies is not exhaustive; it simply illustrates a societal pattern that goes beyond national borders and reveals the influence that the selective behaviour of families has in shaping educational systems.

Braslavsky (1985) was the first researcher to analyse school choice. This research provided an empirical account of socio-economic segregation processes in the educational system, and their connection to educational circuits merging with and becoming based on a student's social background. Stemming from these initial findings, scholars in the early 2000s introduced a series of studies focused on school choice from a variety of perspectives. Del Cueto (2007), Veleda (2012), Ziegler (2004), and Tiramonti and Ziegler (2008) examined the way in which families play an active role in establishing school segregation by selecting or avoiding certain institutions. Thus, schools contribute to the creation of segregated spaces, and assume a significant role in defining the population they choose to serve.

In the current study, findings from parent interviews suggest that one of the explicit factors influencing them to choose an institution is the guarantee of academic excellence, prestige and a 'traditional education'. In these cases, education works as a strategy for strengthening newly rising social groups or by groups that already hold advantageous positions. In terms of elite social mobility (Pareto, 1967), education is a strategy used to maintain gained positions or to compete for new, advantageous positions. Restricting access to certain institutions provides a means by which elites are able to maintain or gain access to new power positions. Clearly, it is not only educational institutions that generate these

206 Sandra Ziegler

conditions, but also the complex interaction of families and schools that reinforce the privileged situation held by certain social groups.

This study demonstrates that the socialising effects facilitated by these schools are based on the student immersion in an institutional structure whereby they experience the ideological imperative of the school rather intensively. This finding resonates with other international studies (Kahn, 2011; Goodson, Cookson & Persell, 2000). Students who attend elite schools seek immersion into a milieu that exhibits a degree of 'social similarity' (Weber, 1984). According to Weber, educational and cultural experiences may favour (apart from class position) the creation of a sense of belonging to a *status group*, whereby students only mix with their own kind. Socialisation among similar individuals results from these groups choosing an educational universe equivalent to their family universe. In choosing the most exclusive schools, actors are guaranteed a certain level of homogeneity (Pinçon & Pinçon-Charlot, 2002). Ball (2003) points to a similar phenomenon in England where social enclosure characterised the school choice of middle-high grades schools. Developing Parkin's work (1974), Ball explains that *social closure* is the way in which social collectives maximise benefits by restricting access to resources and opportunities to a limited circle.

A recurring aspect in family choices is the adherence to traditions as a foundation for school selections. It is thus important to focus on the role that traditions play among families that tend to choose elite schools in my study.

According to Giddens (2001), tradition does not have ancient origins. It is a creation of European Modernity dating back 200 years. Its linguistic roots are derived from the Latin term *tradere*, meaning to transmit or hand something down to somebody for safekeeping. Giddens acknowledges that traditions play a relevant role in maintaining social order in all societies; however, he cautions that more conservative philosophies conceive and associate tradition with accumulated wisdom, thus limiting the possibilities for transformation. In such contexts, tradition defines a truth and a framework for action that cannot be challenged.

The supremacy of tradition guarantees that the strategies that were successful in consolidating elites will be maintained. Minor transformations aside, it would seem that embracing the familiar makes sense when attempting to attain or maintain the most advantageous positions. Preserving traditions is a valued asset as it helps maintain the status quo. In deeply uncertain contexts characterised by continual transformation, attachment to the familiar seems to be the path by which most local elites tread. Faced with the perception that rules are vulnerable and institutions are weak in terms of supporting authority vis-à-vis the new generations, families and schools double their stakes by offering a strong socialisation framework, resort to the legacy of traditions, and resist deinstitutionalisation processes (Dubet, 2006).

Nevertheless, we argue that when families discuss tradition they allude to distinct aspects, thus reflecting disparities within these groups. Even though it is not possible to assert emphatically that these educational institutions target different sections of local elites,[4] we note that families choosing particular schools exhibit different orientations and group memberships within the social, cultural, and economic space in question. In the case of private schools, there is a mutual reinforcing choice represented by a "two-way selection" mechanism between schools and families (Martínez, Villa & Seoane, 2009. Thus, elite schools exhibit preferences to the families they tend to target, and families restrict their choices to a very limited range of institutions. This dynamic leads to the conclusion that even though all the schools share the same aspiration to form elites, not all elite students could attend the elite school of their choice. Hence, it is the traits that distinguish each institution which clearly map the position it holds within the privileged groups' formation.

Tradition Based on Religious Education

In the first case a group of parents selected an institution in downtown Buenos Aires City, a private school that typically emphasises both academic and religious education. Tradition is linked to the school's prestige and history, as well as to the imprint it has left on many generations of students. A noteworthy number of enrolled students are the children and grandchildren of ex-alumni.

According to the parents I interviewed, this school's teaching system is rigorous, demanding and emphasises discipline. Its rhetoric stresses the importance of Catholic doctrine in education while the ultimate goal is to prepare students to excel in all aspects of university life.

Parental attraction to this institution is based on the desire for an academic education that holds students in a controlled environment where values are upheld. In contrast to families that choose other institutions, it is not the value of knowledge in itself that is prioritised here. Gaining access to knowledge is simply utilitarian, as it is expected to help perform well at the university. Parents are attracted to this institution's academic nature because it imposes upon students the dedication to study, thus guaranteeing that children experience disciplinary patterns. Parents seek an institution with strong control of their children as a way to secure their socialisation in the patterns valued by these families. The following interview excerpt, for example, encapsulates the priority parents placed on values:

> Well, as I have already told you, in my opinion, the most relevant aspect of this school is the education it offers as regards values. It is also important that their values be the same as mine, and well, I believe that my choice of a school is based fundamentally on that.
>
> (father: notary; mother: housewife,
> non-university tertiary education complete)

Faced with potential deinstitutionalisation processes, these families expect that a rigorous system will effectively control their children's behaviour and, essentially,

208 Sandra Ziegler

ingrain a link between studying and discipline in their children. According to parents, the daily routine in this institution is highly demanding and characterised by discipline. Owing to significant transformations in contemporary society, these families attempt to safeguard family and religious traditions and customs in order to guarantee their survival in an evolving world.

The parents in the sample included freelance professionals, business owners, families linked to agricultural activities, as well as to military and church hierarchies. It is common to see children as "heirs" of the economic and professional activities of male parents. The personal success they wish for their children's future is linked to a university career, which is necessary for occupying senior positions and to maintain the position of their birth family. Most mothers are housewives who have limited their work activities to the home even though many of them have a university education. Typically, these are large families in which mothers play a prominent role in controlling their children's activities and socialisation networks.

Even though this is a part-time institution,[5] in contrast to other schools, its academic curriculum requires students to dedicate themselves nearly full time. Mothers of students explicitly mention the fact that they are committed to keeping informed about and accompanying the activities conducted by their children after school hours. Control and socialisation are shared by the school and families; mothers are a key component in the reproduction of certain patterns of socialisation, watching over the maintenance of a controlled environment. Additionally, this group tends to seek a social similarity that will guarantee the socialisation of its members among familiar individuals. The following interview excerpt speaks of the tightly exclusive knitted community that families are connected to:

> Interviewer: What purpose serves the school where you send your children, and what purpose do you think it should serve?

> Mother: I think it allows them to move in the same environment which they are used to, I don't know ... to have friends whose parents I know. To give me the possibility of knowing who they are. Within a sector of society, everybody knows everybody. He has got a lot of schoolmates whose dads are friends of mine or whose moms I have known since I was a kid, then you know what circles he frequents.

> > (father: notary public; mother: housewife, secondary education complete)

Finally, these families chose the school from a restricted list and they do not consider non-religious schools as options for them. To conclude, it is an environment whose central aspect is a religious disciplinary model and an exclusive condition connected to school selection. This school is not chosen because of their academic level but the moral education that it provides (Gessaghi & Méndez, 2015).

Tradition: Between a Prestige Acquired in the Past and Modernisation

In the second case parents chose a school located in the northern area of the Conurbano Bonaerense. This institution is rooted in the Anglo-Saxon immigrant tradition and is characterised by its excellent bilingual education. Tuition fees are relatively high compared to other Argentine private secondary schools.[6] Its student body includes groups that are historically linked to the institution, as well as institution "newcomers". Both parents tend to hold university degrees or certificates, and devote themselves to a range of professional activities (freelance professionals, senior government officers, businesspeople, entertainers).

This is a renowned school whose mission is to provide a high-quality bilingual education with an international orientation. Parents discussed the school's high academic standards and attributed the challenges the students face to strict international exams regulations. The school's curriculum includes two mandatory tracks, including the Argentine national curriculum and the International Baccalaureate Diploma.[7] Parents emphasise that their children are rather privileged given their opportunity to attend this school. They frequently urge their sons and daughters to maximise the experience by "taking advantage of" their passage through the school.

> I always tell my children, not only because of the money we pay to send them here, but I really believe that they enjoy the privilege of attending this school, and that's why I tell them: learn everything, take advantage of everything, because you don't know if maybe it will serve you in the future. My son is now taking art classes. I love it because, maybe, through these classes he will get to know if he wants to do something related to art ... because when you are 13, 14 years old, you don't know what your vocation is, so, the more varied the offerings of the school, the more able the kids will be not to make mistakes when choosing.
>
> (mother: lawyer; father: Degree in business administration)

This institution's educational offering combines an appeal to old traditions with modern updates that allow it to adapt to the demands of internationalised competitive societies. The school mixes age-old traditions with curriculum and organisational changes that are directly linked to new social demands. The institutional adaptations developed are grounded in the desire to provide an education that gives students an opportunity to acquire the abilities necessary to be successful in a globalised society (Resnik, 2008).

Families expect the school to prepare students to not only meet, but also surpass international standards. These families include professionals associated with the most dynamic sectors in the economy, including a significant number of mothers who also work full time in commercial organisations or as independent professionals. Parents in the sample include senior executives of both large and

210 Sandra Ziegler

small corporations, as well as business owners. Parents chose this school during the early stages of their children's lives. Additionally, friends and/or family members also tend to send their children here. An additional characteristic is that almost all families live in close proximity to the school, a situation that leads students to socialise in geographically segregated environments, resulting in reproduction strategies marked by social homogeneity.

These families value the fact that this is a "full-time" school whereby they can delegate all their children's socialisation and control.

> This school has one particular trait, a kid that is devoted to school does not have time to do anything else, because the school occupies him seven days a week, that is, they have to devote all their time to school. My daughter plays two sports, she is on the track and field team, she sings in the school chorus, she is involved in community service. She devotes her Saturdays or Sundays to many of these activities.
>
> (father: agronomical engineer; mother: incomplete university education, Political Science)

Such strong sense of belonging facilitates social capital acquisition, and affords status through apparent elitist consumption (i.e., frequenting high-class places and adhering to the group's standards of behaviour (practising exclusive sports, travelling abroad). Studying in this school places these elite groups in a space that need not be won through academic merit or corroborated through demanding entrance examinations.

Unlike the previous group, this school combines the socialisation process present in the most traditional English schools with a modernised curriculum oriented to critical thinking, self-reflection, multiculturalism, self-learning, and flexibility to achieve a "successful" insertion in globalised competitive societies.

Tradition Underpinned by Public Education

In the third case a group of parents chose a public secondary school founded in the 19th century and belonging to a university. Located in Buenos Aires City, this school boasts a long history of educating national leaders and intellectuals. Through a challenging and rigorous admission exam this institution implements a highly selective process that guarantees outstanding intellectual performance. Thus, the school enrols talented students capable of excelling in spite of a highly demanding curriculum.

Although this is not a bilingual school, its curriculum exhibits several traits shared by the other schools examined. First, it offers a diverse array of extracurricular activities resulting in full-time students. The curriculum is designed to deliver a humanist education combining languages, humanities and sciences and strongly linked to the traditional preparation of intellectual elites.

Elites in Present-Day Argentina **211**

The interviewed families stress that their choice is based on the value they ascribe to public education. They recognise that their children are privileged to have the possibility to attend this school. This sample included male and female parents that are professionals and employees working in different economic sectors. In contrast to the families included in the two previous groups, these parents' economic and social backgrounds are more varied while the neighbourhoods where families reside are more dispersed relative to the school's location. Given the school's highly selective entrance examination, most families stress that passing the exam implied hard, arduous work for their children.

> My daughter attends this school following a suggestion of mine. She has always been very smart, in primary school she stood out as a brilliant student, then, well, she took the entrance examination and finally passed it. That year implied a great effort for all of us, for her and for the rest of the family. She saw her friends enjoying their free time, and she could do nothing but study and study to pass the exams. Being just 12, it was a lot of pressure on her.
>
> (mother: lawyer and sworn translator [French]; father: pharmaceutical sales representative, complete secondary education)

Unlike the students in the previous groups whose entire schooling is in the private sector, this school comprises youths who attended public primary schools, and have now chosen this high school. There is a strong public school rhetoric. One important aspect of this case is that the interviewed parents whose children attended primary public schools have a family educational background with recent access to higher education and more exclusive institutions (i.e., parents had access to secondary and higher education). However, their children are the first generation to attend this particular elite school. Results from questions probing educational paths suggest that the educational level attained by previous generations is lower (as opposed to the other schools included in our sample), and that grandparents held lower status positions such as business, factory, and small enterprise employees. Even though parents maintain that the families associated with the school are basically from the upper-middle and upper classes, the family educational paths indicate the presence of middle-class groups that pursued higher education levels as a means to achieve upward social mobility. Despite this school's explicit intention to form elite groups, its enrolment is more heterogeneous with regard to geographical, social and economic backgrounds than that of its private counterparts. The common trait of all students is their possession of, or their potential to access cultural capital; parents send their students to this school due to its promise to provide the latter.

This school exhibits characteristics that distinguish it from the two previous groups. Parents delegate all aspects of socialisation and education to the school, while the institution restricts families from interfering in any school decisions or

212 Sandra Ziegler

activities. The distance established between families and the school forces these youth to engage in a more independent and self-controlled social life at an earlier stage. In turn, this university school, with a selective academic recruitment system and school socialisation processes, targets students that have already demonstrated an ability to work in a meritocratic milieu.

Conclusions

This study demonstrates the nuances of a school selection process whereby families choose a private or a public school with its own characteristic patterns. The differences between individuals attending private and public schools are similar to the distances between institutions that aim to deliver elite education. Among the families that choose private schools there is a stronger orientation towards homogeneity. Such similarity is achieved through not only spatial but also social segregation. For these families the pursuit of social closure[8] guarantees similarity and ensures reproduction according to group norms and ideals. The selectivity and social homogeneity present in these schools provides families the ideal environment for socialisation and makes it possible to adjust school principles based on families' idiosyncrasies. These groups choose schools that provide a resource allowing them to consolidate positions of privilege and guarantee membership in certain social groups in which the scholastic options place individuals in social spaces that form part of a 'lifestyle'. Thus, membership in a private educational sphere oriented towards elites is explained by the families' economic possibilities, which in turn grant them access to such places. In this case, the privileged groups do not prioritise their decision to provide their children with quality 'scholastic knowledge' via a meritocratic system.

In contrast, the families that chose a public elite school opted for a school that selects students based on a meritocratic system that demands high academic skills and knowledge. This school receives students from more diverse social backgrounds and gaining access to this prestigious institution represents a crowning moment for upper-middle-class groups competing for educational resources. Subsequently, the social position of a family is enhanced upon a child's entrance. In comparison to the other elite families, in these cases the 'newcomers' deploy *usurpatory strategies* (van Zanten, 2003) in connection with their children's access to schooling. One important finding to highlight is the tendency for upper-middle-class groups to isolate themselves in the more exclusive university schools instead of their traditional inclination to control the public education system.

The end result of these school selection dynamics is the increase of educational fragmentation, particularly in urban areas where institutional variation is on the rise. The opportunity to attend schools with distinct characteristics diversifies families' aspirations while placing elite members in environments that guarantee separation from lower social classes and social interaction with elite peers.

Scholars have examined school choice in several national contexts; however, the school selection process manifests distinctly in Argentina. No formal, institutionalised, elite selection patterns are evident as the institutional mechanisms and career paths leading to such positions tend to be heterogeneous.

This chapter identifies two co-existing possibilities leading to elite education choice in Argentina. The first is a free public high school based on a meritocratic system and administered by a university. The second are expensive private schools based on the possession of economic resources and located in geographically segregated areas, where the youth's education is increasingly dependent upon the wealth and wishes of parents, rather than the ability and efforts ruled by a meritocratic system.

Gessaghi and Méndez (2015, p. 52) argue that "the study of different elite fractions highlights the work performed by educational institutions not only to reproduce elites but also to produce them. The way in which the different schools described interact with the individuals (and families) that attend them, documents the diversity of the legitimisation criteria for access to elite positions in contemporary societies."

Analysing school choice processes in Argentina reveals what is at stake when opting for an educational institution in a society where access to, and maintenance and legitimation of elite positions are not institutionalised. Thus, families must develop active strategies in order to arrive at and maintain elite positions. Such lack of formality plus the competition to access power and privilege positions explains why families invest in schools according to their preferences, and socio-cultural and economic profiles. They choose schools based on their aspirations, as well as the strategies and opportunities they believe will grant their children advantaged positions. These choices make it possible to acquire social capital and maintain a certain lifestyle while building elite selection mechanisms into a social context where such patterns are vague and less institutionalised and subjects have to combine symbolic and material resources in order to gain access to the elite world.

Acknowledgements

The author thanks two anonymous reviewers for their comments on an early version of this chapter.

Notes

1   Secondary schools in Argentina comprise 13- to 17-year-old students.
2   This study was conducted at FLACSO Argentina, as part of the Research Project "La nueva configuración de la discriminación educativa en la Argentina", directed by Guillermina Tiramonti.

214 Sandra Ziegler

3 Source: Created by author based on data extracted from the Permanent Household Survey, 2011, INDECs. The fifth quintile is the fifth part of the population that concentrates the highest incomes.
4 For such an assertion, it would be necessary to conduct a study tracking schooling processes of individuals who already occupy privileged positions, examining different sections of the elites.
5 Students attend school five hours per day.
6 When we conducted our fieldwork, monthly tuition fees were approximately US$1,000.
7 The International Baccalaureate is an international educational programme managed by an organisation (IBO) based in Geneva that coordinates educational programmes at the international level.
8 Ball (2003) offers a detailed treatment of the social closure that English middle classes tend to seek through their school choices. The author builds on F. Parkin's work to discuss the category of "social closure" more in-depth.

References

Aguiar, A. (2012). Cuando la elección de la escuela es libre: el caso de las élites y clases medias brasileñas. In S. Ziegler & V. Gessaghi (Eds.), *Formación de las elites: Investigaciones y debates en Argentina, Brasil y Francia*. Buenos Aires: Manantial-Flacso.
Ball, S. (2003). *Class strategies and the education market: The middle classes and social advantage*. London: Routledge Falmer.
Braslavsky, C. (1985). *La discriminación educativa*. Buenos Aires: Miño y Dávila.
Crozier, G., Reay, D., James, D., Jamieson, F., Beedell, P., Hollingworth, S., & Williams, K. (2008). White middle class parents, identities, educational choice and the urban comprehensive school: Dilemmas, ambivalence and moral ambiguity. *British Journal of Sociology of Education, 29*(3), 261–272.
Del Cueto, C. (2007). *Los únicos privilegiados: Estrategias educativas de familias residentes en countries y barrios cerrados*. Buenos Aires: Prometeo.
Dubet, F. (2006). *El declive de la institución: Profesiones, sujetos e individuos en la modernidad*. Barcelona: Gedisa.
Gessaghi, V., & Méndez, A. (2015). Elite schools in Buenos Aires: The role of tradition and school social networks in the production and the reproduction of privilege. In A. van Zanten, S. J. Ball & B. Darchy- Koechlin (Eds.), *World Yearbook of Education 2015. Elites, privilege and excellence: The national and global redefinition of educational advantage* (pp. 43–55). London and New York: Routledge.
Giddens, A. (2001). *Un mundo desbocado: Los efectos de la globalización en nuestras vidas*. Madrid: Taurus.
Goodson, I., Cookson, P., & Persell, C. (2000). Distinción y destino: la importancia de la forma del curriculum en las escuelas privadas de elite estadounidenses. In I. Goodson (Eds.), *El cambio en el curriculum* (pp. 161–176). Barcelona: Octaedro.
Heredia, M. (2012). La formación de quién? Reflexiones sobre la teoría de Bourdieu y el estudio de las elites en la Argentina actual. In S. Ziegler & V. Gessaghi (Eds.), *Formación de las elites: Investigaciones y debates en Argentina, Brasil y Francia* (pp. 277–295). Buenos Aires: Manantial-Flacso.

Howard, A., & Gaztambide-Fernández, R. (Eds.) (2010). *Educating elites: Class, privilege and educational advantage*. Lanham, MD: Rowman & Littlefield Education.

Jay, E. (2002). As escolas da grande burguesia: o caso da Suíça. In A. M. Almeida & M. A. Nogueira (Eds.), *A escolarização das élites: Um panorama Internacional da pesquisa*. Petrópolis, RJ: Editora Vozes.

Khan, S. R. (2011). *Privilege: The making of an adolescent elite at St. Paul's School*. Princeton, NJ: Princeton University Press.

Kenway, J., Fahey, J., & Koh, A. (2013). The libidinal economy of the globalising elite school market. In C. Maxwell & P. Aggleton (Eds.), *Privilege, agency and affect: Understanding the production and effects of action* (pp. 15–30). New York: Palgrave, Macmillan.

Kessler, G. (2002). Empobrecimiento y fragmentación de la clase media Argentina. *Proposiciones* Ediciones Sur, Santiago de Chile, 34, 25–34.

Kessler, G. (2014). *Controversias sobre la desigualdad: Argentina 2003–2013*. Buenos Aires: Fondo de Cultura Económica.

Martínez, M. E., Villa, A., & Seoane, V. (2009). *Jóvenes, elección escolar y distinción social: Investigaciones en Argentina y Brasil*. Buenos Aires: Prometeo.

Maxwell, C., & Aggleton, P. (Eds.) (2013). *Privilege, agency and affect: Understanding the production and effects of action*. New York: Palgrave, Macmillan.

Pareto, V. (1967). Forma y equilibrio socialesen. *Revista de Occidente*, Madrid, 12, 33–46.

Parkin, F. (1974). *Marxismo y teoría de clases: Una critica burguesa*. Buenos Aires: Espasa Calpe.

Pinçon, M., & Pinçon-Charlot, M. (2002). A Infância dos chefes: A socialização dos herdeiros ricos na França. In A. M. Almeida & M. A. Nogueira (Eds.), *A escolarização das élites: Um panorama Internacional da pesquisa*. Petrópolis, RJ: Editora Vozes.

Resnik, J. (2008). The construction of the global worker trough international education. In *The production of educational knowledge in the global era* (pp. 147–168). Rotterdam: Sense Publishers.

Stich, A., & Colyar, J. (2013). Thinking relationally about studying 'up'. *British Journal of Sociology of Education*, 36(5), 729–746.

Svampa, M. (2001). *Los que ganaron: La vida en los countries y barrios privados*. Buenos Aires: Biblos.

Svampa, M. (2005). *La sociedad excluyente*. Buenos Aires: Taurus.

Tilly, C. (2000). *La desigualdad persistente*. Buenos Aires: Manantial.

Tiramonti, G. (Ed.) (2004). *La trama de la desigualdad educativa: Mutaciones recientes de la escuela media*. Buenos Aires: Manantial.

Tiramonti, G., & Ziegler, S. (2008) *La educación de las elites: Aspiraciones, estrategias y oportunidades*. Buenos Aires: Paidós.

Van Zanten, A. (2003). Middle class parents and social mix in French urban schools: Reproduction and transformation of class relations in education. *International Studies in Sociology of Education*, 13(2), 107–124.

Van Zanten, A. (2009). *Choisir son école: Stratégies familiales et médiations locales*. Paris: PUF.

Veleda, C. (2012). *La segregación educativa: Entre la fragmentación de las clases medias y la regulación atomizada*. Buenos Aires: Stella-La Crujía.

Waters, J. (2007). Roundabout routes and sanctuary schools: The role of situated educational practices and habitus in the creation of transnational professionals. *Global Networks*, 7(4), 477–497.

Weber, M. (1984). *Economía y sociedad*, Vol. 1, Parte I. (1 ed. 1922). México: Fondo de Cultura Económica.

Weis, L., Cipollone, K., & Jenkins, H. (2014). *Class warfare: Class, race and college admissions in top tier secondary schools.* Chicago, IL: University of Chicago.

Whitty, G., Power, S., & Halpin, D. (1998). *Devolution and choice in education: The school, the state, and the market.* Milton Keynes & Philadelphia: Open University Press.

Windle, J. (2009). The limits of school choice: Some implications for accountability of selective practices and positional competition. *Critical Studies in Education*, 50(3), 231–246.

Ziegler, S. (2004). La escolarización de las elites: un acercamiento a la socialización de los jóvenes de sectores favorecidos en la Argentina actual. In G. Tiramonti (Ed.), *La trama de la desigualdad educativa: Mutaciones recientes de la escuela media* (pp. 73–99). Buenos Aires: Manantial.

Ziegler, S., & Gessaghi, V. (Eds.) (2012). *Formación de las elites: Investigaciones y debates en Argentina, Brasil y Francia.* Buenos Aires: Manantial.

13

THE ECONOMY OF ELITENESS

Consuming Educational Advantage

Howard Prosser

> Haven't we arrived full circle from the myth of the 'rags to riches', the shoeshine boy
> who turns millionaire just by a stroke of luck combined with rather a lot of gumption,
> to a 'new and improved' version of the same myth, though with the shoeshining
> replaced by message kneading? Somewhere along that circular move the promise to
> level up chances by universal, life-enhancing education has been lost ...
>
> Zygmunt Bauman (2012, pp. 38–39)

Introduction

The growing scholarly interest in elites continually reposes a question: what do
we mean by elite? When talking about education, the term elite's elasticity
permits a useful confusion. Does elite point to the quality of the education? Or
does elite indicate the social position of those receiving the education? In this
chapter I unpack some of the issues that lead to such confusion by suggesting that
elite schools and their clientele are well served by this indeterminate descriptor.
The main reason for such indeterminacy is that what is being spoken of, or not
spoken of directly, is class. Within the rhetoric of meritocratic liberalism talking
about class differences has become inappropriate (which in itself is a class issue).
This improper discussion remains the case when it comes to comparing schools,
which is exactly what happens when one school is deemed elite. Calling a school
elite is always already a relational or comparative analysis. But a further
complication is added when the schools themselves disavow the term elite and
replace it with other signifiers like excellence or prestigious (Draelants & Darchy-
Koechlin, 2011). Such alternatives assuage the term elite's classed asperities.

But there's little getting away from the fact that high-end institutions that offer
globally reputed curricula to the wealthy and powerful are called elite schools.

Indeed, calling a school elite is class formation in motion. Class is a process that is continually developing through linguistic and material circumstances. Much like Bauman's shoeshine analogy, elite education has a well-kneaded message that disguises its overwhelmingly classed nature. This message has been softened to a state where such schools do not see themselves as elite and are thus somehow easily accessed or comparable to other schools that cater to different social classes. As a result, elite is a term that obliquely serves class formation. Class should not be regarded as a 'thing' but a relationship that changes over time.

Here I argue that the contemporary celebration of elite schools is integral to a larger 'economy of eliteness' that, in turn, contributes to the ongoing process of class formation. The chapter begins by indicating how class analysis today can find use in a term like elite if it keeps a sense of class being a historical process. This means that scholars studying elites today should be aware of how previous discussion of class can inform their understanding of elites, especially under neoliberal conditions. One way of doing this is by recognising how a syncretic class analysis can cope with the complex economic and cultural factors that influence class formation. From this synthesis, it becomes clear that studying elites is specifically concerned with the ongoing nature of social inequality via the concentration of wealth and power.

As such, I go on to suggest that the economy of eliteness produces an 'elite imaginary' that is now a valuable and exchangeable social currency mobilised in favour of specific class interests. To illustrate this economy I position it in a composite analytical frame with some examples taken from my fieldwork in an elite school in Argentina. Elite schools like this one, the Caledonian School, play a crucial role in representing and reproducing eliteness in both education and society. A school's association with a particular group assists in the institution being seen as elite, while membership of this group is assisted by attendance at the school. A consumer cycle, a virtuous circle, is created. Consequently, the image of eliteness is being made through the consumption of elite education as a commodity.

I end the chapter by suggesting the study of eliteness also has a responsibility to undo such inequality through considered class analysis. Since the economy of eliteness works to assist such concentration, through its cunning quest for greater market value where ever it lays, scholars of elite education should be wary of unwittingly inflating eliteness by celebrating the worth of the schools studied. The 'economy of eliteness' deserves to be exposed as part of a process that produces class power because social and educational advantage is purchasable at a premium. This situation has ramifications for other schools and universities because it mobilises an elite imaginary that is symptomatic of neoliberal times. Schooling is now about emulating the elite institutions of the privileged with little mind to how such privilege was acquired or how, and by whom, such institutions are defined as elite. In other words, an economy of eliteness reinforces a way of thinking about how education is bound to class.

Elite Class Analysis

Elite has become a common term of everyday use. The Anglophone media is rife with the term, especially in the wake of the 2008 economic crash, to describe society's wealthy and powerful. The fascination with elites—as evidenced in celebrity culture of all stripes—replicates previous awe at the aristocracy or royalty. But there is little sense of what constitutes elites status. There is an assumption that various formulations—political elites, intellectual elites, cultural elites, urban elites—are commonly understood. Similarly, those studying the nebulous nature of post-industrial class formations often use 'elite-theory' revenants to compose their analyses (Khan, 2012, pp. 373–374).[1]

Fortunately, these scholars more closely interrogate the term elite than those who deploy it in the popular media. For them elite has come to replace concepts like ruling class or upper class that were bound to specific theoretical traditions (Savage et al., 2013). This shift is representative of a need for a broad-based approach to class as much as to the point that class today seems to manifest itself as a binary between rich and poor, winners and losers, elite and hoi polloi. But society does not work along such simple lines. These binaries may work to highlight, and hopefully reduce, inequality; but they don't show the complexity of the structural processes that lead to class formation.

In the place of such simplification or theoretical rivalry, a more constructive approach is needed. One has been suggested by Erik Olin Wright, who calls for "pragmatist realism" to predominate class analysis (Wright, 2009, p. 101). That is, an approach that combines the richness of various analytical traditions to create a more holistic view of social class as determined by a range of factors. The notion of class as process is the most useful generalisation in to which various theories can be applied. The current consensus of sorts identifies unequal social structures as based on uneven distribution of economic, social, and cultural capital. Accepting such accord means that various theoretical traditions' definitions of class complement each other in different ways, often times through the very conversations they are having with each other about the concept (Wright, 2005).

For this reason the sociology of elites should not be seen as a poor cousin of other theoretical traditions. It is rather a coequal in class analysis by focusing on the problem of understanding systems of economic inequality. We have now arrived at a point where using the term elite no longer means a wholesale acceptance or rejection of other sociological approaches. In fact, syncretic class analysis has long been in place as each theorist or school approached the topic with their own beliefs. This magnanimous approach to class analysis may ignore crucial differences between various social theories that have often led to internecine quarrels. But ongoing pronounced social inequality proves that such quarrels did little to subvert the power they described.

Rather than enter the labyrinth of contemporary class analysis, much less its brutal theoretical past, I want to suggest just one way that current approaches to elite could be strengthened. That is, today's sociology of elites could become more penetrative by selectively drawing on the groundwork of previous discussions of class and ideology. There is a possibility that previous obsessions with class taxonomies can be jettisoned in favour of understanding class formation as a historical phenomenon. Comprehending class means seeing it as a social and cultural formation arising from processes that take place over a significant period (Thompson, 1980, p. 9).

The chief historical virtue of elite theory and the sociology of elites is that they reveal the ongoing dynamics of socio-economic inequality under democratic conditions: the crises of liberalism a century apart. Where in the early 20th century elite theorists were wary of democracy's implications for those with existing power, contemporary scholars now face the conundrum of how well-established democratic conditions, despite championing equality, continue to allow a select few to dominate. Coming to terms with the latter demands some consideration of how elites reinforce and reproduce their position through dominant ideological means that disguise the exploitative nature of their ascendancy. At the current conjuncture this ideology is primarily a version of liberalism, as neoliberalism, that believes humanity is best served by rapacious acts: environmental destruction, food insecurity, worker precariousness and social neglect.

Part of the justification for such ideology comes through an 'economy of eliteness' that works to support the dominant class whatever it may be called. There is, however, a risk that calling such dominators elites will likely assist in the circulation of this economy. To be sure, elite remains a useful convention for those working in the field to group their work around—which is reason enough, for now, to continue its application—but accepting its currency may ignore the larger historical forces at play. Its application may prop up the inequality most scholars of elites seek to upset. This warning makes plain how eliteness is currently a valuable and desirable trait. But the larger issue is that scholars need to be aware of how class is a process that cannot be simply fixed or measured. Eliteness informs the creation of social class through its illusory and nebulous application; it possesses an ambiguity that benefits the interests of those the idea serves.

The economy of eliteness captures this symbolic dynamism by showing how being elite is celebrated within a neoliberal environment. But it also shows how eliteness is linked to the dominance of economic thinking. The achievement of such eliteness is conspicuous through the process of consumption that conceals, thanks to globalised markets and sophisticated culture industries, the exploitative processes of production. The sale and purchase of educational opportunities is but one part of this process. It is an important part because it reveals how primary and secondary education, an experience generally regarded as an important social good, has become a consumable means of social distinction rather than a social leveller. In short, the ability to pay the high price of an elite education for one's children requires collusion with the exploitative processes of global capitalism.

Exchange in the Economy of Eliteness

As a result, the economy of eliteness is shown to be a process based on exchange. There is a reciprocal relationship between the clients and the elite schools that amounts to a form of exchange. For example, confusion around the meaning of elite in elite education serves the institutions and their clients well. By creating an air of grandeur around excellent tuition, through either rumour or marketing, the school becomes more attractive. Likewise, by being able to send your children to a highly regarded and expensive school is a confirmation of social eliteness. These two interpretations quickly become mutually dependent when applied and then circulated among and beyond the schools' locations. The circular logic of this exchange is that educational advantage contributes to the production of eliteness.

To illustrate this economy of eliteness I take some examples from the Caledonian School, an elite school in the greater Buenos Aires region in Argentina, at which I spent six months carrying out ethnographic fieldwork during 2011. This school is highly regarded and is part of a significant group of Argentine elite schools know locally as 'English' or 'British' schools due to their bilingual curricula (English–Spanish) and their association with the Anglo-Argentine community in Buenos Aires (Tiramonti & Ziegler, 2008, pp. 32–33). That community is now in its dotage—its heyday was in the railway boom of the late 19th and early 20th centuries—and has been replaced by families seeking to benefit from the reputation that the school established as a parochial school (Rock, 2008, p. 72).

Today, Caledonian's prohibitive fees mean that only families at a certain income scale can afford to send their children there. This economic definition equates to a classical Marxist analysis that would see class homogeneity based largely on income from entrepreneurial or rentier pursuits.[2] Such homogeneity extends to similarities in political outlook and cultural types. They constitute part of the ruling class that exercises power through wealth and the influence that comes with it, although they remain separated from direct government power.

A definition of the school's clientele can therefore be quite precise. It overwhelmingly stems from Argentina's entrepreneurial elite. The fees of the school, along with relatively few scholarships, mean that only certain families can afford to pay. The overwhelming majority of these families derive their income from their own commercial enterprises that are either directly or indirectly associated with agricultural land use. To be sure, other high-waged professions such as lawyers, engineers, and doctors send their children to the school, but according to the school the overwhelming majority are entrepreneurs usually with family-owned businesses. A 2011 internal assessment of admissions procedures, which surveyed over 100 families, revealed that 40% of fathers were "businessmen" (*empresarios*), with the next largest number being the 8% "employed in the private sector". For mothers, just over 20% were "housewives" (*amas de casa*) and then 12% and 11% were "lawyers" and "businesswomen" (Caledonian School, 2011).

Value in the Economy of Eliteness

Such homogeneity shows how the economy of eliteness works to support specific groups. The school's clientele fits the bill as elite precisely because they are able to afford to send their children to Caledonian, while the decision to do so is because it is seen as an elite school—in terms of its academic quality and its demographic. Thus the school's eliteness is assured by catering to this group; while being associated with the school reinforces the group's eliteness. This mutual relationship is the heart of a virtuous exchange between the school and its clientele. The economics of the situation are crucial since the origins of the wealth comes from privately owned means of production re-invested into the school, and thus the clientele's children, to promote the reproduction of their wealth and class.

Value in the Economy of Eliteness

Here is where the value of the economy of eliteness lies within elite schooling. Such value initially comes from economic arrangements. The ability to purchase an elite education is inextricably linked to exploitative social processes. The façade of educational excellence and beautiful buildings hide their presence in the same way that commodity fetishism disassembles the social relations in the production processes. The ability to pay high fees permits the hoarding of educational opportunities via old-fashioned exploitation of surplus labour.

The main point here is that economic determinants are entwined with a variety of symbolic, moral and cultural factors. Sociologist Beverley Skeggs worked through such a confluence in her *Class, Self, Culture* (2004) to suggest that class is made and given value through culture and how culture is employed as a resource of class power. This cultural production of class is distinct in the way that the value of economic capital is also inscribed with morality. Skeggs (2004, pp. 6–18) discussed a moral economy of class in which cultural resources are ascribed 'value' and 'exchange' potential. In this process, certain characteristics become valuable, at the expense of others, and convertible within a social frame that also legitimises them as morally right.

Elite independent schools in general have to be regarded as institutions for those who predominate in social relations that are ultimately detrimental to others. But this is not something they want to advertise. Here a further notion of value is at work in this economy: eliteness becomes something earned and thus deserved. Elite schools are given a socially defined value by those with an interest in inflating this value. Yet such inflation must be justified and meritocracy provides the perfect means through which to do so. The perfect ruse of the neoliberal moment is that elite social positions are accessible through meritocratic systems—hard work on a level playing field—rather than through access to the elite institutions that assist in class reproduction. Such pretence assists in the propagation of an elite imaginary that is global in its scope: the widespread belief that a sybaritic existence is life's chief pursuit and achieving it is a competitive

Consuming Educational Advantage **223**

activity. The neoliberal dream encourages membership in the social elite at others' expense.

In Buenos Aires, cultural influences lead parents to choose the Caledonian School over others, especially because its elite education has value in Argentina and beyond. Keen parents must make this decision early on in their child's life. This fact alone says something about the value of school choice among this economic elite as a form of symbolic capital. Unlike entry to the selective state schools, which takes place around the beginning of secondary schooling, those students hoping to enter Caledonian are three years old. The demand for places is high and competitive—around three to four prospective students apply for the one position—because of the school's reputation. So parents are aware they make a long-term commitment, and investment, when choosing the Caledonian School—based on the current situation, over 90% of those kindergarteners will graduate as classmates 13 or so years later.

A culture of discussion around the school's reputation facilitates the choice to send one's children there. There are a number of similar schools—often with English or other bilingual curricula—from which these affluent families can choose. The list is limited to no more than 10 alternatives that are seen as in the same league as Caledonian. According to the school's 2011 admissions survey, parents gave three main reasons for choosing Caledonian: the school's academic quality; the values the school imparts; and the excellent level of English taught (Caledonian School, 2011). These responses are certainly in keeping with the way that the school sells itself and thus with the type of clients to which it caters.

Here the value of the school is at its most obvious. Each trait is highly valued in today's global society: academic excellence implies greater tertiary and post-tertiary prospects; solid values instruction points to a well-rounded character befitting a traditional private institution (perhaps as opposed to a public one); and English-language facility suggests a potential mobility as well as a degree of cosmopolitanism. Even these three alone create an aspirational picture of the Caledonian alumnus: a university-educated, bilingual sophisticate.

Producing the Elite Imaginary

And what parent wouldn't want that for their child? When it comes to school choice, if it is available, most parents value highest the school's academic performance (although just how this performance is measured is a different matter). And many do their upmost to give their children educational advantage—as the increasing popularity of charter schools or voucher systems attest. This desire for educational advantage indicates a competitive model within the school system: between schools as well as between students. The commodification of universal education in the past few decades divides public and private systems along class lines. It is a market logic that is governing not just schooling, but most social provisions around the world. This situation manifests in Argentina as a dual system comprising the chief "quasi-state monopoly" (public schools and subsidised Catholic schools) and a much more select marketplace filled by elite independent schools (Narodowski, 2008, pp. 135–138). Consequently, as elsewhere, there is shared presumption among those parents who decide to pay the high fees of elite schools: that a school's quality is proportional to the cost of sending their child there. There are high odds that the educated sophisticate can be bought from Caledonian. In so doing, parents are investing in their child's future.

The notion of investment is crucial here since it combines both the economic means as well as speculation of future returns. Such speculation produces an elite imaginary: an image of what eliteness constitutes. Where the provision of elite education is available social elites will invest in it because it becomes a means of expressing and reproducing their eliteness. Here the elite imaginary of neoliberalism is manifest: the conspicuous consumption of high-priced goods and services is a marker of social worth. At the current conjuncture high social status is measured by one's ability to earn and spend. This scenario leads to what geographer Michael Storper (2000, p. 398) identified as a "new positional inequality in consumption" whereby elites' consumption of goods and services, especially those that used to be publically offered, is deleterious to those on the lowest incomes in society. The illusion is that the consumer economy is equally open to all.

When elite aspirations become 'democratised' through consumption, as normalised in everyday life, then the competition for individual status trumps any calls for social equality (Dardot & Laval, 2013). The democracy at work here fits with the meritocratic value of social positions as something earned in conditions of economic equality. Under this logic, the rich become deserving; but, as a corollary, the poor's position is also justified. Those who profit from positions of influence within this capitalist system paradoxically want to see elite attributes—hyper-consumerism, workaholism, privatisation—democratised to improve their own lot (Gregg, 2011). The outcome is an elite imaginary that is global in its vision of what constitutes success.

The weakening of state formations since the 1980s, especially the reversal of the post-war consensus around the welfare state, has seen an increase in the size of private wealth. This is probably even more pronounced in Argentina, and similar nations, where the state has always been authoritarian or unstable in character. The outcome is a concentration of power in the hands of oligarchies (Echeverría, 2011). Such oligarchies justify their position as legitimately earned through meritocratic systems in much the same way as aristocracies of the past referred to divine law. Indeed, the meritocratic basis to those with power today harks back to divine bases for social exclusion. The ecclesiastical origins of the term elite identify those who are 'the elect' or 'the chosen' (*eligere* in Latin) for eternal salvation. When this notion is extended, across a few centuries, to a Protestant work ethic bound by predestination and then to a liberal sacralisation of capital accumulation, eliteness quickly becomes an earned or deserving status. Meritocracy underpins such deservedness and eliteness is its highest reward.

Social eliteness defined as affluence indicates, at heart, the good fortune of accumulating more capital than others (and usually at these others' expense). This is the economy of eliteness at work. Such meritocracy, originally a term of satire (Young, 1958), is in keeping with visions of society that celebrate those draped in the material trappings of success. Achieving such success is underpinned by a liberal championing of opportunity instead of equality. Using the term elite is using the language of meritocracy in which those who are members of the elite deserve to be regarded as such and, by the same logic, those who are excluded do too. Ultimately, elite became synonymous with deserved power and social righteousness. Such synonymity is a classic self-legitimising function of ruling-class ideology. Indeed, the economy of eliteness itself has a strong historical element that sees eliteness justified with reference to, and especially the imitation of, previously dominant groups.

Argentina's post-neoliberal context certainly questions the celebration of eliteness that seems widespread throughout the world (Wylde, 2012). Since 2003, the Kirchner governments' redistributive and nationalising agenda, arising from the ruins of a neoliberal experiment, condemned those elites that they believe are undermining the national project with their own self-interest (Cohen, 2012, pp. 84–131). Yet an elite imaginary remains. Argentina may be moving toward a post-neoliberal mindset, but its economic elites recognised this position has limited currency within a global domain. Consequently, anthropologist Aihwa Ong's (2007, pp. 3–8) point about neoliberal mobility stands: in Argentina the selective use of neoliberal ideology continues in this specific context in spite of its 'post' status.

Promoting Educational Consumption

Despite this context, schooling's commodification continues in the same way as elsewhere in the world. The symbolic nature of elite schooling—what it represents in class terms—is a product to be consumed by those that can afford it and accepted as superior by those who cannot. Within the process of consumption the symbolic or cultural aspect of elite schooling is directly linked to the material realities that facilitate class difference. A harsher economic underlay supports the softer cultural appearances of social distinction. Instead of seeing eliteness as a position of cultural difference, one ideologically reinforced by its relationship to non-elites, it must be recognised as linked to a process of production and consumption. A prestigious school education is a prerequisite (or, better yet, a perquisite) for a future of privilege. Elite schooling is seen as a means of buying not only educational advantage but class power.

In her 2005 essay, "The Re-Branding of Class", Skeggs calls for the need to rethink class analysis along such consumer lines. The essay pointed to a key aspect of the consumer capitalism system—branding—to show how class today is now a "cultural property" with different value (Skeggs, 2005, p. 47). The dynamics of the culture industries facilitates this process by making certain representations of class acceptable, especially in moral terms like good or bad. Certain classes come to embody these moral judgements through the consumer choices they make. As ethnographer Arjun Appadurai (2013, pp. 230–231) argues, status groups are "defined by lifestyle and consumption rather than by their relationship to the means of production".

There are many instances of this process—from the popularisation of elite culture, via the economy-of-scale manufacturing of luxury goods and services often celebrated by Hollywood and its imitators, to the fictionalisation of finance capital, in which both the purchase and the commodities become abstractions, in both the cause and solution to the 2008 crisis. All of these instances serve to hide the commodity and the production processes that go into it. Such concealment is fetishisation and alienation writ large. The point that Skeggs made about branding now, thanks to economic analysis now returning with a vengeance, can be seen as capturing the symbolic and the material nature of contemporary capitalist exchange.

The global market economy advances the commodity's presence as value—in labour terms, especially—by celebrating consumption and concealing production. The marketing of desirable consumer goods with little mind to how they are made assists with such concealment. This process is made all the easier when the production process takes place in the 'developing' world, as is the nature of manufacturing imports in the post-industrial conditions. Consumption, by contrast, becomes seemingly more accessible via a suffusion of images that appear to make consumers more discerning about what goods and services, including education, they want to buy. And the products seen as elite, or representing the elite imaginary, hold the most value. The economy of eliteness thus supports a larger global capitalist enterprise. This is yet another display of contemporary capitalism's consumerist spectacle—as in Debord's (1994, p. 24) "capital accumulated to the point where it becomes image"—that obscures the exploitation involved in the production and consumption of goods.

How does this apply to the provision of private schooling in Argentina, especially the Caledonian School? Through the economy of eliteness, one's relation to consumption becomes a social marker in the same way that production was in the past. Paying for elite schooling implies membership of a social elite. The process of consumption explains the rationale behind the rise of such schools as markers of not just educational excellence but social worth. Simply put, education's commodification results in echelons of provision throughout society and the way education is consumed indicates social position as well as social gravity. Certain schools (and universities) become the equivalent of luxury goods able to be bought by the very rich. A Caledonian School education is sold alongside its compeers as the best education money can buy for their children.

The uniqueness of the Caledonian situation is that the school has a *very* strong brand within the economy of eliteness. This brand is associated with the school's longstanding history as one of Argentina's oldest private schools; its association with Britishness and, by extension, Anglophone liberalism and commercialism; its status as the Argentine version of the preppy schools envisioned in popular culture, especially from the USA; and an ability to not be held to this history and thus remain mobile, perhaps based on a general process of Argentine reinvention. The decision to send your children to a private school, especially one of the Caledonian's pedigree, signifies something within a broader social context about your commitment to your children's future. It implies a prudent investment in them. In meritocratic logic, which is not dissimilar to consumer therapy, the cost is worth it because the outcome is deserved.

The offshoot, of course, is that *not* sending your child to such schools, to go public, is to misjudge the social landscape and a moral failure in parenting. The act of the purchase, the performance of being able to buy, becomes important. The immorality of the non-private is the ultimate triumph of neoliberal primacy of the individual over the social. Here Skeggs' notion of value as having moral worth is important to the economy of eliteness. School choice is a performance in righteousness in the same way that consuming particular goods—especially those with some social-justice narrative—is now seen as somehow morally superior. But it is a decision still made devoid of thought about the class formation, especially painful processes of wealth extraction, that are at the heart of this consumption process. As Skeggs (2004, pp. 12–13) suggests, by associating a child with a brand, like that of the school, class struggle is engaged "through culture as a form of symbolic violence, through relationships of entitlement that are legitimised and institutionalised, and it is these processes that set limits on who can and cannot belong, be, and have worth on a national and global stage".

Leveraging the Economy of Eliteness

If the economy of eliteness allows consumption to increase the value of eliteness, then purchasing elite education becomes essential to imagined success in global capitalism. The connection between this outcome and the education is not necessarily incorrect. After all, those who receive such educations do better in their accumulation of capital and wealth than others. Yet this fact alone shows how class power is reproduced through a commodified educational process. More than this, class power is not only reproduced but access to greater class power, membership of society's elite, is itself commodified. A confluence of important factors assist in the reproduction of class power of which education is just one; however, the purchase of elite education is a means of gaining leverage in this process.

The Caledonian School holds a symbolic class value that is transferable in both the local and global context. Graduates who either remain in Argentina or move around the globe can draw on their Caledonian background for networks and knowledge that allows them to enter and find comfort in realms of eliteness. Buying

228 Howard Prosser

this alumni status pays future dividends. The means of consumption leads to the production of an elite imaginary. An image of eliteness is being produced through the very process of consumption. In this sense, the consumption of an elite school education can be regarded as part of a cultural production process. That is, students taught at the school learn the correct curriculum, meet the right people, and cultivate the correct tastes for their future success as part of Argentina's economic elite. A Caledonian School education produces alumni—especially the children of the nouveau riche—with the requisite cultural capital for this imagined future.

Elite education is not just about the commodification of education. Paying for prestigious schooling has long been the case. What we see today, within the economy of eliteness, is the commodification of class power through the purchasing of educational advantage. More insidiously, the decision to do so is portrayed as a consumer choice with a morally superior air. The hidden presence of the production and consumption process within this exchange betrays the social inequality at the heart of commodified education. As a result, the surplus of resources available to the elite school means that any comparison with other schools needs to take these resources into account. The consumption of educational advantage, through its purchase, becomes a means of reinforcing inequality because it concentrates educational resources in the minds of the wealthy.

Further, precisely because the quality of education is linked to the demands of global capitalism, those who hold advantage in this system define elite education's eliteness. It works in the schools' interests that this reputation blurs both class definitions and the quality of education. This is elite, or ruling-class, ideology at work in neoliberal times. A marketised version of every social issue means that education becomes a consumer product and the economy of eliteness makes elite schooling all the more attractive. Past mimeses of eliteness—usually manifest in the appropriation of noble aesthetics—now occurs through its purchase rather than mere usurpation.

Consequently, it is incumbent on the sociology of elite education to remain mindful of this situation so that it does not become complicit with this very subtle process of social partitioning. To be sure, elite remains a useful convention for those working in the field to group their work around, but accepting its currency may ignore some of the larger historical processes at play. Its application also runs the risk of propping up the inequality such scholars may seek to upset. Scholars working on social elites and elite education must be wary of how their research upholds the economy of eliteness and thus may contribute to the inequality they seek to reverse.

Notes

1   For ease of understanding, by 'elite theory' I mean that which emerged in early 20th-century Europe, especially Italy, with theorists like Robert Michels, Gaetano Mosca, and Vilfredo Pareto. The current focus on elites fits more neatly into a 'sociology of elites' tradition that began during the 1960s.

2 Less than 5% of students are on scholarships that reduce rates for children of teachers or those alumni with continuing ties to the school community. Such provision points to a difference between the teaching staff and the clientele in terms of income. This is representative of a class difference. However, the teachers' wages are higher than in the public system or the majority of private schools. So too is the staff's cultural capital—English-language fluency, for example—because many teachers are former students of 'English' schools like Caledonian. This connection is part of the overall reproduction of eliteness and class formations.

References

Appadurai, A. (2013). *The future as cultural fact: Essays on the global condition.* London: Verso.

Bauman, Z. (2012). *On education: Conversations with Riccardo Mazzeo.* Cambridge, UK: Polity Press.

Caledonian School. (2011). *Evaluacion del departamento de admisiones* [Evaluation of the admissions department], unpublished report.

Cohen, M. (2012). *Argentina's economic growth and recovery: The economy in a time of default.* Abingdon: Routledge.

Dardot, P., & Laval, C. (2013). *The new way of the world: On neoliberal society.* London: Verso.

Debord, G. (1994). *The society of the spectacle.* New York, NY: Zone Books.

Draelants, H., & Darchy-Koechlin, B. (2011). Flaunting one's academic pedigree? Self-presentation of students from elite French schools. *British Journal of Sociology of Education,* 32(1), 17–34.

Echeverría, B. (2011). Potemkin republics: Reflections on Latin America's bicentenary. *New Left Review,* 70, 53–61.

Gregg, M. (2011). *Work's intimacy: Commercialisation of intimate life.* Cambridge, UK: Polity Press.

Khan, S. R. (2012). Sociology of elites. *Annual Review of Sociology,* 38, 361–377.

Narodowski, M. (2008). School choice and Quasi-state monopoly in education systems in Latin America: The case of Argentina. In M. Forsey, S. Davies & G. Walford (Eds.), *The globalisation of school choice?* (pp. 131–144). Oxford, UK: Symposium Books.

Ong, A. (2007). Neoliberalism as mobile technology. *Transactions of the Institute of British Geographers,* 32(1), 3–8.

Rock, D. (2008). The British in Argentina: From informal empire to postcolonialism. In M. Brown (Ed.), *Informal empire in Latin America: Culture, commerce and capital* (pp.49–77). Malden, MA: Blackwell Publishing.

Savage, M., Devine, F., Cunningham, N., Taylor, M., Li, Y., Hjellbrekke, J., Le Roux, B., Friedman, S., & Miles, A. (2013). A new model of social class: Findings from the BBC's great British class survey experiment. *Sociology,* 47(2), 219–250.

Skeggs, B. (2004). *Class, self, culture.* London: Routledge.

Skeggs, B. (2005). The re-branding of class: Propetising culture. In F. Devine et al. (Eds.), *Rethinking class: Culture, identity, and lifestyle* (pp. 46–68). Basingstoke, UK: Palgrave Macmillan.

Storper, M. (2000). Lived effects of the contemporary economy: Globalization, inequality, and consumer society. *Public Culture,* 12(2), 398–399.

Thompson, E. P. (1980). *The making of the English working class* (2nd edn). Harmondsworth: Penguin.

Tiramonti, G., & Ziegler, S. (2008). *La educación de las elites: Aspiraciones, estrategias y oportunidades* [The education of elites: aspirations, strategies and opportunities]. Buenos Aires: Paidós.

Wright, E. O. (2005). Conclusion: If "class" is the answer, what is the question? In E. O. Wright (Ed.), *Approaches to class analysis* (pp. 180–192). Cambridge, UK: Cambridge University Press.

Wright, E. O. (2009). Understanding class: Towards an integrated analytical approach. *New Left Review*, 60, 101–116.

Wylde, C. (2012). *Latin America after neoliberalism: Development regimes in post crisis states.* London: Palgrave Macmillan.

Young, M. (1958). *The rise of the meritocracy, 1870–2033: An essay on education and equality.* London: Random House.

CONTRIBUTORS

Helena C. Araújo is Professor in the Faculty of Psychology and Education Sciences in the University of Porto (Portugal). She is the Director of the Centre for Research in Education (CIIE/UP). She currently teaches Sociology of Education, Gender Studies and Citizenship and Diversity. She is the Portuguese coordinator of an EU FP7 project "Reducing Early School Leaving in Europe (RESL.eu)" (2013–2018). Her research interests are: Education as a Social Right; School Disengagement; Young People Biographies and Pathways; Gender, Education, and Citizenship; Intercultural Education; Women Participation and Higher Education; Educational Policies and Life Course Research. Email: hcaraujo@mail.telepac.pt.

Caroline Bertron is a doctoral student in Sociology and Anthropology at the University Paris 1 Panthéon-Sorbonne (France) and University of Lausanne (Switzerland). Her research interests include the sociology of elites and elite schooling, the role of transnational mobility and migration for social reproduction and reconversions, and historical sociology. Email: carolinehs.bertron@gmail.com.

Hugues Draelants is Associate Professor at the *Université catholique de Louvain* and member of the Interdisciplinary Research Group in Socialization, Education, and Training (GIRSEF). He was previously a Research Fellow with the *Fonds de la Recherche Scientifique* (F.R.S.-FNRS) in Belgium and Post-doctoral Researcher at the *Centre National de la Recherche Scientifique* (CNRS) in France. He has published on elite and education in several international journals (*British Journal of Sociology of Education, French Politics, Higher Education, Research Papers in Education, Social Science Information*) and in the 2015 *World Yearbook of Education*. He also works on education policy implementation (cf. *Réforme pédagogique et légitimation*, De Boeck 2009) and

232 Contributors

on schools as organisations (cf. *L'identité des établissements scolaires*, co-authored with Xavier Dumay, PUF 2011). Email: hugues.draelants@uclouvain.be.

Christopher Drew, **Kristina Gottschall**, **Natasha Wardman**, and **Sue Saltmarsh** are academics from Australian universities working across education studies, cultural studies, gender studies, and media studies. In recent years they have conducted research into educational marketisation in Australia, through which they have highlighted and challenged the ways that educational marketisation exacerbates competitiveness, elitism, and exclusionary educational practices. Their examinations of promotional materials produced by Australia's elite private schools have focused on the ways that gender, race, geographic location and socioeconomic privilege are invoked in the promotions in the service and maintenance of competitive educational and social hierarchies. Email: christopher.drew@hotmail.com.

Radha Iyer teaches in the School of Cultural and Professional Learning in the Faculty of Education, Queensland University of Technology, Australia. Her expertise and research interests are literacy, English as a Second Language, critical discourse analysis, and sociology of education. Email: radha.iyer@qut.edu.au.

Jane Kenway is Professorial Fellow with the Australian Research Council, Professor in the Education Faculty at Monash University, and elected Fellow of the Academy of Social Sciences, Australia. Her research expertise is in socio-cultural studies of education in the context of wider social and cultural change, focusing particularly on matters of power and politics. Her most recent jointly edited book is *Asia as Method in Education Studies: A Defiant Research Imagination* (Routledge 2015). She currently leads an international team conducting a multi-national five-year research project called *Elite schools in globalising circumstances: a multi-sited global ethnography*. Arising from this project she has recently co-edited special issues of the *International Journal of Qualitative Studies in Education* —'New Directions for Research on Elites and Elite Education: Methodological Challenges'; the *British Journal of Sociology of Education*—'New Sociologies of Elite Schooling: Fresh Theoretical, Methodological and Empirical Explorations'; *Globalisation, Societies and Education*—'Elite Schools in Globalising Circumstances: New Conceptual Directions and Connections'. *Class Choreographies: Elite Schools and Globalisation* is jointly written by the research team (Palgrave 2016). Email: Jane.Kenway@monash.edu.

Aaron Koh is Associate Professor in the School of Education and Professional Studies, Griffith University, Australia. He previously taught in Monash University, Hong Kong Institute of Education, and National Institute of Education, Singapore. He has published in the areas of Global Studies in Education, Cultural Studies in Education and Sociology of Education. He is on the Editorial Boards of *Journal of Adolescent & Adult Literacy*, *Curriculum Inquiry*, *Journal of Curriculum and Pedagogy* and

Contributors **233**

Discourse: Studies in the cultural politics of education. He is also the co-founding editor of a Springer Book Series: *Cultural Studies and Transdisciplinarity in Education.*

Moosung Lee is Centenary Professor at the University of Canberra. Prior to joining the University of Canberra, he held appointments as Associate Professor and Founding Deputy Director of Education Policy Unit at the University of Hong Kong. He has published numerous articles in high-quality academic outlets in the areas of educational leadership and administration, urban education, and comparative education. He is the recipient of the AERA's Emerging Scholar Award in Division A (Administration, Organisation, & Leadership). Email: MooSung.Lee@canberra.edu.au.

Chin Ee Loh is Assistant Professor at the National Institute of Education, Nanyang Technological University. Her research and publications are in reading politics and social class, literature and literacy education at the nexus of globalisation, and teacher education. Email: chinee.loh@nie.edu.sg.

Eunice Macedo is a Research Fellow at CIIE and experienced teacher in adult and teacher training. Currently, she is a Post-Doc in the international project RESL.eu—Reducing Early School Leaving in the EU [FP7-SSH-2012-1]. She is also the Vice President of the board of direction of Paulo Freire Institute of Portugal. She has published in the areas of citizenship, education, youth and gender. Her most recent book is *Cidadania em confronto: Educação de jovens elites em tempo de globalização* [*Confronting citizenship: elite education in a time of globalisation*] (LivPsic & CIIE 2009). Email: Eunice@fpce.up.pt.

Howard Prosser researches and teaches at the Faculty of Education, Monash University, Australia. His research interests include social theory, history of ideas, and ethnography. Most recently he has investigated political culture at an elite school in Argentina and co-edited *In the Realm of the Senses: Social Aesthetics and the Sensory Dynamics of Privilege* (Springer 2015). Email: howard.prosser@monash.edu.

Bertrand Réau is Senior Lecturer in Sociology at the University of Paris 1 Panthéon Sorbonne and researcher at the European Centre of Sociology and Political Science—European Centre of Sociology (Ecole des Hautes Etudes en Sciences Sociales-CNRS-Paris 1). He is a founding member of the seminar 'Tourisme: Recherches, Pratiques, Institutions' at the Ecole des Hautes Etudes en Sciences Sociales (Paris). His work explores the social use of leisure time (both contemporarily and historically), the political function of ethnic tourism in Southeast Asia and the sociology of science. He has published three books: (with François Denord), *La sociologie de Charles Wright Mills* (La Découverte, Paris, 2014); *Les Français et les vacances: Sociologie de l'offre et des pratiques de loisirs* (CNRS Editions, Paris, 2011); and (with Saskia Cousin), *Sociologie du tourisme* (La Découverte, Paris, 2011). Email: breau@univ-paris1.fr.

234 Contributors

Allan Walker is Joseph Lau Chair Professor of International Educational Leadership and Director of the Asia Pacific Centre for Leadership and Change at the Hong Kong Institute of Education. His research focuses on expanding knowledge of school leadership in Chinese and other Asian societies and disseminating this internationally. Email: adwalker@ied.edu.hk.

Yujia Wang has a PhD from Monash University. Her thesis explores elite education and the formation of privileged youthful identities in mobility against the backdrop of globalisation and transnationalism. She is currently rewriting her thesis into a book contracted with Springer. The book is titled, *Making and Remaking a Youthful Chinese Self in an Australian School: The Complex Logics of Culture, Class and Good Life*. Email: tracy.yujia.wang@gmail.com.

Shane Watters is a researcher based in the School of Social Policy, Sociology and Social Research at the University of Kent in the United Kingdom. He has a broad spectrum of research interests in the field of education ranging from social stratification and reproduction to the management of higher education in a global context. Recognition for research conducted for the chapter in this book includes being nominated for a prestigious Faculty research prize within his institution. Email: s.j.watters@kent.ac.uk.

Ewan Wright is a PhD student in the Faculty of Education at the University of Hong Kong. Prior to joining the University of Hong Kong he worked with various think tanks in the UK and Hong Kong including Centre for Cities, Demos and Civic Exchange. His core research interests are based around inequality in education, elite schools and emerging forms of educational distinction. Email: ewantmwright@gmail.com.

Wee Loon Yeo teaches Anthropology at the School of the Arts, Singapore. He completed his PhD in Anthropology at the University of Western Australia. His writing has been published in journals such as *International Studies in Sociology of Education* and *Ethnography and Education*. Wee Loon maintains a keen research interest in the social effects of elite schooling, including class reproduction, gender, and youth identity. Email: weeloon.yeo@sota.edu.sg.

Sandra Ziegler is Senior Researcher at the Department of Education in the Latin American Faculty of Social Sciences (FLACSO, Argentina) and Director of the Centre of Studies on Elites and Educational Inequalities. She is also Professor at the University of Buenos Aires (UBA). She has published several articles and two books on elite education in Argentina. Email: sziegler@flacso.org.ar.

INDEX

Note: Page numbers in *italics* are for tables.

Abrantes, P. 159, 160
academic excellence 175, 176–7, 178, 223
academic performance 44, 148, 151, 223;
    and Asian masculinity 28–30
Ace Institution, Singapore 11–12, 73;
    cosmopolitan outlook 75, 76–7, 78,
    80–2, 83; excellence, discourse of 75,
    78; IBDP adoption 76, 77; institutional
    habitus 12, 75–83; as Integrated
    Program (IP) school 76; meritocracy,
    discourse of 77–80, 82–3; Overseas
    Enrichment Programmes 80–2, 83;
    service aspect 76, 77, 80–2
affect 1–2; *see also* emotions
Afonso, A. 157, 160
agency 78, 79; and privilege 2; and
    structure 72
Aggleton, P. 2, 9, 202
Aguiar, A. 205
Aguiar, L. 116
Ahmed, S. 12, 88–90, 91–2, 94, 96, 97
Alexander, C. 93
Allan, A. 19
alumni networks *see* old boy networks
Ambedkar, B. R. 10
Amelina, A. 8
Annamali, E. 123

Appadurai, A. 8, 9, 36, 226
Apple, M. 9
Araújo, H. C. 159, 161, 165
Argentina 223–4; Caledonian School,
    Buenos Aires 218, 221–2, 223, 226–7,
    227–8; inequality 202; and neoliberal
    ideology 225; poverty 203; privatisation
    of education 203–4; school choice 14,
    203, 204, 205–16 (and discipline
    207–8; and modern curriculum
    209–10; public education 210–12, 213;
    and religious education 207–8; and
    socialisation 203, 206, 207, 208, 210,
    211–12; and tradition 205–12);
social fragmentation 202–3
Arnot, M. 161, 164
Arribas-Ayllon, M. 126
arts and media, as employment destination
    112, 116
Asian/Chinese masculinity 10–11, 19,
    23–30, 43; and academic performance
    28–30; and car culture 26–8; and sport
    24–5, 42, 43; *wen-wu* dyad 11, 23–30, 43
Atkins, G. L. 23
Australian Education International (AEI) 19
Australian elite schools 71; and Asian
    masculinity *see* Asian/Chinese

236 Index

masculinity; Chinese international students *see* Chinese international students; happiness narratives in school websites 12, 87, 90–8
Australian Rules football 25

Ball, S. 4, 9, 75, 104, 146, 157, 161, 205, 206, 214n8
Ballatore, M. 144, 194
Ballion, R. 147
Bamford, T. 104
Barrère, A. 147
Barroso, J. 160
basketball culture 40, 42, 43
Bauman, Z. 217
Beachton Grammar, Melbourne 37–46
behavioural competences 143–4, 152
Belfield, C. R. 160
Bernard, R. 107
Bernstein, B. 161, 164
Bhattacharya, S. 123
Bidart, C. 146, 147
Black, J. 191
Boltanski, L. 176, 183
Boni-Le Goff, I. 178
Börjesson, M. 189
boundary work 6
Bourdieu, P. 2, 6, 41, 46, 79, 105, 113, 114, 122, 124, 130, 139, 140, 148, 158, 162, 163, 183, 189, 203; co-curriculum 39; cultural capital 13, 104, 113, 117, 139, 141–2, 143, 144, 161; habitus 71, 72, 83; social capital 12, 104, 111, 117, 124; symbolic capital 124, 174–5
Boutier, J. 192
Bowles, S. 71
Boyd, D. 101–2, 104, 114
Boyer, K. 94
Bradfield College, UK *109*
branding 5, 13–14, 88, 225–7
Braslavsky, C. 205
Brazil 203, 205
Britain *see* United Kingdom (UK)
British Cohort Study (BCS70) 103
British Household Panel Survey (BHPS) 103
Broady, D. 189
Brooks, R. 5, 33, 124, 125

Brown, P. 115, 144, 152
Brown, W. 5–6
Brummitt, N. 53
Brunold-Conesa, C. 59
Bryanston School, UK *108*, 115
Bryant, D. 57, 61
Buisson-Fenet, H. 148
Bullen, E. 89
Bunnell, T. 53, 71, 77, 133
Burgess, I. 24
business, as employment destination 102
Butler, J. 97

Cain, C. 72
Caldwell, T. 95
Caledonian School, Buenos Aires 218, 221–2, 223, 226–7, 227–8
Canada 124; as university destination for IDBP graduates 57
capital 2, 8–9, 72–3, 104–5, 117, 189; accumulation 6, 14, 226, 227; cognitive 141; cosmopolitan 81, 189; economic 89, 143, 145, 148, 152, 200, 219; finance 226; human 74, 77, 113; linguistic 141; physical 33; transnational/international 53, 189, 193–200; *see also* cultural capital; social capital; symbolic capital
capitalism 4, 8–9; consumer 225, 226; global 10, 220, 227, 228
car culture, and Asian masculinity 26–8
careers 29, 30, 39; *see also* employment destinations; employment opportunities
Carneiro, E. 157, 160
Carneiro, R. 160
Carnoy, M. 125
Carrabine, E. 27
caste system, India 10
Catzaras, N. 193, 194
Cecil, Sir W. 190
Chapman, A. 87
Chapoulie, J.-M. 141
character 22, 53, 70
Charles, C. 19
Charterhouse, UK *109*
Chauvin, S. 184
Chiche, J. 193, 194

China 52–4; international schools 53–4; National Outline for Medium and Long-Term Education Reform and Development (2010—2020) 53; poverty levels 62

China, International Baccalaureate schools 11, 50–69; Creativity, Action, Service (CAS) courses 11, 51, 60–1, 64; and IB Learner Profile attributes 59–60, 61–2, 64 (intercultural understanding 11, 51, 60, 61, 63–4; open-mindedness 11, 51, 57, 61–2, 63–4); school fees 56, 58–9, 63; skyboxification perspective on 51, 52, 56, 59–61, 62–3, 64; and university entrance 50–1, 56, 57–8, 60, 63

Chinese international students, Australian elite schools 10–11; and Asian masculinity *see* Asian/Chinese masculinity; and co-curricular programs 37, 38, 39–47; cultural identity construction 11, 33, 34, 37, 39–46, 47; sports participation 24–5, 39–41, 42; and well-roundedness ethos 37, 39–46

Chinese masculinity *see* Asian/Chinese masculinity

choice of school *see* school choice

Chong, T. 74

Christensen, P. 92

Cipollone, K. 3, 51, 124, 205

citizenship 167–8; global 70, 76–7; *see also* cosmopolitanism

Clarendon, G. 106

class 2, 10, 12, 13, 14, 15, 73, 94, 217–18; and consumption 225–6; as cultural property 225–6; and culture 222; and employment destination 113; hierarchies 167, 168; institutional narratives of 87, 97; moral economy of 222; Singapore 74

class analysis 219–20

class power 225, 227, 228

Clifton College, UK *109*; Old Cliftonian Business Community 113

co-curricular programs: as socialising experiences 39, 43–4; and well-roundedness ethos 37, 38, 39–47; *see also* sport

Coates, H. 59

cognitive ability 103, 105

cognitive capital 141

Cohen, M. 225

Coleman, S. 5

collective learning 29

Collins, R. 70

colonialism 9; and Indian elite schools 12–13, 123–5

Colyar, J. 203

Comaroff, J. & Comaroff, J. 5

commodification 13, 158; of class power 228; of education 63, 88, 132–3, 157, 223–4, 225, 228; of happiness 89, 97

communication: competences 143–4; intercultural 44–5

competitiveness 88, 95, 122, 131, 132, 160, 163–4, 166; economic (India 125; Singapore 74); and hobbies and interests 41, 42; and masculinity 24, 25

conformity 93

Connell, R. W. 9, 10, 19, 20, 21, 23, 24, 25, 30, 47, 132

consumer capitalism 225, 226

consumerism 13, 123, 125

consumption 164, 168, 220, 224; and class 225–6; of elite education 218, 220, 225, 226–7, 228; and happiness 89; inequality 224

Cookson, P. W. 20, 22, 23, 206

Correia, F. 160

Cortesão, L. 157, 161

cosmopolitan capital 81, 189

cosmopolitanisation failures 47

cosmopolitanism 72, 73, 74–5, 83, 189; Ace Institution, Singapore 75, 76–7, 78, 80–2, 83; cultural 11, 33, 34, 35–7, 42–3, 44–6, 47; in-depth 46, 47; Swiss boarding schools 174, 184–5

Cotovio, J. 157

Coulangeon, P. 140, 143

Council of International Schools 129, 133

Courtois, A. 71

Cousin, B. 184, 194

Creativity, Action, Service (CAS) courses 11, 51, 60–1, 64, 65n2

credentials/credentialism 70, 71

Credit Suisse 4

238 Index

Cresswell, T. 94
Crozier, G. 205
cultural autism 166–7, 168
cultural capital 33, 70, 72, 97, 113, 117, 123, 139, 140, 141, 161, 189, 203, 211, 219; attitudinal or 'personal' kind of 144, 152; broad definition of 144–5; co-curricular 38; content of 145; effect of 145; and highbrow culture 140–1, 144, 151–2; informational kind of 144, 152; inheritance of 13, 139, 141, 152; international kind of 144, 152; new forms of 144–5; restricted definition of 144, 145; transmission of 104, 141–3, 152; well-roundedness as form of 33–4, 38, 45, 46
cultural choice 34, 35
cultural cosmopolitanism 11, 33, 34, 35–7, 42–3, 44–6, 47
cultural difference 34, 41, 46, 47; openness to 36
cultural ethics 33, 42, 47
cultural flows 36
cultural globalisation 36
cultural identity 34–5; Chinese international students 11, 33, 34, 37, 39–46, 47; and mediation 34–5
cultural inheritance 162, 165, 167; see also cultural capital, inheritance of
cultural logics 33, 35, 37, 47
cultural logics/power duality 35
cultural meanings 33, 34, 35, 47
cultural mediation 33, 35; of well-roundedness ethos, Chinese international students 37, 39–46
cultural omnivores 140
cultural openness 188, 196
cultural practices 34, 35, 38
cultural rationalities 35, 37
cultural studies, affective turn in 89
cultural univores 140
cultural values 33, 34, 35, 47
culture: and class power 222; as form of symbolic violence 227; highbrow 140–1, 144, 151–2, 153n2, 175; legitimate 139, 140; and masculinity 23; national 36; popular/mass 140; youth 45, 141

culture industries 220, 226
Curzon, G. N., Lord 123

Dale, R. 10
Daloz, J.-O. 1
Darchy-Koechlin, B. 9, 71, 217
Dardot, P. 224
Daverne, C. 142
Davies, S. 125
Davis, M. 75
De Graaf, N. D. 141
Debord, G. 226
Del Cueto, C. 205
Demerath, P. 71, 76
democracy 161, 220, 224
Dezalay, Y. 189
DiMaggio, P. 144
discipline 207–8
disciplines, academic 140
discourse: Foucauldian notion of 126; Indian elite school websites 12–13, 122–3, 125–35; see also happiness narratives
Doherty, C. A. 50, 59
Donnat, O. 140
Donnelly, M. 51
Draelants, H. 71, 148, 151, 217
Drew, C. 88, 96, 125
Dubet, F. 141, 206
Dulwich College, UK 108
Durkheim, E. 175
Duru-bellat, M. 146
Dutercq, Y. 142

Echeverría, B. 224
economic capital 89, 143, 145, 148, 152, 200, 219
economic competitiveness: India 125; Singapore 74
economy of eliteness 14–15, 218; exchange in 14–15, 221–2; leveraging the 227–8; value in 222–3, 227
Edgeworth, K. 88, 125
education multinationals 177, 178, 185n8
educational inequality 7–8, 203
educational travel 14, 188–201; ERASMUS programme 14, 188, 194, 200; Grand Tour 14, 172, 174, 185n3, 188, 190–3; overseas enrichment

Index **239**

programmes 71, 81–2, 83, 131;
peregrinatio academica 14, 188, 190;
Sciences Po students 14, 188, 193–9
Edwards, A. 24
Elias, N. 200n3
elite formation, and school choice,
Argentina 14, 202–16
elite imaginary 218, 222–3, 223–5, 228
"Elite Independent Schools in Globalising
Circumstances" team 71
elitism 6, 13, 88, 90, 94; India 129–30,
131, 133, 135; Portugal 157–8, 160;
Singapore 2, 74, 80
Elliott, J. G. 124
Eloy, F. 141
emo-scapes 8, 12
emotions: and behaviour 89; as discursive
89–90; *see also* affect
employment destinations 101–3; and old
boy networks 12, 101, 111–12, 116–17
employment opportunities,
internationalisation of 115
English medium of instruction 53, 123,
124, 135
English, R. 33, 38, 39
entitlement 175, 227; happiness as 87, 96
Epstein, D. 71
ERASMUS programme 14, 188, 194, 200
Esping-Andersen, G. 105
Estêvão, C. 160
ethno-scapes 8
Eton College, UK *108*, 111, 116
excellence 73, 74, 75, 78, 125; academic
175, 176–7, 178, 223
exchange, in economy of eliteness 14–15,
221–2
exclusion 88, 92, 93–4, 97–8, 131, 133–4,
135
exclusiveness 51, 129, 130, 132, 133, 135
exploitation 220, 222, 226
extracurricular activities 71, 122, 132, 134,
143, 163; *see also* hobbies and interests;
sport

Fabiani, J.-L. 145
Fahey, J. 3–4, 7, 8, 19, 51, 71, 81, 88,
122, 124, 130, 171, 202
Fairclough, N. 90

fairness 63, 64
family: school as 91–4; and Swiss boarding
schools 178–80
family background 14, 71, 72, 103
family transmission of culture 141–2, 143
Farkas, G. 143
Featherstone, M. 36
Feinstein, L. 105
Feldstein, M. 62
Felouzis, G. 143
feminine identity/femininity 19, 92, 93, 165
finance, as employment destination 112,
113, 116
finance capital 226
finance-scapes 8
finishing schools 179
Fisher, R. 87
flow(s) 9; cultural 36; of social science
knowledge 9–10
Forbes, J. 33, 39, 71, 75, 76, 124
foreign languages 144, 188, 189, 192
Forsey, M. 125
Foucault, M. 91, 126, 135
France 71; educational travel *see* Sciences
Po-Paris; school choice 13, 147,
148–51, 152, 205
Freemasonry 115–16
Frey, B. 89

Ganzeboom, H. 143
Garth, B. 189
Gaztambide-Fernández,R. 13, 18, 22, 51,
53, 71, 90, 97, 122, 126, 129, 135,
171, 202
Gee, J. P. 72
Gehring, J. 59
gender 2, 10, 12, 73; conformity 93;
discrimination 167; identity 19;
institutional narratives of 87, 88, 92,
93–4, 97; invisibility 164–6, 167; norms
92, 93, 94, 97; roles 30; *see also*
feminine identity; masculinity
Gessaghi, V. 203, 208, 213
Giddens, A. 206
Gilbert, R. & Gilbert, P. 20, 22, 29
Gintis, H. 71
Glasman, D. 143
global capitalism 10, 220, 227, 228

240 Index

global citizenship 70, 76–7; *see also* cosmopolitanism
global emo-scapes 8
global labour market 115
global nationalism 13
global youth culture 45
globalisation 36, 71, 177, 189
Goh, C. T. 74
Goh, D. P. S. 82
Goldthorpe, J. H. 144
Gombert, P. 142, 147
goodness 90, 91
Goodson, I. 206
Gopinathan, S. 75
Gottschall, K. 88, 125
Grand Tour 14, 172, 174, 185n3, 188, 190–3
Grandes écoles 148, 150, 152, 153n3, 200n4; *see also* Sciences Po–Paris
Green, F. 103, 104, 105, 114
Greene, R. 20
Gregg, M. 224
Gross National Happiness (GNH) 89
Guardian, The (newspaper) 4
Gunter, H. 9

habitus 12, 71–2, 72–3; *see also* institutional habitus
Hall, D. 9
Hall, S. 5, 9
Hallinger, P. 53, 64
Halpern, D. 113
Halpin, D. 87
Hannerz, U. 36, 42, 47, 70
happiness 12, 88–90; commodification of 89, 97; as discursive emotion 89–90, 97; global 89
happiness industry 89
happiness narratives 12, 87, 90–8; exclusionary aspect of 88, 97–8; school as happy family 91–4; winning at sport 94–6
Happy Planet Index 89
hard work 30, 79, 82, 131, 222
Harris, A. 87
Harrow School, UK *109*
Harvey, D. 4, 8
Hay, I. 4

Hayden, M. 53
Hayes, C. 54
Headmasters' Conference (HMC) 104, 106, 116
hegemonic masculinity 11, 20–3, 24, 94
Held, D. 102
Hellerman, P. von 5
Henri-Panabière, G. 142
Héran, F. 147
Heredia, M. 203
Herzfeld, M. 176–7, 180
Hesketh, A. J. 126, 144
heteronormativity 92, 93–4, 97
Heward, C. 105
Heyward, M. 54
highbrow culture 140–1, 144, 151–2, 153n2, 175
Highgate School, UK *108*, 116
Ho, E. 74
Ho, L-C. 74
hobbies and interests 41–2; and competitiveness 41, 42; monitoring of 41
Hobsbawm, E. 185n2
Hofstetter, R. 176
Holland, D. 72, 73, 79
Honey, J. R. D. S. 22
Hong Kong 58, 117, 205
Horne, J. 39
Horvat, E. 105
Howard, A. 1, 9, 71, 72, 73, 77, 79, 162, 202
Hughes, C. 133
Humair, C. 181
human capital 74, 77, 113
Hutchesson, R. 88, 125

identity: construction of 72–3; gender 19; global 70; privilege as 72, 77; *see also* cultural identity; feminine identity; masculinity
ideo-scapes 8
impression management 88
Inci, E. 113
income, distribution of 62; inequality 4, 55, 62
Indian caste system 10
Indian education system 122, 135–6n1

Indian elite schools 12–13; and colonialism 12–13, 123–5; international curricula 50, 122, 125, 132, 133–4; and neoliberalism 125, 132–3; and postcolonial nationalism 13, 124; website discourse 12, 13, 122–3, 125–35 (colonial excellence 127, *128*, 129–30; international excellence *128*, 132–4; metropolitan excellence *128*, 131–2

Indian Public School Conference (IPSC) 131

individualism 13, 161, 166, 168

inequality 13, 54, 55, 160, 202, 218, 219, 220, 228; Argentina 202; consumption 224; educational 7–8, 203; income 4, 55; naturalisation of 166–7, 167–8; as relational process 203; wealth 55, 62, 218

information, and school choice 145–7, 148–51

information processing skills 140

inheritors (of cultural capital) 13, 139, 141, 152

insiders/insider knowledge 13, 140, 145–51, 152

institutional habitus 73; Ace Institution, Singapore 12, 75–83

intellectual ability 21, 22

inter-cultural communication 44–5

inter-cultural understanding 11, 51, 54, 59, 60, 61, 62, 63–4, 134

International Baccalaureate Diploma Programme (IBDP) schools 11, 12, 71, 76; Creativity, Action, Service (CAS) courses 11, 51, 60–1, 64, 65n2; India 50, 122, 133–4; public (state) school sector 64; and university entrance 50–1, 59, 64; *see also* China, International Baccalaureate schools

international capital *see* cosmopolitan capital; transnational capital

International General Certificate of Secondary Education (IGCSE) 123–4, 125, 132

International School of Beijing 53

international schooling sector: China 53; *see also* International Baccalaureate Diploma Programme (IBDP) schools; Swiss boarding schools

international students 19, 33; *see also* Chinese international students

interpersonal competences 143–4

investment 114, 142, 143, 224

Jacquet-Francillon, F. 140

Jarvis, C. 87

Jay, E. 205

Jenkins, C. 59

Jenkins, H. 3, 51, 205

Kaewmukda, D. 64

Kakpo, S. 142

Kam, L. 23, 24, 27, 28, 29, 43

Keeling, A. 53

Kennedy, K. J. 75

Kenway, J. 3, 6, 7–8, 8, 9, 10, 12, 19, 33, 37, 51, 53, 54, 71, 81, 87, 88, 89, 117, 122, 124, 130, 161, 162, 171, 189, 202, 205

Kessler, G. 203

Khan, S. R. 54, 71, 72, 122, 162, 175, 202, 206, 219

Khaopa, W. 64

Kieffer, A. 146

Kings School (Canterbury), UK *108*, 115

Kirk, D. 94, 95

Knowles, C. 93

Koh, A. 3, 8, 9, 10, 19, 33, 51, 53, 71, 74, 77, 117, 122, 124, 161, 162, 189, 202

Kress, G. 91

Krippendorff, K. 107

Krugman, P. 62

Kuriloff, P. 29

labour market, global 115

Lachicotte, W. Jr. 72

Lahire, B. 142

Lapointe Guigoz, J. 181

Lareau, A. 79, 105, 144, 145

Lau, S. S. Y. 64

Lauder, H. 115

Laurens, S. 178

Laval, C. 224

law, as employment destination 102, 103, 111, 112, 113, 116

242 Index

Le Pape, M.-C. 142
leadership 39, 70, 95
learning, collective 29
Lee, A. 91
Lee, J. 47
Lee, M. 50, 51, 52, 53, 56, 57, 59, 61, 64
Leeuwen, T. van 91
Lefebvre, H. 5
Lenoir, R. 180
LeTendre, G. K. 146
Levin, H. 160
liberal education 53
liberalism 220
life skills 38–9
Light, R. 94, 95
Lim, L. 74
Lin, J. 52
Lingard, B. 39, 71, 75, 76, 124, 125
linguistic capital 141
Little, A. W. 123
Little, J. 94
Loh, C. E. 76
Longhurst, B. 27
Lorimer, H. 89
Louie, K. *see* Kam, L.
loyalty 91, 92
Luke, A. 23, 63
Lukes, S. 104, 113
Lynch, K. 124

Mac an Ghail, M. 22
Macaulay, T. B., Lord 123
McCarthy, C. 9
McDonough, P. M. 144
Macedo, E. 160, 161, 165, 166
Machin, S. 103
McIntosh, P. 72, 73
Majumdar, M. 123
Malvern College, UK *109*
Marcus, G. E. 180
marginalisation 88, 202
Marginson, S. 57
marketing 14, 96, 178–9
marketisation 13, 51–2, 54–5, 65, 88, 90
Marlborough College, UK *108*, 114
Maroy, C. 141
Martínez, M. E. 207
Martino, W. 24

masculinity 19, 165; Asian/Chinese *see*
    Asian/Chinese masculinity; and
    competitiveness 24, 25; and cultural
    background 23; hegemonic 11, 20–3,
    24, 94; and sport 24–5, 42, 43, 94;
    teacher's role in formation of 22; and
    toughness 24, 25, 42
mass culture 140
Masse, B. 195
Massey, D. 7
Masy, J. 152
materiality 2
Matthews, J. 33
Maurer, S. 193, 194
Maxwell, C. 2, 3, 9, 202
Maxwell, J. D. & Maxwell, M. P. 124
May, J. 6
Mayer, A. 64
Mayes, R. 94
Mazzarella, W. 34–5
Mead, W. E. 191, 192
Meadmore, D. & Meadmore, P. 71, 125,
    132, 134
media and arts, as employment destination
    112, 116
media-scapes 8
mediation, and cultural identity 34–5
mediation/power duality 35, 37
medicine, as employment destination 102,
    111–12, 113, 116
Méndez, A. 208, 213
merit 14
meritocracy 63, 64, 83, 113, 115, 123,
    124, 175, 222, 224, 225; Singapore 2,
    72, 74, 77–80, 82–3
Messerschmidt, J. W. 30
Mills, C. W. 54
Mingat, A. 146
mobilities 8, 11, 36, 144, 188, 189–90
modernisation: Argentina 209–10;
    Portugal 157
Monkman, K. 125
Mooij, J. 123
moral economy of class 222
moral education, Argentina 208
Moran, M. 124
Mullen, A. L. 124, 161
multilingualism *see* foreign languages

multinationals in education 177, 178, 185n8
Murphy, R. 103
Murphy-Lejeune, E. 144
Murray, W. E. 3
music 22, 141
Muxel, A. 193, 194

Narodowski, M. 224
Nash, R. 105
nation-state 36
National Child Development Study (NCDS) (UK) 103
national culture 36
national perspectives 8
nationalism 13
neo-colonialism 9, 124
neoliberalism 9, 87, 95, 132, 220, 222–3, 224; Argentina 225; and Indian elite schools 125, 132–3; Portugal 13, 160
Ng, V. 53
Nguyen, P. M. 124
Nogueira, C. 164
nonrepresentational theory 12, 89
Nord Anglia 177, 185n8
Nóvoa, A. 157
Nylander, E. 71

Oberti, M. 148
Occupy Wall Street movement 4
OECD 4, 52
O'Flynn, G. 47
O'Halloran, K. L. 91
old boy networks 12, 101, 104, 105–17; and employment destinations 12, 101, 111–12, 116–17; international dimension of 12, 114–16, 117; and job application process 113; maintenance of 114; and positions of power 12, 104, 105; services provided by 112–13; size of 111
Olds, K. 74
oligarchies 224
Oller, A.-C. 143
Ong, A. 8, 34, 35, 47, 70, 225
open-mindedness 11, 51, 57, 61–2, 62, 63–4
openness 175; cultural 188, 196

oppression and privilege, intersection of 158, 161–8
Other 5, 82, 166–7, 168
Oundle School, UK 109
overseas enrichment programmes 71, 81–2, 83, 131

parental influence/investment 142, 143, 152
parentocracy 152
Pareto, V. 205
Parker, S. 113
Parkin, F. 206, 214n8
Pasquier, D. 141, 142
Passeron, J. 71, 79, 139, 148
Pattieu, S. 189, 191
Pearce, R. 54, 63–4
peers: cultural influence of 142, 143; recognition from 29; support from 28–9
People's Action Party (PAP), Singapore 3
peregrinatio academica 14, 188, 190
performativity 13, 163–4, 167, 168
Perrenoud, P. 162
Perroton, J. 143
Persell, C. H. 20, 22, 23, 206
Pestalozzi, J. H. 176, 185n5
Peterson, R. A. 140
physical ability 22
physical capital 33
Piketty, T. 62
Pilot, A. 124
Pimenta, C. 160
Pinçon, M. 206
Pinçon-Charlot, M. 206
Pini, B. 94
place 8, 11; progressive sense of 7; and space distinction 6–7
place-making 7
Platter, F. & Platter, T. 190
Polimeno, A. 1
politics, as employment destination 102
politics of privilege 2, 3
popular culture 140
Portugal: commodification of educational services 157, 158; education system 160–1; liberalisation 157, 158; modernisation 157; and neoliberalism 13,

160; privatisation of education 157–8, 159–60, 161; school choice 157, 160
Portuguese elite schools 13, 157–70; historical overview 159–61; privilege and oppression, intersection of 158, 161–8; research context 158–9
positioning 163–4
positive psychology 89, 91
poverty 62, 202; Argentina 203
Power, S. 87, 146
power 203, 205; concentration of 218, 224; and old boy networks 12, 104, 105
power regimes 35, 47
power/knowledge 9–10
Prasad, A. 123
prestige 14, 53
Prieur, A. 140, 144
privatisation: Argentina 203–4; Portugal 157–8, 159–60, 161
privilege 1–5, 6, 7–8, 9, 13, 14, 15, 73, 77, 82, 87, 88; and agency 2; blindness/inattention to to 79, 82; and colonialism 12–13; discourse of, elite Indian school websites 125–34; as identity 72, 77; multiple geographies of 10; and oppression, Portuguese elite schools 158, 161–8; politics of 2, 3; spatiality of 2
problem-solving skills 140
production, concealment of 220, 226
progressiveness 75, 131–2, 135
promotional websites see school websites
property management, as employment destination 112, 116–17
Prosser, H. 3–4, 6
Public School Lodges' Council 116
public (state) school sector 88, 102; Argentina 210–12, 213; and international bacclaureate 64
Putnam, R. 104

Qian, H. 54
Quaresma, M. L. 159, 160

race 2, 10, 73; institutional narratives of 87, 88
Radley College, UK *109*
Raffles Institution, Singapore 2

Ramesh, S. 77
Ranger, T. O. 185n2
reading 141, 143, 152
Réau, B. 189, 194, 200n1
Reay, D. 75
Reich, R. B. 70
Reichert, M. C. 29
religious education, Argentina 207
Renolds, M. 19
Repton School, UK *109*
Resnik, J. 70, 77, 82, 134, 209
Ridley, J. 116
Rizvi, F. 5, 33, 42, 71, 122, 124, 130, 135, 185n4
Robertson, S. 10
Robinson, K. 92
Roche, D. 189, 192, 200n2
Rock, D. 221
Rose, N. 89, 97
Round Square schools 125, 129, 130, 136n5
rugby 94
Rugby School, UK *109*
Ryan, G. 107

St Andrew's School (Perth), Australia 10–11, 18, 19–23, 28
St Edwards School, UK *110*
St Paul's School, UK *108*, 114, 117, 175
Saltmarsh, S. 87, 88, 125
Sandel, M. 51–2, 54–5, 62, 65
Santiago, R. 160, 161
Santos, B. S. 161
Savage, M. 140, 144, 219
Sayad, A. 199
scale 3, 4–5, 8
scapes 8
Schneider, C. 116
Schön, D. 141
school choice 160, 205, 227; Argentina 14, 203, 204, 205–16; and economic capital 148; France 13, 147, 148–51, 152, 205; and insider knowledge 13, 145–51, 152; Portugal 157
school fees 55; China 54, 56, 58–9, 63
school websites 5; discourse see happiness narratives; Indian elite schools, website discourse; semiotic elements of 5, 12, 88, 90, 91, 94

school-linking 148
Sciences Po-Paris, educational travel 14, 188, 193–9
Scott, J. 104, 105, 114
segregated space 205
self: cultured sense of 35; and the Other 5
self-assertion 167
self-care 38, 39
self-confidence 22
Selwyn, N. 126
semiotic elements of school websites 5, 12, 88, 90, 91, 94
Seoane, V. 207
service: engagement in 76, 77, 80–2; *see also* Creativity, Action, Service (CAS) courses
Seth, S. 123
sexuality, institutional narratives of 87, 92, 93–4, 97
Shaw, M. 4, 6
Sheller, M. 26, 27
Sherbourne School, UK *108*
Shilling, C. 47
Shrewsbury School, UK *110*
Sibley, D. 92
Sidhu, R. 33
Sim, J. B. Y. 82
Singapore 2, 3, 51; class 74; cosmopolitan—heartlander terminology 74–5; economic competitiveness 74; elitism 2, 74, 80; meritocracy concept in 2, 72, 74, 77–80, 82; People's Action Party (PAP) 3; social context of schooling in 74–5; *see also* Ace Institution, Singapore
Skeggs, B. 222, 225, 227
Skinner, D. 72
Skinner, J. 25
Sklair, L. 54
Skrbiš, Z. 36
skyboxification 11, 51–2, 54–5, 56, 59–61, 62–3, 64, 65
soccer 25
social autism 166–7, 168
social capital 12, 14, 33, 72, 104, 111, 117, 123, 124, 143, 145, 147, 152, 189, 190, 200, 203, 210, 219
social closure 206, 212, 214n8
social fragmentation, Argentina 202–3

social inheritance 165, 167
social justice/injustice 63, 81, 82, 160, 227
social networks 104, 146, 147–8; *see also* old boy networks; social capital
social responsibility 166
social status 14, 87, 97, 98, 192, 224
socialisation 143, 144; and school choice, Argentina 203, 206, 207, 208, 210, 211–12
socialising 12, 39, 43–4
soft skills 143–4
space 2, 3, 5–6, 8, 9; and place distinction 6–7; segregated 205; territorial notions of 93–4; *see also* virtual spaces
Spivak, G. C. 123
sport 22; Chinese international students participation in 24–5, 39–41, 42, 43; exclusion from, Chinese international students 39–40, 41; local/overseas hierarchy in 40–1; and masculinity 24–5, 42, 43, 94; Old Boy teams 116; as socializing arena 39; winning at 94–6
Srivastava, S. 122, 124, 125, 130, 135
state schools *see* public (state) school sector
status *see* social status
status groups 206
Stich, A. 203
Stiglitz, J. 62
Stoer, S. R. 147, 159
Storper, M. 224
Stowe School, UK *110*
Stradling, S. 26
Straits Times (newspaper) 2
Stratton, G. 81
Stromquist, N. P. 125
structure, and agency 72
Stuber, J. M. 79
Stutzer, A. 88, 89
Sutton Trust 102, 103, 103–4, 112, 114
Svampa, M. 203
Swiss boarding schools: and academic excellence 176–7; and alternative pedagogies 176–7; cosmopolitan image 174, 184–5; and dialectics of business and education 177–8; as elite schools 171–2; and international pedagogies 177–8; symbolic capital 13–14, 178–87 (family ideology 178–80; international relations

246 Index

as worldview 182–3; national image 176, 183–4; schools as local economic actors 180–1; territorial identification 14, 174, 181–2, 184)
symbolic capital 41, 72, 124, 131, 132, 189; Swiss boarding schools 13–14, 178–87
symbolic capital of recognition 173–5
symbolic violence 41, 162, 227
Symes, C. 87, 88

talent 70, 79
Tan, J. 74, 82
Tan, K. P. 74
Tarc, P. 59, 134
Tavares, O. 160
Taylor, C. 79
teachers: cultural evolution of 141; insider knowledge 147; qualities required of 20–2; social networks 147–8
techno-scapes 8
Teng, A. 2
Terlouw, C. 124
territorial identification, Swiss boarding schools 14, 174, 181–2, 184
Thailand 64
Thompson, E. P. 220
Thompson, J. 53
Threadgold, T. 91
Thrift, N. 6, 74, 89
Tiberj, V. 193, 194
time 2
time-management 39
time/space 6
Tiramonti, G. 203, 205, 221
Tissot, L. 181, 186n11
Tonbridge School, UK *108*
toughness, and masculinity 24, 25, 42
tradition 75; origins of 206; and school choice, Argentina 205–12
transactional activity 63
transnational capital 53, 189, 193–200
travel *see* educational travel
Treanor, J. 4
tuition fees 55, 58; China 56, 58

United Kingdom (UK) 51, 124; employment destinations 12, 101–3, 111–12, 116–17; international influence

of schools 117; old boy networks *see* old boy networks; as university destination for IDBP graduates 57
United States of America (USA) 3, 71, 124, 205; international baccalaureate schools 64; as university destination for IDBP graduates 57
universities, foreign, opportunities to study in *see* ERASMUS programme; *peregrinatio academica*; Sciences Po-Paris
University College School, UK *108*
university entrance 55, 163–4; and International Baccalaureate schools 50–1, 56, 57–8, 59, 60, 63, 64; legacy admission 55; and Swiss boarding schools 175
Uppingham School, UK *110*

Valentine, G. 92
value, in economy of eliteness 222–3, 227
values 207
Van Zanten, A. 9, 132, 142, 143, 144, 146, 147, 161, 212
Veleda, C. 203, 204, 205
Villa, A. 207
Vincent, C. 146
Vincent, S. 142, 143
virtual spaces 5, 12–13; *see also* school websites

Wacquant, L. 72
Wagner, A.-C. 144, 174, 178, 189, 195, 200n1, 200
Walford, G. 18, 102, 104, 105, 106, 125
Walker, A. 53, 54, 61, 64
Walker, L. 26
Walkerdine, V. 92, 126
Walter, F. 186n13
Wang, A. 24
Wang, J. 64
Warde, A. 47
Wardman, N. 88, 93, 125
Waters, J. 5, 33, 71, 124, 125, 205
wealth 4, 227; distribution of 62; inequality 55, 62, 218
Weber, M. 175, 206
websites *see* school websites
Weenink, D. 33, 46, 81

Weiner, G. 33, 39
Weininger, E. 105, 144, 145
Weis, L. 3, 51, 124, 205
well-roundedness ethos 11, 33–4, 93, 223; Chinese international students cultural mediation of 37, 39–47; and co-curricular programs 37, 38, 39–47; teachers' construction of 37–9
Wellington College, UK *110*
wen—wu Asian masculinity 11, 23–30, 43
Westminster School, UK *108*
Whannel, G. 24
Wheeler, B. 1
Whitty, G. 87, 205
Willis, P. 19, 29
Winchester College, UK *110*
Windle, J. 81, 205
winning, and happiness 94–6, 97
Wood, Sir C. 123, 136n3
Woodward, I. 36
work: and economic independence 165–6; hard 30, 79, 82, 131, 222; *see also* careers; employment destinations

Wright, E. 51, 52, 59
Wright, E. O. 219
Wu, X. 52
Wylde, C. 225

Xie, Y. 62

Ye, R. 71
Yell, S. 91
Yin, R. K. 73
Youdell, D. 12, 87, 88
Young, I. 162
Young, M. 225
youth culture 45, 141

Zhang, H. 52
Zhao, Y. 52–3
Zhou, X. 62
Zhu, Y. 103
Ziegler, S. 203, 205, 221

Taylor & Francis eBooks

Helping you to choose the right eBooks for your Library

Add Routledge titles to your library's digital collection today. Taylor and Francis ebooks contains over 50,000 titles in the Humanities, Social Sciences, Behavioural Sciences, Built Environment and Law.

Choose from a range of subject packages or create your own!

Benefits for you
- Free MARC records
- COUNTER-compliant usage statistics
- Flexible purchase and pricing options
- All titles DRM-free.

Benefits for your user
- Off-site, anytime access via Athens or referring URL
- Print or copy pages or chapters
- Full content search
- Bookmark, highlight and annotate text
- Access to thousands of pages of quality research at the click of a button.

REQUEST YOUR FREE INSTITUTIONAL TRIAL TODAY

Free Trials Available
We offer free trials to qualifying academic, corporate and government customers.

eCollections – Choose from over 30 subject eCollections, including:

Archaeology	Language Learning
Architecture	Law
Asian Studies	Literature
Business & Management	Media & Communication
Classical Studies	Middle East Studies
Construction	Music
Creative & Media Arts	Philosophy
Criminology & Criminal Justice	Planning
Economics	Politics
Education	Psychology & Mental Health
Energy	Religion
Engineering	Security
English Language & Linguistics	Social Work
Environment & Sustainability	Sociology
Geography	Sport
Health Studies	Theatre & Performance
History	Tourism, Hospitality & Events

For more information, pricing enquiries or to order a free trial, please contact your local sales team: www.tandfebooks.com/page/sales

Routledge
Taylor & Francis Group

The home of Routledge books

www.tandfebooks.com